Lohia's Quest for Civil Liberty

Court Cases & Judgments

Edited by

Qurban Ali

Foreword by

Justice B. Sudershan Reddy

Former Judge, Supreme Court of India

ANAMIKA PUBLISHERS & DISTRIBUTORS (P) LTD.
4697/3, 21A, Ansari Road, Daryaganj, New Delhi 110 002
Phones: 011-2328 1655, 011-43708938
E-mail: anamikapublishers@yahoo.co.in

First Published 2024

ISBN 978-93-91524-95-1

PRINTED IN INDIA

Published by Anamika Publishers & Distributors (P) Ltd., 4697/3, 21A, Ansari Road, Daryaganj, New Delhi 110 002. Typeset by Shivani Computers, Delhi 110093 and Printed at Vikas Computer & Printers, Tronica City, Ghaziabad

In memory of great freedom fighter
and socialist leader

Madhu Limaye

who was a crusader of freedom and
civil liberties in India.

CONTENTES

FOREWORD

As soon as I accepted the responsibility of writing this Foreword to a publication of decided cases by the Supreme Court of India, in which Shri Rammanohar Lohia's demand for protection of civil rights was adjudicated upon, immediately one difficulty presented itself. Given that he passed away in the year 1967, every one of these cases presented themselves to the Supreme Court, in what can only loosely be termed as its phase of relatively extreme legal positivism. Some visionary jurists, such as Chief Justice, Koka Subba Rao, it must be admitted, did make heroic attempts to making it a principled one in which broader notions of justice – natural, and emanating from instinctual humanism – were often the unstated underlying themes. This necessarily means that the discussions in the cases regarding the status of civil disobedience and of civil rights were muted with respect to evolutionary, sociological, political, moral and philosophical dimensions.

Notwithstanding the above difficult, I submit to the reader that a compilation of such cases is long overdue. While we would expect, in cases decided by the Supreme Court, a total fealty to the norm that law and justice deal with individuals completely impartially and without bending the arc of that principle to the status of the litigant, for those of us who have grown up admiring Lohia, and understand the nature and magnitude of his contributions to freedoms of individuals and expression of demands for justice (especially for the socially and economically disadvantaged), we may see a bend in that arc. Justices, including the greatest of them who have served in the Supreme Court, are undoubtedly not completely immune to an appreciation of the status of the litigant before them in these cases.

The era in which Lohia could incessantly wage his many acts of civil disobedience was informed substantially by the fire of idealism that undergirded the Freedom Movement of this nation. Consequently, even within the framework of legal positivism, substantive concerns came shining through as clarity of thought and exposition of principle. Especially in the judgement authored by Justice Subba Rao (*The Superintendent, Central Jail* vs. *Rammanohar Lohia*), and later substantially followed in *Rammanohar Lohia* vs. *State of Bihar and Others* .

The challenges to the capacity of legal positivism as a framework for achievement of goals of substantive constitutional justice were to come later. Or maybe a wick had always been lit that burnt more to the alleged stability of the State, and less to the dynamic life of the State based on effervescent participation and critique by citizenry. *Kedernath* case of the Supreme Court, in 1962, has been seen by no less an eminent jurist than A.G. Noorani as the reacceptance of "sedition"—in its amorphous spread to any criticism of the government and the powers that be—as grounds to tamper and eliminate the constitutional principle laid down in Constituent Assembly debates that the word "sedition" itself ought to be eliminated from acceptable legal categories. But greater distress took another decade more. As is well known, in the 1970s as the growth of capacity of a State to pick up pace of social transformation and instantiate social justice began to substantively slow down, and with rising aspirations for "inclusion" in the benefits accruing through social action under the aegis of a nominally well-functioning democracy, the elite wielders of power increasingly subscribed to the notions that convenience of governance, along with security of the regime (including even thin skin to robust criticism), trumped both civil rights and the moral rights of civil disobedience. The imposition of an Internal Emergency, in middle of 1970s, and the horrors of butchering the spirit of the Constitution by the abdication of the project of constitutional justice in the*Habeas Corpus* case are all too well described facets of our political experiences. While a reasonable argument can be made that these lessons have been forgotten all too quickly, an equally reasonable proposition can be made that the events of mid nineteen seventies seemed to have shocked even the arbiters of mainstream discourse (who habitually bend more in favour of the rights of the elites—individual entities and groups) into an understanding that their support for the undermining of civil liberties does not affect the poor alone, but that it also scours the freedoms of those belonging to the well to do classes.

For an all too brief period of two decades, it seemed that the discourse of positing free expression of thoughts by citizens as itself being dangerous to the State and members of the elite classes that overwhelmingly filled the roles of the governing class had taken a backward step. At least in the articulations by the Supreme Court. To be sure, there was no overwhelming movement away from the horrors of the poor and the dispossessed in case of strenuous articulation of the constitutional rights beyond the boundaries of norms of mainstream political parties and the sensitive noses of the elite classes dispensing justice. The sorry status of civil liberties in Assam, Kashmir, Punjab (in the 1980s) and tribal belts would always cast a deep shadow over both the institutions of governance as well as the civil society for their indifference to the denigration of human dignity. Nevertheless, at least at the level of high constitutional abstraction, we heard for an all too brief period, the rhythms of unabashed assertion of human dignity and of the indefeasible rights of human beings—of both political liberties as well as what had come to be known as the 3rd generation rights, that find their genesis in notions of uncompromisable linkages between empathy, social obligations and development of both the individual and the society.

However, as the political economy of the country was changed, the Directive Principles of Social Policy were set aside as uncomfortable skeletons of a higher order set of aspirations for humanity. As the ideas that only "trickle down" systems of political economy can be sustained—ascribing a near malevolent persona to human beings as largely responding only to utterly selfish motivations—began to take hold within the dominant discourse of the elites and the sinews of governance, notions of indefeasibility of human dignity, moral necessity of empathetic sharing with fellow citizens and other life forms and consequent moral foundations of civil liberties and existential necessity of acceptance of civil disobedience as feed back loops for governance began to be given a short shrift.

For those suffering compulsions to use their eyes to see, use their ears to hear, use their minds to reason and use their instincts to be reasonable, the mayhem wreaked on the constitutional project, born out of our freedom movement, is all too obvious. From allegations of setting aside of even parliamentary norms of how a bill is enacted into law to threats of arrest and prosecution of a young woman for "daring" to tweet seeking help to procure oxygen for a Covid stricken and dying parent, the current state of political, economic, social and constitutional order seems to present itself as a tableaux vivant of little vignettes of constitutional horrors.

What does all of this have to do with Lohia, a freedom fighter who passed away 54 years ago? Why is it relevant that we recount and recollect five judgements of the Supreme Court that were issued nearly six decades ago? If the purpose is of building a specific legal argument, then surely there would not be a pressing need to compile and make a special mention of cases involving one person?

The answer to the above questions lie not so much in the decisions themselves, as much in the life of Lohia, his extensive writings and exposition of both the processes of democracy as well as of the goals of the nation, and his lived experiences. In the history of any nation there are but a few people who would be deemed to be the founders of constitutionalism in its lived sense. Lohia should be a part of any short list prepared by any serious scholar of constitutional history of this nation.

It is of course well known that Rammanohar Lohia was arrested a total of twenty-five times, and out of that he was arrested 14 times in independent India! It is also well known that he was a charismatic speaker, whose passion for social justice ignited the minds of many a young leader cutting his or her teeth in politics for the first time post-Independence, is also equally well known. Notwithstanding that, the total amount of scholarly attention that Lohia—his personality, his philosophical insights and his programmatic actions and action plans—received is far lesser attention than what is warranted. This has meant that we are seriously impaired in our assessment of Lohia's contributions in historical events by lack of adequate research. Apart from his own writings and a few devoted Lohiaites, his work in the 1942 Quit India Movement, his imprisonment and torture by the British, his involvement in movement for liberation of Goa, and his role in strategizing political & electoral actions based on necessary moral urgency to constantly improve the possibility of justice—political, economic and social—for the downtrodden, disadvantaged and the dispossessed have received scant historical and analytical attention. And I would suggest that this has left the political debate and the practice of democracy to achieve social justice in India impoverished and severely handicapped.

If the publication of the judgements by the Supreme Court, in which Lohia was implicated, were to start the processes of setting right the lacunae, then it would be of immense service. While some literature is available regarding the causes which led to the arrest of Lohia in post-Independence India, very little research is extant about how the Constitutional institutions, in independent India, reacted to a freedom fighter and close associate of Gandhi, engaged in the process of civil disobedience to highlight this or that injustice. I believe, a proper exposition coupled with, and based on, deep forensic historical research, going both backwards about the causes which drew Lohia's attention and acts of disobedience, development of Lohia's own thoughts and then moving forward to tracing the fate of those causes and ideas in actions by other social and political groups as well as institutions of a constitutional democracy, would be of immense help.

A brief methodological point is necessary at this stage. While the broad area of struggles of conscientious leaders and thinkers like Lohia has been broadly characterized as "Civil Disobedience", in respect of the struggles waged by leaders like Lohia, I would suggest might more fruitfully be labelled as "civil resistance". Part of the reason is historical. Gandhi himself rejected the idea that his ideas of civil disobedience were borrowed from Thoreau as the movement that he launched in South Africa was well prior to Gandhi receiving a copy of Thoreau's book. Gandhi suggested the expression "Civil Resistance". In as much as Lohia was, at his core, a Gandhian it is only proper that the expression "civil resistance" be used in the context of Lohia's programmatic actions that led to his arrest more number of times after India won its freedom.

And there are other substantive reasons. The word "disobedience" suggests that law would require obedience, at-least at a moral level, always. The problem is that "law" in its purely positivistic sense could often be, and very frequently was and is, employed to inflict great injustices on human beings. This is more likely to be the case in situations where humanistic impulses might prompt a morally conscientious citizen to protest the existing state of affairs marked by grave injustices—political, economic and social. The word "resistance" suggests a more mature programmatic action, based on an act of courage and conscience as opposed to childlike and willful disregard of the law. And Lohia's programmatic actions were deeply enmeshed in his ideas about what the project of nation-state ought to mean.

A proper analysis of Lohia's contributions to the development of constitutional ideas in India should include his pamphlet "The Struggle for Civil Liberties". In this remarkable document of 43 printed pages Lohia presented a magisterial synopsis of the origins and developments with regard to Civil Liberties in various jurisdictions, particularly United States, England and Europe. To the question of how or why the concept of civil liberties arose, Lohia posits it at the center of the eternal vigil of the citizen against the State.

"Throughout history, the state and its laws have given rise to manifold types of abuses..... " [and] "the citizen groaned and attempted to resist..... [I]n his efforts, however to end oppression and existing evils, he has met with stern repression. The authority in whom state power was vested did not brook defiance.... [T]he wrath of the state fell down on the citizen who tried to be critical...... [H]e, therefore stood in need of a minimum basis of safety from where he could launch attacks on the abuses and evils of his times. The rights of citizens in opposition to the Government as enshrined in the organic and ordinary law of different lands, are an expression of such a minimum basis of safety. If a regime of civil liberties prevails, resistance to oppression is not attended with frightful consequences."

In particular, for Lohia the need for civil liberties is tied toontological assumptions about human dignity and the very project of the nation itself—to progress from horrendous social and economic inequalities, that in turn eviscerate content from any political rights to solicit beneficial attention of the State and its ruling elites. Lohia marks it as vital, particularly in a society marked by great social and economic inequalities:

"Civil Liberties comparatively smoothen society's march towards progress. Society is being eternally pulled between reaction and progress and often degenerates into a state of stagnation. In this pull, the State has more often been controlled by forces of stagnation and reaction.... Lest the

State should turn into a terrible obstruction to progress and continually block it by its repression, its supreme authority over the citizens stands in need of description and curtailment. The entire scheme of citizens' rights is an outcome of the effort to describe and curtail state authority. In this manner orderly social progress becomes possible and society is not continually faced with the choice between tyranny and revolution. The concept of civil liberties is thus a shock absorber of the cruel impact between state tyranny and mass revolts. It enables society's march towards progress to proceed on orderly lives. If a citizen chooses to be critical of the world in which he lives, society permits him to question and to test and experiment without fear of serious reprisals."

In a broad sense Lohia's conception of democracy parallels that of the eminent Australian jurist, Prof. Julius Stone who states that by making the elected representatives (and through them, the executive) subject to, democracy marked by freedoms to change the rulers ensures that a revolution marked by a small "r" is what the society bears as opposed to a Revolution marked by the big "R", of violence and mayhem. Yet, Lohia recognizes that the mammoth inequalities, with vast majorities of the populace condemned to eking out a mere survival, could mean and has often meant the capture of the State by elite interests. With that, Lohia feared, could result in the emergence of a dictatorship of the worst kinds. Consequently, the assertion of the right of the citizen to criticize and oppose the governments (and powers of the day) are vital for the continued existence of a meaningful democracy that is not a dictatorship between two elections.

But, with Lohia, it goes further. He posited a fundamental opposition to "monotonicity" of the kinds found in some religious frameworks: that there is only one truth, that truth has been discovered, and anyone daring to obey that truth is necessarily evil and an enemy to be repressed or eliminated. Every State must perforce order its priorities, in respect of various social groups and citizens, as to who would receive attention first and to what extent might neglect of other individuals and groups might be morally acceptable. But that ordering of priorities cannot be deemed to be set in stone or as the only truth. Epistemic injustices are rampant in such systems, whereby the truth of even extreme suffering by hundreds of millions of citizens have been, and continue to be regularly ignored. Lacking the means to approach the high and the mighty, and further lacking the economic and social means to coalesce and build opinion amongst fellow citizens, civil resistance—open and visible—to the daily injustices becomes the only viable means of registering the need to alter the priorities. At times these issues can be matter of life and death, and quite often a continuous denigration of the human dignity of the dispossessed.

For Lohia the state of being in a "permanent civil resistance" was at once the very raison d'etre of the humanity of a political activist. It fundamentally requires the activist to be ever aware of the intensity of human deprivation, and jealously guard the rights of the dispossessed to solicitous attention by the State. The very act of such a civil resistance is intrinsic to, and an integral part of the very project of nation building. His ideas of "saptakranti"—seven revolutions – were the variable social programmes for pursuit, on a platform of permanent civil resistance. These were meant to be specific and an incomplete list of revolutions needed, and Lohia certainly did not imply that achievement of these goals by themselves would complete the process of revolution. The Gandhian in him recognized the existential facet of all of humanity: a continuous process of becoming, a never ending quest for perfection, both within oneself and also the collectives that individuals comprise as conscious beings. This fact of eternal "becoming" thus necessarily requires eternal vigilance against injustices. And in as much as life experiences of individuals are variegated conscious beings will necessarily have to engage in a dialogue to underscore the moral urgency of those who are relatively or absolutely deprived.

Even a listing of various civil liberties that Lohia identified in his seminal pamphlet of 1936, might strike a chord with those who may be reasonably at unease with the current state of affairs across the world. The first of these that he identifies is "freedom of expression by speech or press", for which the standard that he enunciates is that "no opinion, whatever its revolutionary import, may be punished unless it is accompanied by an overt act of revolt." This he concludes necessarily "imply the abolition of sedition laws and of censorship of press, books, post and radio". Banning of meetings and processions, he stated, in 1936, was impermissible and that "equal rights ... granted to hold meetings in public halls and such areas in towns and villages as are traditionally used for purposes of assembly".

Another important civil liberty that Lohia recognized, which analytically overlaps and is a necessary condition of a human being as a social animal, is the "freedom of association and organization....In order that larger masses of men may translate their keen interest in state affairs and economic management into organized effort to remove existing evils." Consequently, "they must in no event be robbed of their freedom to organize and strike and picket."

Maybe his life in Germany had alerted to certain arguments and trains of thought that accompanied the emergence of Nazism there. So, he warned that the elites in control of the power, and the executive beholden to them, would often "pretend and advertise the fear that such strikes and organizations will eventually lead to breaches of peace and the spread of revolutionary mentality...". For Lohia such attempts were to be resisted and exposed as being detrimental to the very foundations of permanent civil resistance to instantiate a responsible government ever solicitous of the welfare of its citizenry.

If law is indeed an expression of "general will", then for Lohia the democratic control over the government is a continuous and non-negotiable facet of progress. The rights of minorities, racial as well as other kinds who may not be a part of the winning coalition, were to come within "the extent and scope of a civil liberties agitation". "The prosecution of ..... minorities is obviously a reflection of unequal laws as also unequal dispensation of justice and is therefore an attack on the civil liberties..."

The immense foresight of this intellectual and moral giant is marked by two other civil liberties that he places special attention upon. The first is "freedom of conscience and thought and education." How presciently he remarked: "...if a professor or a teacher is dismissed from his job for expressing opinions unsavory to the administration and denominational or communal institutions are encouraged by the Government, the liberties of free conscience and education are directly attacked without serious possibilities of appeal."

Finally, he makes the "demand for release of political prisoners" itself a major plank of the civil liberties of citizens. This flows from his conception of the need for permanent civil resistance, and the needs of the dispossessed to form associations and express their opinions. Consequently, continued incarceration of political prisoners demands a conscientious and continued expression by the citizenry. At that point of time the possibility of indefinite incarceration without even the filing of a charge sheet had not yet been seriously entertained. However, the principle in the following is clearly extendable to the present context:

"Most convictions are based on a legal and judicial system which is too heavily weighted in favour of the Government against the Citizen. A fight against the system would obviously entail protection of its victims and therefor the release of political prisoners is a demand of civil liberties. Pending such release the rights of prisoners in relation to food, accommodation, punishments, intellectual provisions and the like have to be fought for."

We are on the cusp of significant, and maybe even epochal changes. Multiple forces are going to test our capacity, as human beings to cooperate to achieve concerted action to avoid disasters. The on rushing issues of climate change present the potential for disasters on a global scale. The blasé approaches of neoliberal lotus eaters that mankind's ingenuity will enable them to find technical solutions for ever increasing material consumption and also solutions to avert disasters are increasingly shown to be both irresponsible and maybe even criminally negligent about the possibility of catastrophes. The recent pandemic has certainly highlighted the severe limitations imposed on state capacities in respect of health care and extend a helping hand to those adversely affected, potentially leading to the death of many millions. To forget the efforts made by giants of our history, like Lohia, to construct the normative foundations for continuous civil resistance would be to be all too willing participants in the thwarting of human voices even as catastrophes of unimaginable kinds occur.

How do we abide the deaths of millions of fellow human beings, which could have been avoided if concerns for justice and empathy had been given greater priority – or at least greater priority than the demands of short run rationality based on greed as the sole value? Surely, the pandemic that has ravaged much of this world starting with later 2019, was as much the result of ignoring the warnings of impending disasters? And not just warnings but ignoring the signs of incapacities of our collective institutions, as revealed, for instance, by the fact that many millions die every year due to communicable diseases? And due to other avoidable causes such as micronutrient deprivation and hunger? How could we then call ourselves moral beings in any sense, if we do not compel our institutions to stop harassing and imprisoning those who speak up, from the depths of their deprivations? Or those who speak up on their behalf are labelled and persecuted by those who control the levers of the State?

In addition to issues of climate change, we are also likely to face immense challenges posed by automation, applications of artificial intelligence, and biotechnology. How we deal with those issues, without losing our instinct for humanity and empathy for each other, can be informed by what giants like Lohia of our history. Justice Koka Subba Rao (as then was) writes in *The Superintendent, Central*...vs. *Rammanohar Lohia*":

"It is said that in a democratic set up there is no scope for agitational approach and that if a law is bad the only course is to get it modified by democratic process" (meaning electoral politics) "and that any instigation to break the law is in itself a disturbance of the public order. If this argument without obvious limitations be accepted, it would destroy the right to freedom of speech which is the very foundation of democratic way of life". (Emph. supplied).

The tight formulation of Justice Subba Rao (as then was) recognized the imperative of an understanding that an agitational approach might itself be needed to protect a democracy in its truest sense and purport. The life and agitations of Rammanohar Lohia were real life examples of proving that judicial wisdom, and in fact went beyond, to make constitutional institutions and popular discourses realize that agitations, by and on behalf of the deprived, are vital for survival of democracy itself.

I congratulate Sri Qurban Ali and his associates for deciding to publish this book and place it before the public all over again. I trust that those who are deeply troubled about the content and direction of democratic politics, all across the world, would be enriched as much by researching the causes that Lohia stood for, and the philosophical underpinnings of his action.

Justice B. Sudershan Reddy
Former Judge, Supreme Court of India
15th August 2021
Hyderabad,
Telangana 500033, India.

PREFACE

CHAMPION OF THE CIVIL LIBERTIES

Dr. Rammanohar Lohia has been a fighter for civil liberties all his life. While he was Secretary of the Foreign Department of the Indian National Congress, he wrote a pamphlet "the Struggle for civil liberties." It was published by AICC in 1936 and Pt. Jawaharlal Nehru wrote its forward. He writes:

> "There has been much talk of civil liberties in India during recent months. That is not surprising for the suppression of civil liberty here has assumed prodigious proportions and become a public scandal of the first magnitude. It affects all of us intimately and mere self-interest would prompt us to combat this suppression. And yet, in spite of all this talk and interest, there are not many persons who think clearly about it or are aware of the full significance of the idea. Questions are frequently put to us which betray an amazing ignorance of the subject, and economic and social questions are mixed up with it. Dr. Rammanohar Lohia has done well to prepare this pamphlet on the subject, to tell us what the concept of civil Liberty is and how it has grown in western countries. I hope that many will read it and that it will help us in combating the suppression of civil liberties here and the ever-increasing encroachment by the State on what little remains".
>
> Jawaharlal Nehru, December 21, 1936.

This pamphlet is given as appendix in the book. (See pp. 301)

First Satyagraha and Imprisonment in Free India

Dr. Rammanohar Lohia regarded Satyagraha and civil disobedience as a great contribution by Mahatma Gandhi to mankind. He himself practiced and preached it throughout his life. While agitating for the democratic rights of the people of Nepal, he was arrested in Delhi. This was his first Satyagraha and arrest in free India.

The epalese people were struggling for freedom and democratic rights. The Nepalese National Congress was formed from the inspiration given by Dr. Lohia. The Nepalese Congress was fighting for freedom and Democracy against the autocratic Rule of Ranashahi in Nepal. The freedom struggle in Nepal was supported by Dr. Lohia, as it was a part of his Himalayan policy. Hundreds of workers of the Nepali Congress were imprisoned in the struggle and were languishing in jail for a long period. The former President of the Nepali Congress B.P. Koirala had begun his fast unto death in May 1949.

On the 25th of May 1949, a meeting in support for Nepali's cause was organized by the Socialist Party at Connaught Circle in Delhi to express India's sympathy and support for the struggle for Democracy in Nepal. After the meeting, a march led by Dr. Lohia was taken out to the Nepalese Embassy to present to the Ambassador a Memorandum in respect of the Nepali Congress demands. The morcha was stopped by the police at 500 feet from the embassy and was prevented from presenting a memorandum to the embassy. The authorities told the people in the morcha that a prohibitory order under Sec.144 was given and therefore they cannot be allowed to proceed to the Embassy. The workers squatted on the road and gave slogans for an hour or so. Suddenly the authorities ordered the busting of tear gas. The tear gas used by the police against the demonstrators was so strong that the meeting held at Constitution Club, one mile away from the scene of Satyagraha had to be abandoned. All but fifty workers dispersed because they could not bear the tear gas. Some were injured. The remaining workers who refused to dispense along with Dr. Lohia were arrested at 9 p.m.

This was Lohia's first arrest since the advent of freedom. The two minor boys and girls were released and the remaining were charge-sheeted and were released on bail. When the trial started on June 2, 1949, the Government Pleader prayed that the bail order of Satyagrahis be cancelled. The reason given by the Pleader was that they were likely to participate in another meeting. The Court cancelled the bail order. All the Satyagrahis were sent to jail. They were arrested under the Punjab Security Act. The trial lasted for one month.

In his statement before the Court Lohia stated "The plea of an emergency would be raised by the Government in order to suppress the discontent of the people, he stressed the need to set up people Court, as in Sweden, where the people could challenge injustice perpetuated by the Government and seek the protection of Fundamental Rights. He further said that it was also necessary to set up a committee to clear the prevalent jungle of laws. He pointed out that the Punjab Security Act under provisions of which they were arrested was emergency legislation and it was unjust to use those provisions against them. He further argued that the right to offer Satyagraha had been recognized in the Gandhi-Irwin Pact. He argued that the demonstration was perfectly peaceful and there was no necessity to use the tear gas. All of them were sentenced to two months imprisonment and a fine of Rs.100/- each, in default of payment of fine, and a further six weeks of imprisonment was awarded to them. All of them were sent to prison.

This was the first instance of Satyagraha in Free India when Jawaharlal Nehru was the Prime Minister The Press as well as the people discussed the detention of Dr. Lohia in Jail. An article in the Statesman newspaper was also published. Naturally, the Government was a bit upset because of all these happenings. In a letter addressed to Sardar Vallabhbhai Patel, who was then the Home Minister, on 9th June 1949 by Jawaharlal Nehru, he said, "There is general disapproval of Lohia's action, but this general disapproval has now taken place of a widespread sympathy - not for his action but because of the prolonged proceedings and detention in prison for over a month for a relatively trivial offense. People unconnected with politics have come to know and asked me why you are continuing this matter, it is being given publicity daily and that has excited sympathy. Normally such offenses are lightly treated in foreign countries and we are going much further than is usually done". The article in the Statesman was not a balanced article but it represented a widespread feeling in progressive circles in England and our Government is considered more and more as a police state indulging in detentions, police actions, and our reputation is low abroad.

He further wrote that "we are rapidly getting out of touch with public opinion and becoming just a Government and nothing more. The police are an essential force. But the police view of anything is seldom a right or balanced view. It is not the politician's or the Statesman's view. As for conditions in Nepal, they have been very bad, and we have addressed strong representations there. I think there is likely to be an upheaval there before a very long time. I am greatly concerned with what I see happening all around me in the Congress world and find that we are progressively alienating many vital sections of the community. There are hardly any young people with us. The people who are still with us are either some relics of the past or some others who have no influence in molding public opinion or some against whom there is a great deal of public feelings. It is in this context that I view Lohia's case and consider its prolonged session unfortunate and harmful to our cause".

On 11th June 1949, Acharya J.B. Kripalani wrote to Jawaharlal Nehru, "I feel that the trial and the continued detention of Lohia and his Party will be of no advantage to the authorities. They are giving the affair an importance that it does not deserve. I may tell you that I do not approve of Dr.

Lohia's conduct, and I have told him so. If it is not too late and if it is not a question of prestige or if it is only a question of prestige, I think that the case should be withdrawn and they should be released. My analysis may be wrong, but I have ventured to place my view before you."

When Dr. Lohia was in Jail, he was elected to represent the Indian Committee of the One World Movement. As such, he was to attend the conference in Stockholm. In his letter dated 29th June 1949, Jawaharlal Nehru wrote to Vallabhbhai, "I heard today that some time ago Lohia was elected to represent the Indian Committee of One World Movement, as such he is supposed to go to the One World Conference in Stockholm. The Promoters of the One World Business are some British M.Ps. as well as others like Lord Boydorr, the Food Experts, etc. They are inclined to be faddists and impractical, but they are good-intentioned people."

He further wrote, now that Lohia has been chosen by the Committee to go to Stockholm, the question of his going will arise. We can of course allow matters to drop and let him remain in prison and thus prevent him from going to one conference. I think this will be a wrong policy and will have bad effects. It would be good for him to go there. A visit abroad will probably do him good. I suggest, therefore, that you might allow his tour or whatever the number of the socialists in prison in Delhi to be released unconditionally i.e., the remaining part of their term of imprisonment and fine might be remitted."

That is the correspondence that took place between the Prime Minister and the Home Minister and some others and ultimately the Government of India issued a communication. The communiqué stated "the Government of India has considered the case of Dr. Rammanohar Lohia and other persons who were convicted for the breach of the Lawful order of the District Magistrate of Delhi in connection with Nepal Day. The so-called reasons for such breach have been given by the accused in the Court. The Chief Commissioner, Delhi has explained the position relating to these orders in his press conference held on 29th June 1949. It must be emphasized that the continuation of these regulations for holding a public meeting and taking out processions is necessary in the interest of peace and orderliness of the capital city, the population of which has increased enormously during the last five years and consists of heterogeneous segments and some of whom are anti-social. The number of meetings held and the nature of the speeches delivered; however, indicate clearly that such regulations have never been used by the Government to settle political opposition or to ban their activities. It has never been Government policy to make any political advantage out of the transgressions of their opponents, nor do they feel that in such cases, the accused persons should be punished more severely than what the indication of law and authority demands. After a review of these cases on merits, the Government considered that the ends of justice would be served by the imprisonment already undergone and have, therefore, decided to remit the remaining part of their sentences and the fines imposed on them by the Court".

THE KISAN STRUGGLE AND ARREST AT SAGAR-KARNATAKA

Socialists had repeatedly tried to organize Kisans of the Country since 1936. Ultimately in 1949 in a convention at Patna, an All India Hind Kisan Panchayat (HKP) was formed with Dr. Lohia as its chairman. The first session of the All India Hind Kisan Panchayat was held on 20 February 1950 at Rewa in Madhya Pradesh. The awakening among the Kisans in the country had been increasing and the formation of the strong organization raffled the government. The Vindya Pradesh government tried to place all kinds of abstraction at the time of the country with a view to foil the plan to hold the rally. It declined to provide water facilities to the delegates. The government denied even the facility for buses. Lohia told the government that the Kisan would accept the challenge of the government. They will walk the distance of 40 miles from Satna to Rewa. They would live under open sky unmindful of the obstacle. The Kisan conference despite the obstacles was a great success to the discomfort of the ruling government.

In the year 1951, the Kisans of Kagodu, a village in Sagar taluka of Shimoga district in Mysore, had launched a struggle against injustice. Seventy Kisans had been ejected from their land forcibly, because of selfish middlemen and vested interests of zamindars of the village. The zamindars were recovering from them rent, at Rs.30/- per acre, while they paid the government only Rs.2/- per acre. The zamindars used to smuggle food grains into the then Bombay state, for sale in the black market. The Kisans refused to pay rent at such a high rate. All the land in the village belonged to a single zamindar family, and one of its members was a congress leader. Kisans offered satyagrah under the leadership of the Socialist party. Lending his powerful support to the satyagrah, Lohia said that it was possible that Kisan tilling the land for the generation were being ejected illegally and the zamindars might be just trespassers. It was surprising that the Mysore government had come forth to protect the trespassers. All the members of the executive of the Mysore State Socialist Party were arrested and 400 Kisan had been thrown behind prison bars. Atrocities were being committed against the Satyagraha. The state government was determined to suppress the struggle, while the Kisan were equally determined to fight until they secured justice. Their demands were: (1) the land must be restored to the Kisan who were the legitimate owners, (2) a judicial committee should be appointed to settle the dispute, and (3) all the satyagrahis must be released. Provoked by the Mysore government's anti-Kisan policy, Lohia declared that he was proceeding to Kagodu, which had become the symbol of the Kisan's struggle against injustice, to express his solidarity with the satyagrahis and to participate in the campaign. He said that he proposed to enter the village with such party colleagues as wished to support the struggle launched by the legitimate owners of the land.

Lohia was arrested at the resthouse at Sagar railway station at midnight and taken to Bangalore and produced before a magistrate. The magistrate remanded him to custody till 20th June 1951. Lohia asked the magistrate as to the charges against him. The magistrate replied that he could make a statement before the court. "This means that you are not the court. Then how are you remanding me to custody?" Lohia asked him. When the magistrate offered to release him on bail, on the production of surety, Lohia remarked: "As you have not told me the charges against me, the question of producing a surety does not arise."

The Socialist party observed "Kagodu Day" all over the country to protest against Lohia's arrest. Socialists London organized a demonstration in front of the Indian high commissioner's office. Dr. Lohia was scheduled to leave India for Stockholm to attend an international conference and to visit Yugoslavia. The foundation of the World Government had also invited him to visit the U.S. Lohia's arrest had become the subject of comment in the U.S. Lohia filed a Habeas Corpus petition, and the government realized that the high court's ruling would go against it. To avoid the resultant discomfiture, he was released on 21st June, while the hearing was still in progress.

In independent India, Rammanohar Lohia confronted the government and Judiciary and challenged his illegal arrest through 'Habeas Corpus' many times and himself argued his cases from lower courts to High Courts and in the Supreme Court and was invariably successful. There is a long list of his court cases where he challenged the arrest made by the administration and police to help the ruling party to crush its political opponents or protest its anti-people policies. He strongly disapproved of the unconstitutional methods adopted by the government to curtail the civil liberties of the citizens.

AUGUST 1954 SATYAGRAH IN UTTAR PRADESH

In the year 1954, the Congress Government in Uttar Pradesh had enhanced the irrigation cess sevenfold in 13 districts of the State. The burden was beyond the capacity of the persons to bear. The State Government had resurrected the U.P. Special Powers Act, a draconian measure enacted by the British, to ruthlessly put down any resistance to the increased levy. The executive of the U.P. Units of Socialist Party met to consider the situation. Dr. Lohia was present at the meeting. Besides opposing the enhancement in the levy, the executive condemned the state Government's resort to the Special Powers Act and decided to launch Satyagraha in the 13 districts of U.P.

Earlier in 1954 as General Secretary of the Party, Dr. Lohia had issued an open letter to the Members of the Party and referred to the reports received by him about acts of injustice perpetuated by the Government against people. He said that all these acts cried for resistance and called upon the Party men to set in motion the "Wheel of Satyagraha" campaign launched by the Party in Rajasthan. Vindhya Pradesh, Bihar, and U.P.

The U.P. Government unleashed a reign of terror in the State to suppress the agitation. By June 1500 persons had been arrested in connection with the agitation from 12 districts. Dr. Lohia toured the State to mobilize support from the people. He urged the people to express through Satyagraha their anger and resentment against the injustice meted out to them. He was scheduled to address two meetings on 4th July, at Kaimganj in the evening and at Farrukhabad at night. The City Magistrate of Farrukhabad and the Sub Divisional Magistrate of Kaimganj under the Special Powers Act, at the place where he had been for dinner in Kaimganj, arrested Lohia. The police remanded him to custody for two days. Two days after the arrest, the Magistrate went to the Prison where Lohia had been lodged and wanted to hold the trial there. Lohia opposed the proposal, which he described as strange, and applied to the Allahabad High Court under article 436 of the Constitution that should be tried before it. The request was granted.

Lohia wrote a letter to the Chief Justice of the High Court. In the said letter, Dr. Lohia contended that; (1) he should be tried in an open court and not in a prison; (2) he was produced before the Magistrate 48 hours after the arrest; (3) He had sent a telegram each to the Chief Justice of India and Chief Justice of Allahabad High Court, immediately after his arrest, seeking their intervention, but the City Magistrate did not forward it to them and told him (Lohia) the next day that he did not do so because it was for Lohia to bear the telegram charges. He had pointed out to the Magistrate that by not doing so, he had committed contempt of the Court, but he had ignored the warning; (4) it was unjust to arrest a person in a free country just for having delivered a speech. The government's offence would be even graver if the speech did not contain incitement to violence. The U.P., Special Powers Act violated Article 19 of the constitution; (5) he did not know which of the issues raised by him came under the jurisdiction of the Supreme Court and which came under that of the High Court. Even so, he prayed that the Supreme Court should take up the issue raised by him about the validity or otherwise of the Special Powers Act. He submitted that every hour of his detention in custody constituted an encroachment on his fundamental rights and an encouragement to violence for 1500 to 1600 persons who were undergoing severe sentences under this unjust Act; (6) prisoners in the ordinary class were being supplied unwholesome food; (7) he said that he had dispatched the letter on July 7.

Lohia was transferred from the Fatehgarh prison to the Naini jail. Speaking to newspaper reporters who met him at the Allahabad station on the way Lohia said, "After arresting political leaders, Sardar Patel had at least the decency to keep quiet and not to talk too much, but the Prime Minister must talk on all occasions and on every matter. He ought to know that we too had a hand in placing him where he is today. Small men, whom luck and Gandhiji pitchforked into high positions in one of the most ancient and populous countries, are tragically proving that they are really small men, and the verdict of history will also record it."

Though he was ill, Lohia was taken to the prison in an old ramshackle van. From the Naini Prison, in a letter to the President, Dr. Rajendra Prasad, he wrote, "As a citizen of the republic over which you preside, and as one who was first put in prison and later hit below the belt, at least three times at Nangyal, Allahabad, and Mirzapur by your First Minister. I am writing to you, not in expectation of a remedy, nor even in the hope of publication of the wrong done to me unless it be through some fortunate change, but only to go on record. Your First Minister has observed that the practice of civil disobedience in a free country is senseless. He may have specifically meant conditions of democracy and the adult vote. Even in that case, all war resisters, all tax resisters and all peasant and labour fighters, from whom he earlier drew inspiration, have been senseless. The illiteracy of the Prime Minister's remark can only be matched with its astonishing irresponsibility, the scattering away of this contribution, and the invitation to violence in place of civil disobedience. The law under which I have been arrested makes signs and gestures, for instance, the open palm uplifted so usual with Mahatma Gandhi, punishable with imprisonment of six months and a fine. Your ministers, Sir, have no conception of "Maryada" or limited authority. Your Ministers are using against us a law which was called the black law by Mahatma Gandhi. Your First Minister has justified without shame this trampling underfoot of the Indian constitution and the guaranteed liberties of the republic. The tyrants do not even care to conceal their tyranny. Your First Minister has forgotten, too soon, that he is where he is, not alone by virtue of what he and his companions did, but also because of what we did. This ungrateful person has proved that a stung liberal can be worse than a blunt conservative. There was a time when the Congress Party also spoke in too many voices and then it was alive. Today it is dead. It speaks with the voice of Nehru alone, who has successfully stifled all voices. I have only two wishes and ambitions. One is to travel throughout the world without a passport. Secondly, I wish Your First Minister to live along, so long that the people send him again into a prison for his numerous offences against the Republic. I do not like being in a prison, I have always disliked prisons and hate them now. They are a mortifying reminder to me of my impotence, the impotency of justice against injustice. If tyrants roam the earth, prisons will be filled with those who hate them. I apologise for writing to you at such length and more so far writing it in a foreign language that I do not know well enough. But I remember the fate of the People's Charter, which was written in Hindustani, and your Government obviously transacts most of its business in a foreign language."

Dr. Lohia's arrest caused resentment among the people in general and in the Party in particular. Newspapers also criticized the Government's actions in arresting him. The British Labour Party leader Fenner Brockway wrote to Nehru expressing his distress over Lohia's arrest. But the Socialist Party failed to channelise the people's resentment and anger. It directed its units all over the country to observe 'Lohia Day' on 18th July. Some state units decided to send jathas of Satyagrahis to U.P., but some of the party leaders like Jayprakash Narayan were opposed to the agitation against the enhancement in irrigation cess. An attempt was also made to see that the agitation did not develop into a massive popular struggle. When Acharya Kripalani met him in prison, Lohia urged Acharya to intensify the struggle. Kripalani's reply was astounding. He asked Lohia; "should I commit a murder to court imprisonment?" The subject of intensifying the struggle was raised at the meetings of the party's General Council held at Indore the same month, but no decision could be taken. Madhu Limaye, joint Secretary of the Party wrote to Lohia on

August 4th; "I have an impression that some of our colleagues are not serious about the U.P. struggle. Kripalani did not even want our all-India day to be observed. Moreover, as for jathas, he does not like the idea of outsiders offering Satyagraha in U.P. The Party and people have responded enthusiastically, and a record number of meetings were held throughout the country on the occasion."

The hearing of Lohia's petition began before a Divisional Bench of Justice Chaturvedi and Desai on 26th August. A huge crowd had gathered to hear the proceedings. Lohia was brought to the Court under a heavy police guard. Lohia's counsel Shri Khare addressed the Bench first. The Advocate General followed him. Lohia made his statement on August 28th. He said, "I have come here not as an offender but as an accuser. I am an accuser, and the Government the defendant. Whether the Special Powers Act, 1932 is offensive to the Indian constitution or not is the issue before the Court." He said that between August 15, 1947, when India became free, and July 4, 1954, he had been arrested several times. Then he was comparatively certain about his personal freedom because he had been arrested on all those occasions for his acts in disobedience of the law. He had never been arrested on the charge of making a speech, he pointed out. The Special Powers Act, he said, was "a rusted sword that the Government had brought from the armory of the British suppressive laws". The Advocate General had during his address, contended that as the civil disobedience affected law and order, it was necessary to impose restrictions on personal freedom. Incitement by an individual could cause the beginning of civil disobedience. Lohia referred to the argument and asked, "Has or has not, any political leader preached civil disobedience or refusal to pay a tax in a democracy before?" He cited three well-known examples in that respect, one each from India, the U.S., and Greece. The three men he was referring to, Mahatma Gandhi, Socrates, and Thoreau, were universally acknowledged as great men. Two of them were assassinated and the third courted imprisonment. Each of them was far greater than all the persons, whom the Advocate General had quoted in the Court, put together, Lohia remarked. He said Magistrate who was a great believer in democracy tried Socrates. After he was awarded the death sentence, Socrates's friends had prepared a plan for him to flee Athens. But Socrates refused to flee. Athens was then a free and democratic state. He was the first great man in the world who called upon the people to disobey bad laws but insisted that they must obey just and progressive laws. Thoreau called upon the people not to pay unjust taxes. He contended that if they found the laws enacted by the Government, which the people voted to power once in five years, meaningless, the people must defy such laws. Even if 999 persons out of thousand supported such laws, the remaining solitary citizen could resist such legislation. This was Thoreau's conception of social civil disobedience. Lohia said Mahatma Gandhi was the greatest man born during the last five centuries, not only in India, but also in the world. He was never unequivocal in expressing his views. He had said that to refuse to pay a tax was man's most ancient birthright. It was his view that the people had this right not only under an alien rule, but they had this right irrespective of the character of the regime. It became the people's legitimate right to refuse to pay a tax if the levy was oppressive and all other means available to secure its withdrawal had proved of no avail. Civil disobedience was Gandhiji's legacy to humanity for all time to come. Its gospel must be spread all over the world, Lohia said. He also referred to satyagrahis like Pralhad and Charvak in that context. He said that humanity had progressed from Socrates to Gandhi after a long and arduous journey. Only select persons resorted to civil disobedience before Gandhiji's advent on the world scene. Gandhiji made the weapon available to millions of the common people.

Lohia said he made a distinction between the preaching and the practice of civil disobedience. Socrates, Thoreau, Gandhiji, and others like them willingly underwent the sentence imposed on them for disobedience of unjust laws. However, none of them had been penalized for having preached civil disobedience. On the contrary, their writings preaching of civil disobedience are available in books. Section 3 of the Special Powers Act, sought to prohibit the preaching of civil disobedience, and that he would have no objection to the provisions, had it sought to prevent violent resistance. He pointed out that under that section of the act, the Government would be able even to proscribe the works of Socrates, Thoreau, and Gandhiji. Lohia told the Court that he spoke quite openly before thousands of Americans, against the law then in force in the U.S. discriminating citizens based on colour. He was not prevented from doing so, if he restricted his opposition to the law, to its verbal expression. He referred to the Advocate General's contention that civil disobedience could not be practiced against a democratically elected Government and said that to say that civil disobedience had no place in democracy amounted to denouncing Gandhiji's legacy of satyagraha to humanity. India had become barren in political thought and action after Adi Shankaracharya. For the first time since then, India had contributed to the world thought, through its practice of satyagraha on a broad, mass basis. Closure of the avenue of peaceful civil disobedience would amount to an invitation to a violent insurrection he pointed out to the court and submitted to the Judges that they are custodians of the entire legal system of the country, and not merely of Section 124 of the I.P.C. He said that he was perhaps the first satyagrahi to be tried for having preached civil disobedience. He had not actually committed a breach of any law through any action. He said that freedom of speech also meant the right to make a wrong speech. A speech which a government and the people regarded as wrong or improper today might be regarded as right and proper after the lapse of some time. The weapon of civil disobedience was invaluable. Its practice would cause no harm to the nation. Lohia pointed out that he had remained in prison for more than 50 days and said that it was necessary to lay down rules to facilitate expeditious disposal of Habeas Corpus petitions.

The judgment of the bench was postponed to 12th August. The two Judges constituting the Bench could not reach unanimity. Justice Desai held that the Special Powers Act was ultra vires of the constitution. He was of the view that when actual refusal to pay the irrigation cess could not undermine public order, mere incitement not to pay it, could not bring it in jeopardy. Justice Chaturvedi, however, held that Section 3 of the Act, as amended, did not offend the constitution and, therefore its violation constituted a grave offense. The matter was, therefore, referred to a third judge, Justice Agarwal. He struck down section 3 of the Special Powers Act as ultra vires of the constitution. He agreed that abiding by the laws was a necessity for the success of democracy. But one could imagine circumstances when the most law-abiding and the greatest believers of truth among the people, would find it necessary to disobey unjust laws and might consider it as their duty to disobey them.

His Lordship referred to the martyrdom of Socrates in the cause of freedom of thought and expression, and to the advice, Socrates gave to the citizens of Athens at his trial. He also alluded to what Thoreau had said while preaching civil disobedience, as also to Gandhiji's concept of civil disobedience outlined by the Mahatma during his deposition before the Hunter Committee in 1918 and said that though a person practicing it was liable to conviction, it did not mean that a civil resister must necessarily be convicted in every case. The preaching and practice of civil disobedience was an action in the exercise of the right to freedom of expression. This freedom could be curbed only under circumstances contemplated by clause 2 of article 19 of the constitution, he said and observed that in his opinion, the constitution protected the right of every citizen to preach satyagraha. Allowing Lohia's petition, the Court also ordered the State Government to pay him Rs.500/- as costs.

In this case, the bench of Allahabad High Court observed in its judgment that "The applicant (Rammanohar Lohia) is the General Secretary of the Praja Socialist Party of India. The Government of Uttar Pradesh has increased irrigation rates for water supplied from canals to cultivators and the Praja Socialist Party of Uttar Pradesh is carrying on an agitation against the increase on the ground that it places an unbearable burden upon the cultivators who are adversely affected by the progressive fall in prices of foodgrains. The applicant visited Farrukhabad in connection with the agitation and addressed two public meetings on 4-7-54, one at Kaimganj at 4 p. m. and the other at Farrukhabad at 8-30 p. m. In the speeches, he incited cultivators not to pay "the enhanced irrigation rates" to the Government. He also severely criticised the state Government, but we are not concerned with that criticism as it does not form the basis of the charges which he has to answer at the trial. The Station Officer, Kaimganj, followed him from Kaimganj to Farrukhabad and lodged a report against him for the offence under Section 3, U. P. Special Powers Act, at the police station, Farrukhabad, and asked the Station Officer, Farrukhabad, in writing to arrest him. Consequently, the Station Officer, Farrukhabad, arrested the applicant the same day at 10 p.m. and informed him of the reason for the arrest, and showed him the written authority. Just then there arrived Sri, A. H. Drummond, City Magistrate of Farrukhabad and Sub-Divisional Magistrate of Kaimganj; the Station Officer produced the applicant before the City Magistrate there and then and the City Magistrate granted a remand for two days. The applicant was then sent to the District Jail.

After a careful hearing judges of the Allahabad High court gave their judgment "We differed on two points of law in this petition and referred them to a third Judge. The third Judge has given his opinion and he has answered both the questions in favour of the petitioner. The result is that this petition must be allowed. We consequently, allow the petition, hold that the petitioner's detention is illegal and we release him forthwith.

The petitioner shall be entitled to receive from the respondents a sum of Rs. 500/- as costs of this petition. We certify that the case involves substantial questions of law as to the interpretation of the Constitution".

This judgment was challenged by U.P. Government in the Supreme Court. But the Supreme Court also decided in favour of Dr. Rammanohar Lohia. Delivering this historic judgment Justice K. Subba Rao and five other judges of the bench wrote in "The Superintendent, Central Prison, Fatehgarh vs Rammanohar Lohia" on 21 January 1960: Fundamental Right-Infringement of-Enactment imposing restrictions on freedom of speech-Constitutional validity-Test-"In the interest of public order". Meaning of-Doctrine of severability-Applicability-Constitution of India, Arts. 19(1) (a), 19(2)U.P. Special Powers Act, 1932 (U.P. XIV Of 1932).HEADNOTE: Section 3 of the U.P. Special Powers Act, 1932, provided as follows:- "Whoever, by word, either spoken or written, or by signs or by visible representations, or otherwise, instigates, expressly or by implication, any person or class of persons not to pay or to defer payment of any liability, and whoever does any act, with intent or knowing it to be likely that any words, signs or visible representations containing such instigation shall thereby be communicated directly or indirectly to any person or class of persons, in any manner whatsoever, shall be punishable with imprisonment which may extend to six months, or with fine, extending to Rs. 250, or with both." The appellant, who was prosecuted under the section for delivering speeches instigating cultivators not to pay enhanced irrigation rates to the Government, applied to the High Court for a writ of Habeas Corpus on the ground, amongst others, that the said section was inconsistent with Art. 19(1) (a) of the Constitution and as such void. The High Court decided in favour of the appellant and he was released. The State appealed to this Court and the question for determination was whether the impugned section embodied reasonable restrictions in the interests of public order and was thus protected by Art. 19(2) of the Constitution. Held that even though in a comprehensive sense all the grounds specified in Art. 19(2) of the Constitution on which any reasonable restrictions on the right to freedom of speech must be based can be brought under the general head "public order", that expression, inserted into the Article by the Constitution (First Amendment) Act, 1951, must be demarcated from the other grounds and ordinarily read in an exclusive sense to mean public peace, safety and tranquility in contradistinction to national upheavals, such as revolution, civil strife, and war, affecting the security of the State.

The learned judges of the Supreme Court led by K. Subba Rao dismissed the appeal filed by U.P. State. The judges further observed:

"The constitutional validity of a section cannot be made to depend upon such an uncertain factor. Whether the principle of the first two decisions is applied or that of the third is invoked, the constitutional validity of the section cannot be sustained. We, therefore, hold that section 3 of the Act is void as infringing Art. 19(1)(a) of the Constitution. The entire section therefore must be struck down as invalid. If so, the prosecution of the respondent under that section is void. The learned Advocate General made an impassioned appeal to persuade us to express our view that though the present section is void on the ground that it is an unreasonable restriction on the fundamental right, in the interests of public order the State could legitimately re-draft it in a way that it would conform to the provisions of Art. 19(2) of the Constitution. It is not this Court's province to express or give advice or make general observations on situations that are not presented to it in a particular case. It is always open to the State to make such reasonable restrictions which are permissible under Art. 19(2) of the Constitution. In the result, the appeal is dismissed.

SATYAGRAH IN LUCKNOW IN NOVEMBER 1957 AND HIS ARREST

On 2nd November 1957, Rammanohar Lohia was standing in the verandah of the Sales Tax office, Lucknow. When a postman arrived to deliver mail, Dr. Lohia told him, "please do not enter this office, Sales Tax is the cause of soaring prices of food items.". Immediately Lohia was arrested for threatening, violence, and obstruction, none of which was involved in his action. He was taken to the district jail with a fortnight's remand.

Lohia's offering of satyagraha was a part of an All India campaign of his Socialist Party for redressal of various grievances of the people and certain other demands. One of these was the removal of statutes of the earlier British rulers in public places. The U.P. Government concealed this demand and declared that the statues would be removed before 15 August 1957. Earlier his colleague Raj Narain and other socialists were arrested in an attempt to offer satyagraha for this demand. Logically, following this decision, those who had sought arrest for this demand should have been released from jail. Lohia said; "If Raj Narain who demanded the removal of statues gets 18 months of jail, surely Sampurnanand (then Chief Minister of the State) who ordered it should get a sentence for 29 months". Over five thousand Satyagrahis had been jailed in this movement, since May 10, 1957. One party worker Kamesh Prasad Raj had died due to police torture, another Ram Singh died for want of medical aid. Satyagrahis had been given two to two and half years' imprisonment. In Lohia's opinion, peaceful demonstrators should never have had to undergo jail terms longer than 6 months. Hence, his counsel was that appeals against the injustice perpetrated by governments and courts were not proper in order if made after six months. Earlier announcing his decision to court arrest, Lohia said in a public meeting. "Of late, courts, particularly at lower levels, have become unreasonable and shameless. True, socialists should not have appealed, but judges of higher courts have themselves remarked that sentences of lower courts were extreme and severe.

Socialist Party branches observed 16 November as 'Lohia Day'. His arrest was condemned, and the state government's repression was placed before the people as also the significance of the path of satyagraha. Lohia had been remanded after arrest without being presented before a magistrate. He was given copies of the warrant as well as a remand order on the 16th. Lohia wrote to the High Court, seeking redress. He said, "The Seventh clause is neither constitutional nor in force in U.P. Further, it becomes operative only after a declaration under clause four, and it is not applicable to government offices. A remand has to be just and granted in the presence of the accused. A remand granted in his absence is illegal. Remand has come into being for the convenience of the accused as well as prosecution."

It was clear that remand was granted in Lohia's absence. Refusing to appear in court on 18th Lohia remarked: "Judicial and Jail authorities run a remand factory in collusion. Undated blank forms are kept in readiness and any dates are written - according to convenience." Thousands had been put behind bars. under clause seven of the criminal amendment law. While this unconstitutional law was being used for months and thousands were being arrested under it, Parliament and other self-styled civil rights organizations had not lifted a finger. To Lohia, all these institutions seemed stagnant, lifeless, and meaningless

On November 30, the Magistrate visited the jail to take up Lohia's case. Neither Lohia nor his attorney had been advised of this, so Lohia would not come into the jail verandah to participate in the court proceedings. In the afternoon the Jail superintendent accompanied by warders and prisoners approached Lohia and informed him that orders had been received to present him before court forcibly, Lohia replied that the court might please be reminded of his petition filed in the High Court. If despite this, they wish to force things, it will be another matter. The Superintendent withdrew but returned with 30-35 prisoners and 18-20 warders. They mounted a cane charge on the Satyagrahis around Lohia. More Satyagrahis gathered on hearing the noise around Lohia. The attackers also called for reinforcements. Satyagrahis thrashed severely. Some even got hurt on their genitals. After all the Satyagrahis were pushed into their cells, Lohia was tied in chains and carried to the Magistrate. When Lohia could not even speak, his thumb impression was secured on a piece of paper, by force. As the news of all these events reached outside, Raj Narain approached the Court and Justice Randheer Singh of Lucknow Bench of High Court and filed a petition on his advice, with Justice Beg, for permission to act as an amicus curiae. He ordered the civil surgeon of Lucknow and his assistants to examine the Satyagrahis and submit a report.

Lohia's Habeas Corpus case to the High Court was fixed for hearing on the 3rd, 5th, and 6th December 1957. Judicial Magistrate Jaiswal explained to Justice M.H. Beg and Justice Anand Narain Mulla that because Lohia twice refused to attend the court, the third time around he had to be brought to the court and his thumb impression secured by force. Justice Mulla queried as to the need to secure the thumb impression. The government prosecutor replied that this was because Lohia would not answer any questions. Justice Mulla exclaimed, "How ridiculous, And the Magistrate was a silent witness to this episode. Taking a thumb impression by force is sheer stupidity and utter impropriety! On 5th December, Lohia himself participated in the proceedings with the Court's permission. He narrated the whole story beginning with the illegal remand. The City Magistrate replied that he could not recall whether the reasons for arrest had been explained to Lohia. The argument made on behalf of Lohia was that Article 22(2) of the Constitution and Section 344 and 367 of the I.P.C. had been violated. The remand was illegal and hence the accused was released forthwith, Justice Mulla asked if a second order for Lohia's detention had been issued after the expiry of remand on November 16th. The Government prosecutor replied that the Magistrate's calling the case for hearing is deemed as a remand order. When Justice Mulla asserted that an explicit order was essential, the prosecutor only replied that the traditions of the U.P. Jails are followed. Justice Beg commented that the detention of an individual was a serious matter, and the tradition seemed a dangerous one. When the prosecutor continued to defend his point, Justice Beg thundered: "What preposterous tradition! How does the court tolerate this? Mr. Prosecutor, you better destroy the constitution itself so that everything will become legal. Are you a law unto yourselves? If these things continue, the courts will become superfluous. Your entire affair seems fabricated," After examining the warrant register of the jail, Justice Bég said, "This is indeed a long series of misdeeds. Every law has been transgressed there." Similar was the reaction of Justice Mulla. Justice Beg told the argumentative prosecutor that his justification amounted to yet another link in the same chain, "This is a vicious circle of glossing over errors." Lohia argued in the Court that in his case Article 22(2), 22(1), 19(1) 19(A) and 21 of the Constitution had been violated. Describing his entire experience Lohia remarked: "I am not given to a habitual lawbreaking. However, the Government arrests mean in an erroneous manner. My only hope is that the High Courts of the country. Not as a leader, but as a common man it is my request to the Court that the encroachment upon civil rights should not be allowed. I hardly enjoy jail terms. I have suffered enough in the British raj. Now even a minute's detention becomes unbearable. However, I am helpless. Having been brought up in the Gandhian tradition I cannot but resist injustice and exploitation." Justice Mulla interrupted Lohia and told him that he was only indulging in demagogy. 12th December was the day of the verdict. Justice Beg opined: "Lohia's arrest is illegal. Even if all the irregularities in the matter are overlooked any further detention of Lohia would be against law. There is no provision by which he could be kept in jail." Justice Mulla however found Lohia's arrest a normal matter. Due to the difference of opinion, the case was delegated to the third Judge.

On 13th and 16th December, the case was heard by Justice Raghuvir Dayal. Lohia was present to make a statement, despite his illness. Article 341(1) of the Constitution provides that the language of the Indian government is Hindi and Article 351 specifies that the spread of Hindi is a duty of all governments. Lohia, calling attention to these articles, began to address the Court in Hindi. However, Justice Dayal taking advantage of article 343(2), which makes English the language of transactions in High Courts for 15 years, forced Lohia to switch to English. Lohia repeated the whole story. However, on 17th Lohia's Habeas Corpus petition was rejected. A writ petition was filed in the Supreme Court on 21st December challenging this decision. The Government chose to retreat on the eve of the Supreme Court hearing, by releasing Lohia.

All Citizens Shall Have The Right To Move Freely Throughout The Territory of India

This right to travel in our country is a Fundamental Right of a citizen and in fact, no restrictions should be put on this right. Dr. Lohia who was a firm Democrat believed in this principle. In fact, he preached that a person should be allowed to travel anywhere on the surface of this earth without a passport. Of course, this was his idea which only the future knows when it will come into existence. In our country in the Northern part i.e., the Part regarded as a NEFA, presently known, a person is not allowed to enter and travel without the permission of the Central Government. The right to free movement in the country should not be obstructed for that would violate the spirit of the constitution. Right to free movement is subject alone to reasonable restrictions are in the interest of the public and scheduled tribes. No restrictions can be deemed reasonable if it does not specify the circumstances under which they come into operation. The restrictions must be specifically mentioned, and they should not be unlimited, undefined, and purely arbitrary. Dr. Lohia never called these areas as NEFA, but he had coined his own word for the area Urvasim. The word was his own creation. That the territory restricted for entrance was around 35000 sq miles i.e., it is even larger than West Bengal. If you restrict the entry into this territory, the Government must prove the fact it is dangerous in the interest of Scheduled Tribes and the public. No such thing has been done by the Government and such restrictions continued for years together.

He pointed out that the India-China dispute has on the contrary even proof and urgency to his view that both these interests are impaired by these unreasonable restrictions. The Hill Tribes are kept in isolation and without contact with the rest of India, except through Government servants and contractors and under these circumstances; it becomes a ripe fruit for foreign plucking. It was precisely such isolation which finished Tibet and which might yet finish Bhutan and Urvasim. To deny to these hill tribes and the rest of India, the right to hear and talk to each other, is not only to abridge the fundamental right but also to impair the unity and security of the Country. Further, more an Indian Citizen possesses an inalienable right to know himself and keep his country united by visiting all places of history, mythology, and natural beauty. When in the year 1958 he tried to visit this part of the country, he had said that my primary interest was tourism, the desire to see the land of our ancestral Rukhimini, the land of the Mismis. He further pointed out that the said interest is still uppermost, and I do not see why I should be blocked in that desire. He further pointed out that it is not sufficiently appreciated that the Chinese are seeking to make a powerful appeal to all mostly the entire northern frontier of India and are calling the Indian Frontier men, their brothers and are advancing a fraudulent plea of black noses slanting eyes and yellow complexion. Films, Documentaries, posters, and all kinds of other publications are indeed called for, which would reveal the truth that all the people right up to Thailand are far more related to India than to China in their language, script, ways of thought, religion and even their physiognomy and racial makeup.

It is on this background and in the interest of national integration and unity, Dr. Lohia insisted on the removal of such restrictions, which have continued for years. In 1958, he had visited the area, but he was not allowed to enter the same since he did not hold a valid permit. Thereafter he made an application to the concerned Authorities but in a years' time he did not receive the necessary permission, therefore, as promised earlier he had decided in the year 1959 to enter Uravasim and before entering that territory, had said, "I do not intend to defy any bans, or restrictions nor to practice Satyagraha, but I propose simply to attempt to enter Uravasim which is part our country". In last November, I had declared that I would do so after a year and I must keep my word. My request of last year for a permit must still be with the Government, which has now had a year to consider the question. There need be no fuss and all that the Government must do is to let me go into a part of my own country. Should the Government act otherwise, it would violate the constitution."

After issuing the said statement, he proceeded to enter Uravasim on November 23, at Tinsukia. This he said is to exercise the right of unrestricted travel in NEFA, which is a part of my country. But his entry ended up in his arrest, as he attempted to get into the prohibited area at Deonalin, a small check post on the Bank of Namsang, about 38 miles from Tinsukia at 12.30. Two armed sentries were guarding the check post as Dr. Lohia accompanied by his followers, arrived at Deonamali where he halted for a night. Soon after he alighted from his Car, Dr. Lohia was held by the third armed constable who inquired of his purpose and told him that he could not enter into NEFA territory without the permission of the authorities.

In another case related to civil liberty, Rammanohar Lohia was wrongfully arrested in Imphal (Manipur) on 11th April 1955, and he challenged his arrest in the Gauhati High Court as a writ of 'Habeas Corpus'. This case was known as Rammanohar Lohia And Ors. vs V.S. Sundaram.On 26th April 1955, justice Brij Narain observed in his judgment order that:

> "This is an application by Dr. Rammanohar Lohia and six others for a writ of Habeas Corpus. The petitioners alleged that they were wrongfully and illegally arrested on 11-4-1955 at about 5.30 P.M. in the Tikendrajit Park, Imphal when Dr. Rammanohar Lohia was delivering a speech on the ground that the holding of public meetings was prohibited by an order on the analogy of Section 144, Criminal P. C, dated 17-12-1954, passed by the District Magistrate, Manipur, within a radius of two miles from the Court of the District Magistrate, Manipur and this order was subsequently substituted by another order dated 21-12-1954 by which the area was increased to 4 miles and both those orders were proclaimed without being published in the Manipur Gazette, from the police van. On 15-2-1955 the Chief Commissioner, Manipur, published the Notification No. HP/83/54 whereby this order analogous to Section 144, Criminal P. C, was extended for another period of 3 months within the radius of 4 miles from the Court of the District Magistrate, Manipur. According to the petitioners the people of Manipur, after the illegal abolition of the Manipur State Legislative Assembly, have been exercising their right Under Article 19 of the Constitution of India in assembling peaceably and in giving expression and making speeches on the subject, but the executive Government has denied them their above-mentioned fundamental rights and arrested various persons under various sections of the Indian Penal Code.

Accordingly, they formed a reception committee of which S. Nabakumar Singh was elected the Secretary for inviting the petitioners for holding a public meeting on the 11th instant the Tikendrajit Park, Imphal. to discuss whether the Legislative Assembly and the Council of Ministers were rightly abolished and whether those should be reinstated. S. Nabakumar Singh applied to the District Magistrate, Manipur on 7-4-1955 for holding the said public meeting but the District Magistrate wanted a guarantee illegally that there would be no disorder, but as no such guarantee could possibly be given as the petitioners could not become responsible for any action of other people present, the District Magistrate refused permission on 11-4-1955. The petitioners held a meeting in, which exercise of their fundamental right under Article 19 of the Constitution, and when even though there was nobody else except 3 or 4 persons who also hurriedly left the place at the sight of the Inspector General of Police and the District Magistrate coming near them, the District Magistrate told the petitioners that as there was an order Under Section 144, Criminal P. C, prohibiting assemblage of 5 or more persons within a radius of 4 miles from the office of the District Magistrate, Manipur, in which lay the place of their meeting, tire meeting was unlawful and he ordered them to disperse. No time was given to them to disperse and the petitioners were arrested Under Sections 143, 145, and 188, IPC.I have already shown above that the petitioners were exercising their right of speech and assemblage without arms in a peaceful manner in order to vindicate their rights for enforcement of public rights adumbrated in the Manipur State Constitution Act, 1947, and so the assembly of 7 persons could not be deemed to be an unlawful assembly within the meaning of Section 141, IPC and the present petitioners could not legally be deemed to be members of any unlawful assembly. An assembly to be unlawful must be of 5 or more persons if the common object of the persons composing of that assembly is First: To overawe by criminal force, or show of criminal force, the Central or any Provincial Government or Legislature, or any public servant in the exercise of the lawful power of such public servant; or Second: To resist the execution of any law, or of any legal process, or Third: To commit any mischief or criminal trespass, or other offence, or Fourth: By means of criminal force, or show of criminal force, to any person to take or obtain possession of any property or to deprive any person of the enjoyment of a right of way, or of the use of water or another incorporeal right of which he is in possession or enjoyment, or to enforce any right or supposed right, or Fifth: By means of criminal force, or show of criminal force, to compel any person to do what he is not legally bound to do, or to omit to do what he is legally entitled to do. The present petitioners numbering seven were trying to get the provisions of law (Manipur State Constitution Act 1947) acted upon and they were not using any criminal force and so their assembly could not possibly be deemed to be an unlawful assembly, and their rights to freedom of speech and rights of assemblage could not legally be curtailed as was done in this case. As the order Under Section 144, Cr. PC issued in this case was not a legal and valid order no prosecution Under Section 188, IPC could legally ensure for disobedience of this order. The result is that the present petition must be allowed, and the petitioners are set at liberty, and the commitment order Under Sections 143, 145, and 188, IPC against them is quashed. As the petitioners raised several pleas which were found to be without force, it is ordered that the parties will bear their own costs".

Civil Disobedience in America as a World Citizen

On 16 April 1964, Dr. Rammanohar Lohia began his second world tour 13 years after his first. He was in the U.S.A. for two weeks. On 28th April he landed in Tucson International Airport on his way to the University. He was welcomed by Richard A Hairille of the University and Dr. Ruth Stephen, founder of Ruth Poetry Center. In his lecture at the Poetry Center, he said, "My understanding of Gandhiji has become a little deeper with the years. I sometimes feel that he sacrificed India at the alter of the world and added "In his pursuit of non-violence and civil disobedience, Gandhiji did a number of things which had temporarily brought harm to the country, but if the tenets of non-violence and civil disobedience become universally adopted, this temporary harm to India would result in the good of the world and Gandhiji would be remembered along with the Jesus and Buddha. Up to now, we have had a Jesus and Gandhiji of non-violence. If president Johnson aspires to become Bis Mark of the non-violence, he should ask for a summit conference with Khrushchev, not for discussing negative issues, but positive issues like the removal of poverty. I have no criticism of America's motive in foreign aid, but I am somewhat sceptical of the west's ability to distinguish between the modernization of consummation. Aid to foreign countries should be based on how these countries use the aid they receive and what these countries need.

It was 26th of May 1964, Lohia was in Jackson, a town of Mississippi, this southern state was notorious for its extreme poverty and racialism while going from Jackson Airport to Tangelo College along with the writer friend Ruth Stephen, the president of the college, Mr. Beitles, his wife and Lohia stopped at the Morison cafeteria for lunch. Looking at the black man, Lohia, the manager of the cafeteria declined him to serve food. Lohia was naturally full of indignation, full of feeling for resistance. However, he calmed himself and intimated the manager "I shall come back tomorrow. That night discussion in the Tougaloo College with agitating students. Beitles and Edwin and Janek king on the situation in the state went on till late. After these, Lohia announced his intention of going out of the cafeteria the next day. It was explained to him that he might be arrested in New Orleans or Atlanta, and that there was even the risk of facing a Hazing gun. He told his friends "Backing out now! would be against my notion of non-violence. If I stay, it will mean I am a coward and unconcerned about the treatment meted out to the Blacks". The next day officers of Morrison Company were intimated. The king escorted him, in his Indian dress, and entered, the restaurant as planned. The white manager told him "we do not wish to do business with you. This is private property. Please leave the place. Lohia firmly but politely refused to oblige. The police lieutenant asked him if he heard the manager and asked him to leave. Lohia reiterated his stand upon which the police officer announced that he had no choice but to arrest him, Lohia extended his hand in a friendly gesture forwards to the officer who easily brushed it aside.

Lohia was taken in the police van. The van left the place but did not go to the police station. Instead, it drove aimlessly through the streets of the town for about an hour. Obviously, the police official of the town was still undecided whether they should arrest Lohia are not. Probably they were consulting the Home Department in Washington. At last, after some more time, Lohia was released.

In the press conference held thereafter, he said "I want to make it clear that my purpose was not all that of highlighting a dark corner of American life. Such wretched places are everywhere including India. Normally I would promptly leave the place where I am not welcome. However, in this situation to leave America while the upheaval is going on is to encourage injustice and oppression. If entering a public place is a breach of Law, arrest me. I break such laws deliberately as a member of humanity. I have therefore not intimated my consulate or Parliament". This was his act as a world citizen, he. said and added, "The reference of my action is obvious. I shall always practice civil disobedience. I bow to the welfare and inspiration of the United States which is squarely facing the challenge of an apartheid".

A prolonged discussion between Lohia and some young activists developed that night. Many young participants of the Mississippi movements had gathered to attend the conference on Civil liberties at a house on Beach Street in Jackson. Volunteers and citizens exchanged ideas and experiences of the mass movements. Lohia was all praise for the non-violent efforts for social change. His interest in the movement pleased the audience. Lohia inquired about the plans and advised them to be conscious of the past as well as the future. After the first round of discussions, Lohia sensed restlessness among the young activities. Therefore, he invited the question about India. However, no one knew enough to ask anything. Realizing this he narrated the thrilling story of the Indian freedom movement, enunciated non-violence as its strategy as well as the philosophy of life, and explained the limitations of the movement and its victories. During the discussion, a black woman asked him with a surprise how Lohia could describe Nehru and his great contribution to the Indian freedom struggle in such growing terms when Lohia had suffered an electoral defeat at his hands. Lohia smiled and explained that he knew Nehru and his associates very well and hence their severe criticism, but this by no means implied that their good deeds should not be appreciated.

Lohia advised the activists about the need for a careful conceptualization of the objectives of their movement strategies. and long-term perspective. These must stand the test of time. Edwin King, his wife Janet and their associates in S.N.C.C. were highly impressed. The discussion continued till the late hours, the participants absorbing many ideas. Lohia remarked that perhaps he might return to the U.S. to join the movement. On receiving the news of Lohia's arrest, under Secretary of State, George Ball, issued orders to the Mississippi state Government for his release and sent a regret note to the Indian Embassy. Officials of the foreign Ministry contacted Lohia on the phone and apologized for the mistreatment. Lohia's response was typical, "I expect the same treatment as an American Citizen. If my experience in Jackson is that of a common black American citizen, I want nothing else". The news came from New York. Adlai Stevenson the U.S. Representative in the United Nations would meet Lohia and discuss the latter's arrest. Lohia laughed and said, "I will ask the Sternsons to apologise to the statue of Liberty". Lohia asked, "Why apologies to me? President Johnson should similarly offer apologies.

In public meetings leaders of various sections criticized Lohia's arrest. Lohia had made his own small contributions to the anti-apartheid movement in which Kennedy had become a martyr, following Lohia; Martin Luther King arrested was along with 17 associates. The struggle was getting intense, and consequently, on 20 June, the U.S. Senate passed by a thumping majority, the civil rights bill to put an end to discrimination in American Public Life. The bill empowered the Government to take all necessary steps that Blacks were to get every right enjoyed by the whites, thus at least on a legal plane, the demand for equality by blacks was conceded! Gandhiji's civil disobedience was thus victorious and a true Indian Gandhian Dr. Lohia participated in it as a citizen of the world.

DR. RAMMANOHAR'S ARREST IN BIHAR IN 1965

The President of India declared a state of emergency by issuing a proclamation under Article 352 of the Constitution dated 26 October 1962. The proclamation of emergency gave rise to certain extraordinary power to the State and Central Government. The powers are to be found in Part XVIII of the Constitution entitled Emergency Provisions. As a result, of the order of 26 October 1962, made under Article 359 of the Constitution, the right of any person to move any Court for the enforcement of Rights conferred by Article 21 and 22 of the Constitution remained suspended. If any such person is deprived of any such rights under the Defense of India

Ordinance of 1962 (Thereafter replaced by Defence of India Act of 1962) or any order made thereunder, he would not get any redress from Court. Out of this ordinance, two things stand forth. The first is that only the enforcement in a Court of Law of rights conferred by Article 21 and 22 is suspended. The second is that the deprivation must be under the Defence of India Act or any rule or order made thereunder. The word "thereunder" shows that the Authority of Defence of India Act must be made out in each case when the deprivation is by rule or order.

An order of detention under the Defence of India Act and rules can also be challenged on the ground of want of good faith on the part of the detaining authority. Such a plea is not shut out by the Presidential order. When the Presidential order was promulgated, it gave vast powers to the Central and State Governments. Once a person was arrested under the Defence of India Act, he could not seek any relief or could get justice from the Court because Article 21 and 22 were suspended. The order under the Defence of India Act could not be challenged in the Court of Law. Making use of this enactment, hundreds of persons were arrested and detained without trial since no specific charge was necessary. In Maharashtra, several persons who were doing trade of illicit liquor were arrested and detained under the Defence of India Act. The Law had really become draconian for it gave Government Authority to arrest any person under the said Act without assigning any reason for his arrest and could detain him. Taking advantage of this promulgation many persons who were not in any way connected with the defence of India were also arrested and detained.

Dr. Lohia went to Bihar on his tour and was in Patna on 9th August 1965. A meeting was organized in Patna and Dr. Lohia addressed a large gathering. Thereafter he was proceeding to Delhi to attend the session of Parliament. In transition, he stayed at the circuit house in Patna. He was arrested in the Circuit House of Patna under the Defence of

India Act. District Magistrate Patna passed the order of his arrest on 9th August 1965. The order was in the following terms:

> "Whereas, I, J.N. Sahu, District Magistrate, Patna, am satisfied with respect to the person known as Dr.Rammanohar Lohia, Circuit House Patna that with a view to preventing him from acting in any manner prejudicial to the Public Safety and the maintenance law and order, it is necessary to make an order that he be detained.Now therefore in exercise of the power conferred by clause (B) of Sub-clause I of Rule 30 of the Defence of India Rules 1962 read with notification No. 180/CW dated 20th March 1964 of the Government of Bihar Political (Special) Department. I hereby direct that the said Dr. Rammanohar Lohia be arrested by the police wherever found and detained in the Central Jail of Hazaribagh until further orders."

On the basis of this order, Dr. Lohia was arrested in the Circuit House of Patna on 10th August 1965, lodged in the Hazaribagh Central Prison, and detained there on the same day. Thereafter he addressed a letter in Hindi to the Chief Justice of the Supreme Court. Along with the letter, he had also filed an affidavit sworn in the Hazaribagh jail. The Supreme Court received the said letter and the affidavit on 13th August 1965. Although the Petition was somewhat irregular that is not conforming to the Rules it was treated as a petition and the Court issued a rule to be served on the Government of Bihar. As no objection was taken on the ground of form of the petition, the Court did not say anything about it.

Dr. Lohia had filed his petition to the Supreme Court under Article 32 of the Constitution. Art 32 of the Constitution reads as under:

Remedies for enforcement of rights are conferred by this. Part,

1. The right to move the Supreme Court by appropriate proceedings for the enforcement of the rights conferred by this Part is guaranteed.
2. The Supreme Court shall have the power to issue directions or orders or writs, including writs in the nature of Habeas Corpus, mandamus, prohibition quo warrantor, and certiorari whichever may be appropriate for the enforcement of any of the rights conferred by the Part.
3. Without prejudice to the Powers conferred on the Supreme Court by clause (1) or (2) Parliament may by law empower any other Court to exercise within the local limits of its jurisdiction all or any of the powers exercised by Supreme Court under Clause (2)
4. The right guaranteed by this article shall not be suspended except as otherwise provided by the constitution.

Dr. Lohia filed his petition to the Supreme Court under the above Article of the constitution. His petition was supported by an affidavit in which he submitted that he was arrested at the midnight of August 9, 1965, and was told that it was on charges of arson. However, later on, he was served with the order of detention, and that in this way his arrest for a substantive offence was turned into preventive detention. He further stated that the order of detention showed that he was to be detained in Bankipur Jail, but the name of the jail was scored out and "Central Jail Hazaribagh" was substituted which led him to conclude that typed copies of detention were kept ready and that the District Magistrate did not exercise his mind in each individual case. He contended that his detention under Rule 30(1)(B) of the Defence of India Rules was illegal because according to him, that rule dealt with prejudicial activities in relation to the Defence of India and Civil defence and not with the maintenance of Law and order of a purely local character. He alleged that the order was malafide that it was made to prevent him from participating in the House of People, which was to go in session from 16th August and particularly to keep him away from the 'Kutch issue' (Kutch Satyagrah). He further alleged that he had only addressed a very large gathering in Patna and had disclosed certain things about the Bihar Government, which incised that Government and caused them to retaliate in the manner and that detention was made to prevent further disclosures by him.

In answer to Dr. Lohia's affidavit, two affidavits were filed on behalf of the State. One affidavit was filed by the District Magistrate.

In this case a bench of the Supreme Court judges comprising Justice A.K. Sarkar, Justice M. Hidaytullah, Justice Raghubar Dayal, Justice J.R. Mudholkar, and Justice R.S. Bachawat observed in a historic judgment on 7th September 1965:

> In this case the District Magistrate, Patna purported to make an order under r. 3 0 (1) of the Defence of India Rules. The State has placed on record copies of two orders: one is said to have been recorded by the District Magistrate on his file and another which was served on Dr. Lohia. We are not concerned with the former because the operative order must be the one served on the detenu. The District Magistrate may well keep the former in the drawer of his table or alter it as often as he likes. It cannot, therefore, be regarded as anything more than a draft order. The order which finally emerged from him and was served on the detenu would thus be the only one which matters. The grounds for detention given in the latter order are that Dr. Lohia's being at large is prejudicial to public safety and maintenance of law and order. Under r. 30(1) an order of detention of a person can be made "with a view to preventing him from acting in any manner prejudicial to the defence of India and civil defence, public safety, the maintenance

> of public order, India's relations with foreign powers, the maintenance of peaceful conditions in any part of India, the efficient conduct of military operations or the maintenance of supplies and services essential to the life of the community".

Under r. 30(1) no power is conferred upon that authority to detain a person on the ground that it is necessary so to do to prevent that person from acting in a manner prejudicial to the maintenance of order in a local area. What is it that the District Magistrate, Patna had in mind when he ordered the detention of the petitioner? Was the apprehension entertained by the District Magistrate that Dr. Lohia, if left at large, was likely to do something which will imperil the maintenance of public order generally or was it that he apprehended that Dr. Lohia's activities may cause disturbances in a particular locality? There is thus an ambiguity on the face of the order and, therefore, the order must be held to be bad. No doubt, the order also refers to the apprehension felt by the District Magistrate about Dr. Lohia's acting in a manner prejudicial to public safety. But then the question arises, what is it that weighed with the District Magistrate, the apprehension regarding public safety or an apprehension regarding the maintenance of law and order? Again, would the District Magistrate have made the order solely on the ground that he felt apprehension regarding the maintenance of public safety because of the activities in which he thought Dr. Lohia might indulge? It could well be that upon the material before him the District Magistrate would have refrained from making an order under r. 30 solely upon the first ground. Or on the other hand, he would have made the order solely upon that ground. His order, however, which is the only material based on which we can properly consider the matter, gives no indication that the District Magistrate would have been prepared to make it only upon the ground relating to public safety. In the circumstances, I agree with my brethren Sarkar and

Hidayatullah that the order of detention cannot be sustained. I have not referred to any decisions because they have already been dealt with fully in the judgments of my learned brethren. In the result, therefore, I allow the petition and direct that Dr. Lohia be get at liberty.

ORDER

In view of the majority opinion, we allow the Petition and order that the petitioner be set at liberty.

DR.RAMMANOHAR LOHIA'S ARREST IN UTTAR PRADESH IN 1966

In another case of wrongful arrest and illegal detention, Dr. Rammanohar Lohia was arrested in Agra on 11th July 1966, when he was supposed to address a public meeting in connection of "UP Bandh" organised by his Samyukta Socialist Party(SSP). Lohia challenged his arrest in Allahabad High Court as a writ of 'Habeas Corpus'. Although his writ was dismissed by the court but judges recognised the necessity for the right to freedom of speech and expression and to assemble peaceably and without arms in a democracy. The judges' observed in their judgment in Rammanohar Lohia And Ors. vs State Of U.P. And Ors. on 15/3/1967:

This is a petition for writ of Habeas Corpus by seven persons who were confined as undertrial prisoners in the district Jail of Agra at the time of making the petition. Petitioner No. 1 is Dr. Rammanohar Lohia who is a member of the Lok Sabha; petitioner No. 2 is Sri Brij Raj Singh who, according to the petition, is an old worker of the Samyukt Socialist Party and who was a member of the Lok Sabha from 1957 to 1962; petitioner No. 3 is Sri Baloji Agarwal, who is a member of the Uttar Pradesh Vidhan Sabha from the Agra City Constituency; and the remaining petitioners are Sri Hukum Singh Parihar, Sri Ram Sanehi Lal Yadava, Sri Kitab Singh Yadava and Sri Ganga Prasad Sharma who, according to the petition, are active workers of the Samyukt Socialist party.

The opposite parties to the petition are the State of Uttar Pradesh, Sri Ravi Shanker Johri, District Magistrate Agra, and Sri K. C. Seth, Additional District Magistrate (Judicial), Agra. The facts which led up to the petition are briefly as follows: Some political parties including the Samyukt Socialist Party were trying to organise 'U.P. Bandh' on July 12, 1966. In view of this situation, Opposite party No. 2, the District Magistrate of Agra, acting under Section 144 Cr. P. C. passed an order the relevant portions of which are as follows: "To The General Public residing or frequenting Agra District. Whereas information has been received that in connection with U. P. Bund Agitation there is the likelihood of some sections of the public indulging in violence and lawlessness to force the closure of shops, offices, etc. and thereby causing breach of the peace and Whereas immediate prevention and speedy remedy is desirable for maintaining public peace and tranquility; Now, Therefore in the exercise of the powers under Section 144 of the Code of Criminal Procedure 1898, I, R.S. Johri District Magistrate, Agra hereby order as follows: (i) No procession or demonstration of any kind shall be organised or taken out anywhere in the district without a special permit from me or from the Sub- Divisional Magistrate concerned or the Superintendent of Police Agra. (ii) No assembly of five or more persons shall gather at any public place. Any such assembly shall be deemed to be unlawful and shall be liable to be dispersed by necessary force without further warning if it does not disperse upon command by a Magistrate or an officer in charge of the Police Station. Exception -- This prohibition does not apply to bona fide religious assemblies at places of worship like temples, mosques, gurdwara, churches, etc. No person shall indulge in any inflammatory speech as may be likely to cause disturbance of the public peace. (vii) .. .. (viii) No person shall shout or make use of any slogans in public streets of public places likely to cause a breach of the peace. (ix) This order shall come into force at once and shall remain in force for a period 15 days unless withdrawn earlier.

(x) This order is passed ex parte in view of the emergency. (xi) This order shall apply to the limits of Agra District; (xii) A breach of any of the provisions of this order is punishable under Section 188 of the Indian Penal Code. (xiii) .... Given under my hand and the seal of the Court this Tenth day of July 1966. Sd/- R.S. Johri, District Magistrate, Agra.

The Judges observed in their judgment order that:

> "Relying on the observations of Hidayatullah, J. Dr. Lohia contended that the decision in AIR 1966 SC 740 (supra) in 1966, modified the earlier view of the Supreme Court that "public order" was synonymous with public safety and tranquillity. This contention is without force. In the judgment of Hidayatullah, J. in AIR 1966 SC 740 (supra), the judgment of Subba Rao, J. in AIR 1960 S C 633, was mentioned and the specific observations of Subba Rao, J. quoted were "public order" is synonymous with public safety and tranquillity;. ....". Hidayatullah, J. did not dissent from these observations in so far as the meaning of the phrase "public order" used in Article 19(2) of the Constitution was concerned. Consequently, whatever meaning might be attached to the word "tranquillity" standing alone, when the word "tranquillity" is qualified by the word "public" in Section 144, Criminal Procedure Code, we are clearly bound by the decision of the Supreme Court in (1960) 2 SCR 821: AIR 1960 SC 633 (Supra) that "public order" is synonymous with public safety and tranquillity. Hidayatullah, J. himself went on to place "law and order" in the largest concentric circle and "public order" in the next circle and security of State in the smallest circle and the reason for placing "public order" in a smaller circle than that of "law and order" was the use of the word "public" before the word "order".

However, Judges also observed:

While on the one hand the necessity for the right to freedom

> of speech and expression and to assemble peaceably and without arms in a democracy is there, it cannot be denied that this right itself cannot be properly exercised by all without permitting a law which imposes reasonable restrictions in the interests of public order. No democracy can exist if "public order" is freely allowed to be disturbed by a section of the citizens. That was the background in which Clauses (2) and (3) of Article 19 of the Constitution had to be amended by the insertion of the words "public order" In view of the decision of the Supreme Court equating "public order" with "public safety and tranquillity" the provisions in Section 144, Criminal Procedure Code for the issue of directions which are likely to prevent or tend to prevent a disturbance of the public tranquillity cannot be said to be ultra vires. Dr. Rammanohar Lohia also contended that Section 188 Indian Penal Code itself was ultra vires. For the reasons mentioned by my learned brother and which I need not repeat I am also of the view that Section 188, Indian Penal Code is constitutional and not ultra vires. I would, therefore, agree that the petition be dismissed. We dismiss the petition.

In this book, we have published judgments of five of his important court cases delivered by various High Courts and the Supreme Court. The first one is "Rammanohar Lohia vs. The Superintendent, Central prison Fatehgarh" delivered by a bench of Allahabad High Court on 27th August 1954. In this case, Rammanohar Lohia challenged his arrest on 4th August 1954 by U.P. Government under U.P. Special Powers Act section 3, and of 14 of 1932 through a writ of 'Habeas Corpus'. In his plea, Dr. Lohia contended that the Act, and particularly Section 3 of it, stands repealed under Article 13 of the Constitution of free India on account of its being inconsistent with the provisions of Article 19.

A bench of Allahabad High court allowed his 'Habeas Corpus' and consequently, declared his detention illegal and released him immediately. The Court also entitled him to receive a sum of Rs. 500/- as costs of this petition from U.P. Government and also declared that 'this case involves substantial questions of law as to the interpretation of the Constitution.'

This judgment was challenged by U.P. Government in the Supreme Court. But the Supreme Court also decided in favour of Dr. Rammanohar Lohia. Delivering this historic judgment Justice K. Subba Rao and five other judges of the bench wrote in "The Superintendent, Central Prison, Fatehgarh vs Rammanohar Lohia" on 21 January 1960, that it involves "Fundamental Right-Infringement of-Enactment imposing restrictions on freedom of speech and Constitutional validity. Meaning of-Doctrine of severability-Applicability-Constitution of India, Arts. 19(1) (a), 19(2)U.P. Special Powers Act, 1932 (U.P. XIV Of 1932). The learned judges of the Supreme Court led by K.Subba Rao dismissed the appeal filed by U.P. State and observed in their order:

> "The constitutional validity of a section cannot be made to depend upon such an uncertain factor. Whether the principle of the first two decisions is applied or that of the third is invoked, the constitutional validity of the section cannot be sustained. We, therefore, hold that section 3 of the Act is void as infringing Art. 19(1)(a) of the Constitution. The entire section therefore must be struck down as invalid. If so, the prosecution of the respondent under that section is void. The learned Advocate General made an impassioned appeal to persuade us to express our view that though the present section is void on the ground that it is an unreasonable restriction on the fundamental right, in the interests of public order the State could legitimately re-draft it in a way that it would conform to the provisions of Art. 19(2) of the Constitution. It is not this Court's province to express or give advice or make general observations on situations that are not presented

> to it in a particular case. It is always open to the State to make such reasonable restrictions which are permissible under Art. 19(2) of the Constitution. In the result, the appeal is dismissed.

The second case is also related to civil liberty and illegal detention. In this case, Rammanohar Lohia was wrongfully arrested in Imphal (Manipur) on 11th April 1955, and he challenged his arrest in the Gauhati High Court as a writ of 'Habeas Corpus'. The Court accepted his writ and declared his arrest illegal. This case is known as Rammanohar Lohia And Ors. vs V.S. Sundaram.On 26th April 1955, justice Brij Narain observed in his remarkable judgment order that:

"This is an application by Dr. Ram Monohar Lohia and six others for a writ of Habeas Corpus. The petitioners alleged that they were wrongfully and illegally arrested on 11-4-1955 at about 5.30 P.M. in the Tikendrajit Park, Imphal when Dr. Ram Monohar Lohia was delivering a speech on the ground that the holding of public meetings was prohibited by an order on the analogy of Section 144, Criminal P. C, dated 17-12-1954, passed by the District Magistrate, Manipur, within a radius of two miles from the Court of the District Magistrate, Manipur and this order was subsequently substituted by another order dated 21-12-1954 by which the area was increased to 4 miles and both those orders were proclaimed without being published in the Manipur Gazette, from the police van.

The present petitioners numbering seven were trying to get the provisions of law (Manipur State Constitution Act 1947) acted upon and they were not using any criminal force and so their assembly could not possibly be deemed to be an unlawful assembly, and their rights to freedom of speech and rights of assemblage could not legally be curtailed as was done in this case. As the order Under Section 144, Cr. PC issued in this case was not a legal and valid order no prosecution Under Section 188, IPC could legally ensure for disobedience of this order. The result is that the present petition must be allowed, and the petitioners are set at liberty, and the commitment order Under Sections 143, 145 and 188, IPC against them is quashed".

The third case of Dr. Rammanohar Lohia is also related to civil liberty and his illegal arrest in Patna(Bihar) on 9th August 1965, under Defence of India Rules, 1962. He was arrested by an order of District Magistrate Patna and put in Central Jail, Hazaribagh.

Dr. Rammanohar Lohia challenged his arrest and filed a petition in the Supreme Court under Article 32 of the Constitution. Dr. Lohia's petition was supported by an affidavit in which he submitted that he was arrested at the midnight of August 9, 1965, and was told that it was on charges of arson. However, later on, he was served with the order of detention, and that in this way his arrest for a substantive offence was turned into preventive detention. He further stated that the order of detention showed that he was to be detained in Bankipur Jail, but the name of the jail was scored out and "Central Jail Hazaribagh" was substituted which led him to conclude that typed copies of detention were kept ready and that the District Magistrate did not exercise his mind in each individual case. He contended that his detention under Rule 30(1)(B) of the Defence of India Rules was illegal because according to him, that rule dealt with prejudicial activities in relation to the Defence of India and Civil defence and not with the maintenance of Law and order of a purely local character. He alleged that the order was malafide that it was made to prevent him from participating in the House of People, which was to go in session from 16th August and particularly to keep him away from the 'Kutch Issue'. He further alleged that he had only addressed a very large gathering in Patna and had disclosed certain things about the Bihar Government, which incised that Government and caused them to retaliate in the manner and that detention was made to prevent further disclosures by him.

In this case, a bench of the Supreme Court judges comprising Justice A.K. Sarkar, Justice M. Hidaytullah, Justice Raghubar Dayal, Justice J.R. Mudholkar, and Justice R.S. Bachawat gave a historic judgment on 7th September 1965 and observed:

> "In this case the District Magistrate, Patna purported to make an order under r. 3 0 (1) of the Defence of India Rules. The State has placed on record copies of two orders: one is said to have been recorded by the District Magistrate on his file and another which was served on Dr. Lohia. We are not concerned with the former because the operative order must be the one served on the detenu. The District Magistrate may well keep the former in the drawer of his table or alter it as often as he likes. It cannot, therefore, be regarded as anything more than a draft order. The order which finally emerged from him and was served on the detenu would thus be the only one which matters. The grounds for detention given in the latter order are that Dr. Lohia's being at large is prejudicial to public safety and maintenance of law and order. Under r. 30(1) an order of detention of a person can be made "with a view to preventing him from acting in any manner prejudicial to the defence of India and civil defence, public safety, the maintenance of public order, India's relations with foreign powers, the maintenance of peaceful conditions in any part of India, the efficient conduct of military operations or the maintenance of supplies and services essential to the life of the community".

Under r. 30(1) no power is conferred upon that authority to detain a person on the ground that it is necessary so to do to prevent that person from acting in a manner prejudicial to the maintenance of order in a local area. What is it that the District Magistrate, Patna had in mind when he ordered the detention of the petitioner? Was the apprehension entertained by the District Magistrate that Dr. Lohia, if left at large, was likely to do something which will imperil the maintenance of public order generally or was it that he apprehended that Dr. Lohia's activities may cause disturbances in a particular locality? There is thus an ambiguity on the face of the order and, therefore, the order must be held to be bad. No doubt, the order also refers to the apprehension felt by the District Magistrate about Dr. Lohia's acting in a manner prejudicial to public safety. But then the question arises, what is it that weighed with the District Magistrate, the apprehension regarding public safety or an apprehension regarding the maintenance of law and order? Again, would the District Magistrate have made the order solely on the ground that he felt apprehension regarding the maintenance of public safety because of the activities in which he thought Dr. Lohia might indulge? It could well be that upon the material before him the District Magistrate would have refrained from making an order under r. 30 solely upon the first ground. Or on the other hand, he would have made the order solely upon that ground. His order, however, which is the only material based on which we can properly consider the matter, gives no indication that the District Magistrate would have been prepared to make it only upon the ground relating to public safety. In the circumstances, I agree with my brethren Sarkar and Hidayatullah that the order of detention cannot be sustained. I have not referred to any decisions because they have already been dealt with fully in the judgments of my learned brethren. In the result, therefore, I allow the petition and direct that Dr. Lohia be set at liberty.

ORDER

In view of the majority opinion, we allow the Petition and order that the petitioner be set at liberty.

The fourth case is also related to the illegal arrest of Dr. Rammanohar Lohia and six of his party colleagues at Agra in Uttar Pradesh on 11th July 1966. Dr. Lohia also challenged this illegal act of the U.P. Government through a writ petition of 'Habeas Corpus' in Allahabad High court. Although High Court rejected Dr. Lohia's petition but discussed the issue of civil liberty at length and observed:

> "While on the one hand the necessity for the right to freedom of speech and expression and to assemble peaceably and without arms in a democracy is there, it cannot be denied that this right itself cannot be properly exercised by all without permitting a law which imposes reasonable restrictions in the interests of public order. No democracy can exist if "public order" is freely allowed to be disturbed by a section of the citizens. That was the background in which Clauses (2) and (3) of Article 19 of the Constitution had to be amended by the insertion of the words "public order" In view of the decision of the Supreme Court equating "public order" with "public safety and tranquillity" the provisions in Section 144, Criminal Procedure Code for the issue of directions which are likely to prevent or tend to prevent a disturbance of the public tranquillity cannot be said to be ultra vires. Dr. Rammanohar Lohia also contended that Section 188 Indian Penal Code itself was ultra vires. For the reasons mentioned by my learned brother and which I need not repeat I am also of the view that Section 188, Indian Penal Code is constitutional and not ultra vires. I would, therefore, agree that the petition be dismissed. We dismiss the petition.

We are immensely grateful to Justice B. Sudershan Reddy, former judge, Supreme Court of India, for beautifully writing the foreword on the quest of Rammanohar Lohia's fight for civil liberties. He painstakingly went through all the judgments related to the illegal arrests and detentions of Dr. Lohia during his politics of civil disobedience and Satyagrah in independent India. We are also grateful to Prof. Anand Kumar who relentlessly persuaded Pankaj Sharma of Anamika Publishers to publish this book and who requested Justice Sudershan

Reddy to write the foreword of the book. Gratitude is also due to Pankaj Sharma and his team for publishing this book of immense legal value and for the cause of civil liberties and freedom of speech and expression, as well as to veteran socialist, late Shri Haribhau Limaye for providing us glimpses of Lohia's fight for civil liberty through a book "Dr. Rammanohar Lohia-Battle for liberty and Justice", published by Rammanohar Lohia Smrutikendra and Sadashiv Bagaitkar Smrutimala, Pune. This book was provided to me by dear friend Anant Bagaitkar.

We dedicate this book to the memory of great freedom fighter and Socialist leader late Madhu Limaye, who was also a crusader of freedom and civil liberties in India.

Qurban Ali

SHORT PROFILE OF RAMMANHOR LOHIA

Dr. Rammanohar Lohia was born on 23rd March 1910. After completing his education by obtaining a Doctorate in Economics from Berlin University in Germany in 1932, he came back to India. He joined the freedom movement at an early age. His interest in politics gained further momentum owing to the atmosphere he had found at home. The final choice of politics as a career was made when the Congress Socialist Party (CSP) was formed in 1934. Lohia was one of the founding members of CSP, and its Drafting Committee and elected a member of its National Executive(1934-1947). He was also appointed the Secretary, AICC Foreign Department, 1936-38. With his selection as Secretary of the Foreign Department of the Indian National Congress at the Lucknow session, he changed his headquarters from Calcutta to Allahabad and began to take more interest in international affairs. As Foreign Secretary of the Congress, Lohia was instrumental in laying the foundations of the foreign policy of India. He maintained close contacts with the freedom movements then going on in other parts of the world and developed close relations with progressive organisations in Asia, Africa, and Latin America. As Secretary, he had written a pamphlet "The Foreign Policies of the Indian National Congress and the British Labour Party" which was described as a "Work of outstanding merit" by Pandit Jawaharlal Nehru.

Lohia was aware of the problems faced by the overseas Indians and he told the Indian people about their pitiable conditions. He had also drawn the attention of the world towards the suppression of civil liberties in India and other countries. He was arrested for making anti-Government speeches, on 24 May 1939, in Calcutta, his first imprisonment, but was released the next day on bail. The possibility of World War II led him to suggest to Congress in 1939 the launching of a Satyagraha for India's independence. He did not want Britain to gather men and materials from India for the War. He was of the view that the country would not get freedom automatically. He created awareness among the people by writing articles and pamphlets. During the Second World War, he supported the view that India should not extend any support to the British and advocated complete non-cooperation. He said that the supply of men and money to the then Government should be refused. When the All-India Congress Committee passed a resolution in 1939 supporting Britain in the war effort, Lohia opposed it and wrote an article "Down with Armaments".

He was arrested second time from the premises of the A.I.C.C., at Allahabad on 7th June 1940, for making anti-war speeches. Mahatma Gandhi did not like it and reacted very strongly. Deploring the action, Gandhiji said that imprisonment of patriots like Rammanohar Lohia and Jayaprakash would not be tolerated, and he would not be a silent witness to this increasing encroachment on popular freedom. Lohia was released in July 1942. During these years he did not approve of either the Gandhi-Viceroy Statement of 9th September 1939 or of the attitude of Subhas Chandra Bose to the War. The individual civil disobedience campaign launched by Gandhiji in 1940 was designed to assert the people's right to democratic freedom. National and international events in 1941-42 brought Lohia closer to the other sections of the Congress. Rammanohar Lohia opposed the Crips Mission of 1942 and participated in the 'Quit India' Movement launched by Mahatma Gandhi. Welcoming the Quit India resolution of 8th August 1942, he played a significant role in the 'Quit India' Movement of 1942.

He went underground along with Smt. Usha Mehta and Ms. Aruna Asif Ali and started a secret 'Congress Radio' and broadcast it from Bombay and Calcutta in 1942. He utilised the time by writing booklets and articles full of inspiration like "How to establish an Independent Government?", "I am Free", "Prepare for the Revolution", and "Brave Fighters March Forward". Another scholarly article "Economics after Marx" was also written by him while he was underground.

He along with Jayaprakash Narayan worked for the 'Azad Dasta' in Nepal for some time. He eluded the grasp of the police since 9th August 1942 but was finally arrested on 20th May 1944 in Bombay. Lohia was interned at Lahore and Agra Jail under an extremely hostile environment and faced the inhuman torture and cruelty of Britishers at Lahore Fort. He was released from Agra prison on 11th April 1946. He directed the Movement while remaining underground and could not be detected for nearly two years.

His original and creative mind attracted writers and artists and inspired young generations. He instilled the spirit of self-respect among the classes, victims of the caste system and enabled them to assert their will to power which transformed the political scene in India. In international politics, he associated with World Government Movement, civil-rights movements for African Americans, Afro-Asian, Socialism and Third World movement, etc. He traveled abroad in many countries. In 1951 he attended the first International Conference of Socialists at Frankfurt (Germany). He also organised, though he did not attend, the first Asian Socialists Conference at Rangoon in 1953.

After the Independence of India, Dr. Lohia started Liberation Movement for Nepal's freedom in 1948. He also fought for the civil liberty and freedom of Goa and was arrested twice. He was arrested twenty-five times for participation in the freedom movement of India, Goa, and Nepal and civil disobedience movements in free India and in Mississippi, America against racial discrimination in 1964. He vehemently criticised the foreign policy of the Government of India and campaigned against the Chinese occupation of

Indian territory in 1962.

He believed in Gandhiji's philosophy of Satyagraha and Civil Disobedience. In fact, he had dedicated his life's activities with Satyagraha and Civil Disobedience for the fight against poverty, injustice, and for the protection of civil liberties, freedom of speech, and Democracy. In his first visit to America in 1951, he had advised Negroes (Blacks) to adopt these principles in their fight against Racialism. In his next visit to America, he defied laws and was arrested. He was a fighter and militant in his approach to problems and fought hard all his life for others. He was constantly at war against the prejudice, which distorts human values. A relentless fighter for the common man he was uncompromisingly dedicated to their betterment.

1. RAMMANOHAR LOHIA VS. THE SUPERINTENDET., CENTRAL PRISON, FATEHGARH AND ANR.

JUDGMENT
27/8/1954

Desai, J.

1. This is an application by Dr. Rammanohar Lohia for a writ of '*Habeas Corpus*'. He is being prosecuted on two charges, each of committing an offence under Section 3, U.P. Special Powers Act, 14 of 1932. He contends that the Act, and particularly Section 3 of it, stands repealed under Article 13 of the Constitution on account of its being inconsistent with the provisions of Article 19.

2. The applicant is the General Secretary of the Praja Socialist Party of India. The Government of Uttar Pradesh has increased irrigation rates for water supplied from canals to cultivators and the Praja Socialist Party of Uttar Pradesh is carrying on an agitation against the increase on the ground that it places an unbearable burden upon the cultivators who are adversely affected by the progressive fall in prices of foodgrains. The applicant visited Farrukhabad in connection with the agitation and addressed two public meetings on 4-7-'54, one at Kaimganj at 4 p.m. and the other at Farrukhabad at 8-30 p.m. In the speeches he incited cultivators not to pay "the enhanced irrigation rates" to Government. He also severely criticised the state Government; but we are not concerned with that criticism as it does not form the basis of the charges which he has to answer at the trial.

The Station Officer, Kaimganj, followed him from Kaimganj to Farrukhabad and lodged a report against him for the offence under Section 3, U.P. Special Powers Act, at police station, Farrukhabad, and asked the Station Officer, Farrukhabad, in writing to arrest him. Consequently the Station Officer, Farrukhabad, arrested the applicant the same day at 10 p.m. and informed him of the reason for the arrest and showed him the written authority. Just then there arrived Sri A.H. Drummond, City Magistrate of Farrukhabad and Sub-Divisional Magistrate of Kaimganj; the Station Officer produced the applicant before the City Magistrate there and then and the City Magistrate granted a remand for two days. The applicant was then sent to the District Jail.

The Station Officer, after investigation submitted a charge sheet against the applicant for two offences, each of Section 3, for making the two speeches, in the Court of Sri. P.R. Gupta, a Judicial Officer, where the case is pending. The Magistrate went to the Jail on 6-7-'54 to try the applicant who protested against his trial within the jail premises. The Magistrate rejected the protest. Then the applicant made an application for referring the case to the High Court under Section 432, Criminal P.C., and that application also was rejected. Thereupon the applicant applied for an adjournment of the case on the ground that he wanted to move this Court for transfer of the case and the Magistrate adjourned it to 7-8-'54. Though the offence of Section 3 is bailable, the applicant has not applied for bail. He filed the present application on 9-7-1954.

3. The only grounds urged by the applicant are that the Act is 'ultra vires' because it contravenes Article 19 of the Constitution and that his arrest and detention are illegal and contrary to Article 21 of the Constitution. Two counter-affidavits have been filed in reply to the application, one by the Assistant Jailor of the central prison where the applicant is being confined at present and the other by the Station Officer of police station, Farrukhabad. The Assistant Jailor affirms that the applicant has been arrested for the offences of Section 3 of the Act, that he was produced before the Court inside the jail on 6-7-54, that the case was adjourned to 19-7-1954, and that

he is being confined in the jail under the orders of the Judicial Officer. The Station Officer, police station Farrukhabad, in his counter-affidavit mentions the circumstances in which the applicant was arrested and affirms that he is being confined as an under-trial on charges of Section 3 of the Act.

4. Though the applicant mentioned Article 21 as having been contravened by his detention in the jail, he meant to rely on Article 22. Under that Article a person on being arrested must be informed of the grounds for his arrest and must be allowed the right to consult and be defended by a legal practitioner; also he must be produced before the nearest Magistrate within 24 hours and no arrested person can be detained in custody beyond 24 hours without the authority of a Magistrate. I find that none of these provisions was infringed in the present case; the applicant was informed of the reasons for his arrest by the Station Officer, Farrukhabad, at the time of the arrest and was produced there and then before a Magistrate and had been detained from the date of his arrest in custody with the authority of one. Magistrate or another. Sri A. H. Drummond remanded him to custody for two days on 4-7-54 and Sri P.R. Gupta commenced his trial in the jail on 6-7-'54 and, when adjourning it to 19-7-'54, passed an order for continuing his detention in the jail.

In the warrant directing the Superintendent of the Central Jail to keep him in custody, the Magistrate has ordered that he should be produced before him in Court on 19-7-'54. It amounts to his authorising the applicant's detention in jail custody. Ordinarily Magistrates write in the order-sheet of the case, when adjourning it to the next date, that the accused should remain in custody as before; but Sri P.R. Gupta or (sic) did not say in the order passed on 6-7-'54 that the applicant should remain in custody up to 19-7-'54. That omission does not matter when the warrant contains the magistrate's authority for the detention. One authority for detention is enough. Moreover whether there existed any magisterial authority for detaining the applicant in custody after 6-7-'54 or not is a question of fact which cannot be permitted to be raised for the first time in argument. Had it been the applicant's case that there existed no authority, he should have alleged it in the affidavit and given an opportunity to the opposite party to contest the allegation. He simply pleaded in his application that his detention contravened the provisions of Article 21 without stating the facts constituting the contravention.

5. Sri S.C. Khare contended that the applicant was not produced before a Magistrate within 24 hours of his arrest within the meaning of Article 22. His argument was that Sri A.H. Drummond went to the spot of arrest of the applicant in his capacity of an executive officer (probably to see that there was no disturbance of public order) and not to exercise any judicial or magisterial functions such as of granting a remand and authorising the detention of an arrested person in custody.

It is true that Sri A.H. Drummond and the Sub-Divisional Magistrate, Kaimganj, closely followed the Station Officer of Farrukhabad when he proceeded to arrest the applicant and arrived at the place of arrest within a few minutes of the arrest. They might have gone there for the purpose of seeing that the arrest did not result in any disorder. They might have gone there to exercise their executive authority. But it cannot be disputed that they had also magisterial powers and were not prevented from exercising them if an occasion arose for the same, merely because they had gone to the place primarily for the purpose of exercising executive powers. There were absolutely no restrictions upon the exercise of magisterial powers by Sri A.H. Drummond and when the Station Officer, Farrukhabad, produced the arrested applicant before him, he was fully competent to authorise his detention in custody within the meaning of Article 22.

Swami Hariharanand Saraswati vs. *The Jailor I/C, District Jail, Banaras*, AIR 1954 All. 601(A) on which Sri Khare relies does not support his contention at all. There the Swami was arrested by a Magistrate inasmuch as he was taken into custody by the police under his orders and under his direct supervision, and was produced before the same Magistrate who remanded him to custody; and it was held that he should have been produced before another Magistrate. A person can be arrested not only by a police officer, but also by a Magistrate. If he is arrested by a police officer, he must be produced before the nearest Magistrate within 24 hours. If he is arrested by a Magistrate, then also he must be produced within 24 hours before the nearest Magistrate, that is, before another Magistrate.

There is nothing to suggest that Article 22(2) will not apply if the arrest is made by a Magistrate. Since it must apply also to an arrest by a Magistrate, the arresting Magistrate must produce him before the nearest Magistrate. He cannot refuse to produce him before another Magistrate by saying that he has produced him before himself as a Magistrate. This argument would amount to not applying the provision to an arrest by a Magistrate. If a person arrested by a Magistrate is not required to be produced before another Magistrate by reason of the fact that the person arresting him is himself a Magistrate, it would mean that the arresting Magistrate has to do nothing after arresting him, in other words, that he is not bound by Article 22(2). The Magistrate who arrested the Swami was, therefore, bound by Article 22(2) to produce him before the nearest Magistrate, that is, before another Magistrate.

In the present case, the arrest was not made by Sri A. H. Drummond, nor was it made under his orders or supervision. It was the Station Officer, Farrukhabad, who had arrested him on his own authority, and he could be produced before Sri A. H. Drummond who, being at the spot, was the nearest Magistrate. Therefore, full compliance with the provision of Article 22(2) was done.

6. Now, I come to the main question whether the U.P. Special Powers Act is inconsistent with Article 19(1)(a) of the Constitution which is:

> "All citizens shall have the right to freedom of speech and expression."

It is laid down in Clause (2) that the above provision cannot affect the operation of any existing law, insofar as it imposes

> "reasonable restrictions on the exercise of the right in the interests of the security of the State, public order, decency and morality, or in relation to contempt of Court, defamation or incitement to an offence."

Article 13 lays down that all laws in force immediately before the commencement of this Constitution, insofar as they are inconsistent with the provision of Part III (which includes Article 19) shall, to the extent of such inconsistency, be void. The following questions arise:

> "(1) What is the meaning of "freedom of speech", whether it means freedom limited only by the expressed limitations or freedom limited in addition by unexpressed limitations?
> (2) Whether the impugned Act is inconsistent with, or restricts the applicant's right to, freedom of speech and expression?
> (3) If so, is the restriction on the exercise of his right in the interests of the security of the State etc.? and
> (4) Is the restriction reasonable?"

7. Before I deal with the above questions, I shall dispose of a preliminary objection raised by the learned Advocate General. He argued that there arises no question of the freedoms enumerated in Article 19 in respect of a citizen who has been deprived of his total freedom by being detained in custody either for punitive or for preventive purposes. The argument is based on a misapprehension of what was decided by the Supreme Court in *A. K. Gopalan* vs. *State of Madras*, AIR 1950 SC 27(B), on which he exclusively relies, and on a misunderstanding of the applicant's grievance. A. K. Gopalan was detained by an order passed under Section 3, Preventive Detention Act, 1950, by the Madras Government on the ground that it was necessary to detain him with a view to preventing him from acting in a

manner prejudicial to the security of the State or the maintenance of public order. He applied for a writ of 'Habeas Corpus' against his detention, contending that the Preventive Detention Act contravenes the provisions of Article 19. In the words of Kama C. J.:

> "As the preventive detention order results in the detention of the applicant in a cell it was contended on his behalf that the rights specified in Article 19(1)(a), (b), (c), (d), (e) and (g) have been infringed. It was argued that because of his detention he cannot have a free right to speech as and where he desired and the same argument was urged in respect of the rest of the rights mentioned in Sub-clause (b), (c), (d), (e), and (g). Although this argument is advanced in a case which deals with preventive detention, if correct, it should be applicable in the case of punitive detention also to any one sentenced to a term of imprisonment under the relevant section of the Indian Penal Code."

That argument was repelled by the Supreme Court. Kama, C. J., observed at p. 35;

> "... the legislation to be examined must be directly in respect of one of the rights mentioned in the Sub-clauses. If there is a legislation directly attempting to control a citizen's freedom of speech or expression, or his right to assemble peaceably and without arms, etc., the question whether that legislation is saved by the relevant saving clause of article 19 will arise. If, however, the legislation is not directly in respect of any of these subjects, but as a result of the operation of other legislation, for instance, for punitive or preventive detention, his right under any of these Sub-clauses is abridged, the question of the application of Article 19 does not arise. The true approach is only to consider the directness of the legislation and not what will be the result of the detention otherwise valid, on the mode of the

> detenu's life."

At p. 36 the learned Chief Justice observed:

> "Reading Article 19 as a whole, therefore, it seems to me that that it has no application to a legislation dealing with preventive or punitive detention as its direct object."

Patanjali Sastri, J., observed at p. 70 that:

> "...Article 19 guarantees to the citizens the enjoyment of certain civil liberties while they are free."

By reason of the preventive detention A. K. Gopalan might have been prevented from exercising the rights enumerated in Article 19(1), but in the words of Mukerjea, J., at p. 96:

> "... this would not make the law providing for preventive detention a legislation taking away or abridging the rights under Article 19(1)(g) of the Constitution...."

When the learned Judge stated at p. 93 that:

> "On the other hand, Articles 20, 21 and 22 are primarily concerned with penal enactments or other laws under which personal safety or liberty of persons could be taken away in the interests of the society and they set down the limits within which the State control should be exercised."

and at p. 94 that they

> "embody the entire protection guaranteed by the Constitution in relation to deprivation of life and personal liberty both with regard to substantive as well as to procedural law",

be only meant that the validity of a penal enactment not directly infringing the rights enumerated in Article 19 depends upon the provisions of Articles 20, 21 and 22. If the penal enactment does not directly infringes the rights but an infringement arises incidentally out of an action taken under it, its validity is not affected thereby. The Preventive Detention Act, 1950, does not directly infringe the rights mentioned in Article 19 and is not inconsistent with it. If on account of an action taken under it (e.g. detention under Section 3) a person is deprived of certain freedom, that is only an incidental effect of the working of the Act and the Act cannot be said to be inconsistent with Article 19. The quintessence of the decision in the case is that arresting a person, whether for doing something or for preventing him from doing something, is not infringing any of the rights conferred by Article 19(1).

The Constitution makes a distinction between the right of personal liberty and the right of freedom of speech, expression, trade, forming association, interstate movement, acquiring property etc. Only the former is infringed by confinement or detention which is nothing but confining within four walls and not allowing to go out without permission. This is certainly a restriction on movements, but it does not infringe the rights mentioned in Article 19(1)(d), which is the right of moving freely from one State to another. Depriving a person of his personal liberty (by arrest) does not deprive him of the rights conferred by Article 19(1), which in theory, he can still exercise. If he cannot utter some words or cannot hold certain property or cannot practise a profession while he is in confinement, it is the result not of the confinement but of the prison regulations. The prison regulations may be said to prejudice his rights but not the confinement. Therefore A. K. Gopalan's grievance that on account of his detention he was deprived of the rights enumerated in Article 19 was without substance.

The present case is different from *A. K. Gopalan's case (B)*. The applicant's contention is that the Special Powers Act itself infringes the freedom of speech and expression; he complains of the arrest on the ground that the Act under which he was arrested is unconstitutional and not on the ground of any consequences arising out of his detention. He could have complained about the unconstitutionally of the Act even if he had not been arrested, or had been released on bail. A. K.

Gopalan was not detained by way of punishment for any speech made by him; he was detained in order that he might not act prejudicially to the public safety and the maintenance of public order. If a person is punished for a certain speech, it means that the freedom of speech is directly abridged; but the same cannot be said if he is detained so that he may not speak in a certain manner.

In *Ram Singh* v. *State of Delhi*, AIR 1951 SC 270(C), the decision in *A. K. Gopalan's case (B)* was followed and the Act was held constitutional, even though it allowed Ram Singh's detention with the express object of preventing him from making certain speeches. Section 3 may contemplate that a person is to be detained so that he may not make certain speeches, still it cannot be said to be a provision directly affecting the freedom of speech and consequently inconsistent with Article 19(1). I find that there is no reason, and no authority, for saying that the bare fact that an action taken under a certain enactment results in a person's being deprived of his personal liberty, prevents him from challenging the constitutionality of the provision on the ground of its being inconsistent with Article 19.

8. There is an observation in AIR 1954 All. 601(A), that:

> "the true position in regard to the scope and nature of a petition of *Habeas Corpus* excludes the possibility of a challenge in regard to the constitutionality of an enactment. It is clear that the petitioners can challenge the validity of the impugned Act in proceedings which have been initiated under the Act against them. They have, therefore, another and a more appropriate remedy open to them for that purpose."

I, think it was only a dictum by way of obiter. The Swarn's application for *Habeas Corpus* was none the less allowed. With great respect to my learned brothers I do not think that the law prohibits the constitutionality of an Act being challenged in a 'Habeas Corpus' proceeding. The applicant complains against his arrest and not against conviction, and the writ of *Habeas Corpus* is the only remedy available to him. He can undoubtedly challenge the constitutionality of the Special Powers Act during his argument at the end of his trial, but that must necessarily take, time. If the Act is unconstitutional, he could not be arrested by the police without a warrant and he must not be permitted to remain in jail even for one moment and he has a right to be released instantaneously. Therefore, he cannot be told to await the result of his trial. Article 21 guarantees that he shall not be deprived of his personal liberty except according to procedure established by law. This guarantee is broken the moment he is arrested for doing an act that is made penal by a Statute which is unconstitutional, and this Court has, not only the power, but also the duty to issue a writ of *Habeas Corpus* to enforce his right to personal liberty. The function of a writ of*Habeas Corpus* does not extend beyond an enquiry into the jurisdiction of the Court by which the warrant of arrest was issued and the validity of the warrant upon its face. Jurisdiction is the power to hear and determine the subject-matter in controversy between the parties to a suit. But proceedings under an unconstitutional Act are absolutely void and the Act, being void, has no effect to confer jurisdiction. An unconstitutional law is no law and an offence created by it is not a crime. If a Court tries a person for an act which is made penal by a void Act, it transcends its jurisdiction and he is entitled to a discharge just the same as if the non-jurisdiction of the Court were apparent in any other manner; see *Bailey on Habeas Corpus*, Vol. I, paragraphs 30, 31 and 37. Mere error in judgment or proceedings constitutes no ground for the issue of a writ of 'Habeas Corpus'. *In Ex Parte Siebold*, (1879) 25 Law Ed 717(D), it was laid down that the only ground on which relief can be given to a prisoner on 'Habeas Corpus' is the want of jurisdiction over the person, or the cause, or some other matter rendering the proceedings void, and that if the validity of a judgment is assailed on the ground that the Act under which the applicant was charged was unconstitutional, it affects the foundation of the whole proceeding, and the conviction is not only merely erroneous but illegal and void and cannot be a legal cause for imprisonment. If no appeal lies the judgment may be final, but

> "personal liberty is of so great moment in the eye of the law that the judgment of an inferior court affecting it is not deemed so conclusive but that, as we have seen, the question of the court's authority to try and imprison the party may be reviewed on 'Habeas Corpus' by a superior court." (Per Bradley J. at p. 719 of Law Ed.)

Miller J. stated in *Ex. Parte Yarbrough*, (1883) 28 Law Ed. 274 at p. 275(E),

> "If the law which defines the offence and prescribes its punishment is void, the court was without jurisdiction and the prisoners must be discharged."

In *Ex Parte Nielsen*, (1888) 33 Law Ed. 118(F), it was stated by Bradley, that it is firmly established that if the law under which the proceedings are taken is unconstitutional, the court has no Jurisdiction to render a judgment and that if it still renders one, it is void and can be questioned collaterally in 'Habeas Corpus' proceedings. It is stated in *Corpus Juris Secundum*, Vol. 39 "Habeas Corpus", paragraph 18 that:

> "The unconstitutionality of a statute or ordinance under which a person is detained generally is ground for relief on 'Habeas Corpus'."

If relief can be given on 'Habeas Corpus' even after conviction and imprisonment it can certainly be given during the pendency of the case. Then even the question of going up in appeal will not arise. The British Parliament being supreme, an Act of Parliament cannot be challenged as unconstitutional; so there should not arise any occasion for challenging the constitutionality of an Act on a 'Habeas Corpus' application in England. But there also the law is that:

> "If it appears clearly that the act for which the party is committed is no crime...the Court discharges him."

Upon the return to the writ of 'Habeas Corpus'; see *Halsbury's Laws of England*, 2nd Edn., Vol. 9, Section 1215. I have not come across any authority stating that a *Habeas Corpus* application cannot be on the ground of invalidity of an Act. It is, therefore, not correct to say that the scope and nature of a petition of *Habeas Corpus* excludes the possibility of a challenge in regard to the constitutionality of an Act. In the end I should mention that the learned Advocate General did not plead that this Court had no jurisdiction to enter into the question of the constitutionality of the Act in these proceedings.

9. Every supply of canal water is deemed to be given at the rates and subject to the conditions prescribed by the rules made by the State Government, (see Section 31, Northern India Canal and Drainage Act, (1873)). If any sum lawfully due under the provisions of the Act remains unpaid after the date on which it becomes due, it can be recovered by the Collector from the person as if it were arrears of land revenue under Section 45. Section 70 is the only section dealing with the offences under the Act. It punishes certain acts such as damaging or obstructing canals, interfering with the supply of water, fouling water of a canal and destroying a level mark or water gate, etc., but not the non-payment of any sum due under the Act or inciting its non-payment.

Violation of a rule made under the Act, for breach whereof a penalty may be incurred, is also an offence, the non-payment of a sum due under the Act or inciting its non-payment does not violate any rule made under the Act for breach whereof a penalty may be incurred. No penalty is incurred for not paying the sum due under the Act on the date on which it falls due; if it is not paid the Collector can recover it but the defaulter is not subject to any penalty. Therefore, not paying any sum due under the Act, or instigating its nonpayment, is not an offence under the Northern India Canal and Drainage Act. It is not an offence under any other enactment also.

10. The U.P. Special Powers Act was enacted in 1932 in order "to make provision against and to take powers to deal with instigation to the illegal refusal of the payment of certain liabilities" (vide the preamble). Originally it was to remain in force for one year, but the period was extended and ultimately in 1940 it was made permanent. The provisions of the Act were to come into force in those districts to which the Act was extended by a notification in the State Gazette. Between April and June, 1954 the provisions of the Act were extended to 33 districts, including the Farrukhabad district. Section 3 of the Act is as follows:

> "Whoever by words either spoken or written or by signs or by visible representations or otherwise instigates expressly or by implication, any person or class of persons not to pay or to defer payment of any liability, shall be punishable with imprisonment which may extend to six months, or with fine, extending to Rs. 250/-, or with both."

The word "liability" is defined in Section 2 to mean—

(1) land revenue,
(2) any sum recoverable as arrears of land revenue,
(3) any tax, rate, cess or other due or amount payable to government,
(4) as above, payable to any local authority,
(5) rent of agricultural land,
(6) anything recoverable as arrears of, or
(7) along with rent of agricultural land.

We are not concerned with any other provisions of the Act. Section 3 punishes several acts. It punishes certain words either spoken or written. It punishes certain signs. It punishes certain representations. It punishes instigation of nonpayment of liability to one person. It punishes instigation of non-payment of liability to a class of persons. It punishes instigation of deferment of payment. It punishes as many as 40 different acts. When one has regard to the fact that "liability" comprises seven different kinds of dues, it follows that in all 280 different acts are punishable under Section 3; in other words that the section contains as many as 280 provisions each punishing an act. All these provisions are separate from one another. For the sake of convenience they have been put together in one section, but each could have formed a separate section. If any provision is unconstitutional, it can be ignored, as if it did not exist, without affecting the enforcement of the others. If good and bad provisions are joined together by using the word "and" or "or", and the enforcement of the good provision is not made dependent on the enforcement of the bad one, i.e., the good provision can be enforced even if the bad one cannot be, or had not existed, then the two provisions are severable and the good one will be upheld as valid and given effect to. On the other hand, if there is one provision (as distinct from several joined together) and it hits valid objects as well as invalid ones which cannot be separated without altering the language (which is beyond the jurisdiction of courts) and is capable of being used for a legal purpose as well as for an illegal one, it is invalid and cannot be allowed to be used even for the legal purpose. In *Herndon* vs. *Lowry*, (1936) 301 US 242 at p. 259 (G), Roberts J. said—

> "Where a statute is so vague and uncertain as to make criminal an utterance or an act which may be innocently said or done with no intent to induce resort to violence or on the other hand may be said or done with a purpose violently to subvert government, a conviction under such a law cannot be sustained."

Similar view was expressed in *Stromberg* vs. *California*, (1930) 283 US 359 at p. 389 (H), and *Thornhill* vs. *State of Alabama*, (1939) 310 US 88 at p. 97 (I). In *Romesh Thapar* vs. *State of Madras*, AIR 1950 SC 124, at p. 129 (J), it was stated:

> "Where a law purports to authorise the imposition of

> restrictions on a fundamental right in language wide enough to cover restrictions both within and without the limits of constitutionally permissible legislative action affecting such right, it is not possible to uphold it even so far as it may be applied within the constitutional limits, as it is not severable. So long as the possibility of its being applied for purposes not sanctioned by the Constitution cannot be ruled out, it must be held to be wholly unconstitutional and void."

Mahajan J. (now C.J.) observed in the case of *Chintaman Rao* vs. *State of Madhya Pradesh*, AIR 1951 SC 118, at p. 120 (K):

> "The law ... cannot be held valid because the language employed is wide enough to cover restrictions both within and without the limits of constitutionally permissible legislative action affecting the right."

The provision in Section 3 of the Act that instigating a class of persons by spoken words not to pay to Government any sum recoverable as an arrear of land revenue is an offence is distinct and severable from the other provisions in the same section punishing other acts. Its validity does not depend upon the validity of the other provisions. It is not of such a nature as to be valid if applied for one purpose and invalid if applied for another purpose. It does not matter if the applicant instigated the non-payment of only the excess over the irrigation dues that were previously payable by the cultivators. We are not concerned with what the applicant did. Our concern is with the question whether the particular provision is against the Constitution or not. There is nothing to suggest that the disturbance of public order depends upon the nature of the liability, the non-payment of which is instigated. As regards that question, if public order is likely to be disturbed by instigation of non-payment of 'takavi', it is likely to be disturbed by instigation of non-payment of the excess of the irrigation dues.

Consequently the unconstitutionality of a provision

punishing one act will not affect the constitutionality of another provision punishing another act. The punishment of one act does not depend upon the punishment of another act. The applicant is being prosecuted for the act of expressly instigating by spoken words a class of persons not to pay money recoverable as arrears of land revenue. That act is punishable under Section 3. What we have to sec is whether the particular provision of Section 3 penalising that act is inconsistent with Article 19(1)(a) or not; we are not concerned with the other provisions of the section. Even if they are consistent with Article 19(1)(a), the particular provision penalising the act done by the applicant may be inconsistent and consequently void; on the other hand, the other provisions may be inconsistent and still the particular provision penalising the act may be consistent and consequently be upheld as constitutional. If there is any illegality in any of the provisions penalising an act, it is not a contagious illegality and the other provisions do not become infected by it merely on account of their juxtaposition in the same section or being contained in the same Act.

11. The learned Advocate General vehemently argued that the freedom of speech guaranteed by Article 19 is not absolute and is subject to limitations such as that nobody can incite the breach of a law. He relied upon numerous decisions of the Supreme Court of America such as—*Benjamin Gitlow* vs. *State of New York*, (1924) 268 US 652 (L); (1930) 283 US 359 (II),—*Terminiello* vs. *Chicago*, (1948) 337 US 1 (M) and—*American Communications Asso.* vs. *Douds* (1949) 339 US 382 (N). In (1924) 268 US 652 (L), Sanford J. stated at p. 666:

> "It is a fundamental principle, long established, that the freedom of speech and of the press which is secured by the Constitution does not confer an absolute right to speak or publish, without responsibility, whatever one may choose, or an unrestricted and unbridled license that gives immunity for every possible use of language, and prevents the punishment of those who abuse this freedom. That a state,

> in the exercise of its police power, may punish those who abuse this freedom by utterances inimical to the public welfare, tending to corrupt public morals, incite to crime, or disturb the public peace, is not open to question. A state may punish utterances endangering the foundations of organised government and threatening its overthrow by unlawful means. **** It does not protect publications or teachings which tend to subvert or imperil the government, or to impede or hinder it in the performance of its governmental duties."

In *American Communications Asso.* vs. *Douds*, (N), Vinson C.J. observed at p. 394:

> "Freedom of speech thus does not comprehend the right to speak on any subject at any time."

In the case of *Terminiello*, (M), it was stated by Douglas J. at p. 4;

> "That is why freedom of speech, though not absolute, is nevertheless protected against censorship or punishment, unless shown likely to produce a clear and present danger of a serious substantive evil that rises far above public inconvenience, annoyance, or unrest,"

In the *Selected Essays on Constitutional Law,* Vol. 2, at p. 1033 is quoted an observation of Judge Hamersley of Connecticut that:

> "The liberty protected is not the right to perpetrate acts of licentiousness, or any act inconsistent with the peace or safety of the State. Freedom of speech and press does not include the abuse of the power of tongue or pen, any more than freedom of other action includes an injurious use of one's occupation, business, or property."

At p. 1050 it is stated:

> "Judge Hand places outside the limits of free speech one who counsels or advises others to violate existing laws. It is

true, he says, that any discussion designed to show that existing laws are mistaken in means or unjust in policy may result in their violation, but if one stops short of urging upon others that it is their duty or their interest to resist the law, he should not be held to have attempted to cause illegal conduct."

Dicey in his *Law of the Constitution*, 9th edn., p. 579, refers to the *King* vs. *Aldred*, (1909) 22 Cox C. C 1 (O), as containing a summary of the law of seditious libel and quotes the following from the charge of Mr. Justice Coleridge to the Jury:

> "A man may lawfully express his opinion on any public matter, however distasteful, however repugnant to others, if of course he avoids defamatory matter or if he avoids anything that can be characterised either as blasphemous or as an obscene libel. Matters of State, matters of policy, matters even of morals—all these are upon to him. ********* If he makes use of language calculated to advocate or to incite others to public disorders, to wit, rebellions, insurrections, assassinations, outrages, or any physical force or violence of any kind, then whatever his motive, whatever his intentions, there would be evidence on which a jury might, on which I think a jury ought to, decide that he is guilty of a seditious publication."

12. But the case is governed not by the law prevailing in America or England, but by the law contained in our written Constitution. When the First and the Fourteenth Amendments to the American Constitution protect the freedom of speech against interference by the Union and the States, they refer to the freedom of speech as understood at the time of the Amendments and not absolute freedom. Unlike our Constitution, they do not prescribe the limitations on the right of free speech, though no one can have an absolute freedom to say anything he likes at any time or any place. In the interests of the States and the public, there must be some limitations on

the right of free speech. Consequently freedom of speech guaranteed by the Amendments has got to be understood as subject to implied or inherent limitations. Our Constitution, on the other hand, prescribes the limitations expressly, vide Sub-clause (2) of Article 19. When in Sub-clause (2) it is stated how far the freedom of speech can be interfered with, it follows that the freedom guaranteed under Sub-clause (1) is absolute freedom and that it is not subject to any limitations that are not to be found in Sub-clause (2).

The enquiry before us is simply whether the alleged restriction on the freedom of speech is covered by Sub-clause (2) of Article 19 or not. In AIR 1950 SC 27(B), Kania C.J. uttered a warning against reading Article 19 with a pre-conceived notion and observed at p. 35 that:

> "It clearly means that the legislation to be examined must be directly in respect of one of the rights mentioned in the Sub-clauses."

In the same case Patanjali Sastri J. observed at p. 69:

> "Liberty has, therefore, to be limited in order to be effectively possessed. Accordingly, Article 19, while guaranteeing some of the most valued phases or elements of liberty to every citizen as civil rights, provides for their regulation for the common good by the State imposing certain 'restrictions' on their exercise."

Das J. pointed out at p. 109 that:

> "....none of the seven rights enumerated in Clause (1) is an absolute right, for each of these rights is liable to be curtailed by laws made or to be made by the State to the extent mentioned in the several Clauses (2) to (6) of that Article."

These observations make it clear that whatever limitations exist on the freedom of speech in this country are those mentioned in Sub-clause (2) and no other. The limitations that are supposed to be inherent in the idea of freedom of speech guaranteed by the American Constitution are specifically expressed in our Constitution. Most of the limitations mentioned in the American decisions are to be found in Sub-clause 2. If there were any doubt on the point, it is removed by the latest amendment to Sub-clause (2), by which the words "incitement to an offence" have been added. With reference to the First Amendment. Black J. stated in *Bridges* vs. *California*, (1941) 86 Law Ed. 192 at p. 203 (P) that:

> "It must be taken as a command of the broadest scope that explicit language, read in the context of a liberty-loving society, will allow."

With reference to Article 19(1), I would say that it must be taken as a command of the broadest scope that explicit language, read in the context of Sub-clause (2), will allow.

13. I am unable to agree with the learned Advocate General that S. 3, Special Powers Act, does not infringe the guarantee of the freedom of speech. He argued that the preamble of the Act shows that it was not designed to put any restriction on the freedom of speech. What the preamble does is really to supply the motive behind the enactment of the Act. The Act prohibits certain speeches by penalising the making of those speeches. Freedom of speech means freedom from subsequent punishment; see *Terminiello* vs. *Chicago*, (M), and (1939) 310 US 88(I). In the latter case Murphy J. observed at p. 102 that:

> "Freedom of speech and of the press guaranteed by the Constitution embraces at the least the liberty to discuss publicly and truthfully all matters of public concern without previous restraint or fear of subsequent punishment."

The Act clearly and expressly infringes the freedom of speech by prohibiting the uttering of certain words. The preamble only supplies the reason or intention behind the prohibition. When an Act is impugned on the ground that it runs foul of the guarantee of free speech, the Court is only concerned with the question whether it does so or not; it is not concerned with the reason why it does so (unless the case is sought to be brought within the prescribed limitations).

The object behind the Act might have been to facilitate the collection of certain dues by prohibiting the encitement of illegal refusal to pay them, but there is no difference between enacting a law to collect dues by limiting the freedom of speech and enacting a law to restrict a speech so that Government dues may be collected. A legislature cannot enact a law infringing the freedom of speech, whether the infringement is its primary object or is a subsidiary object or is an unintended effect. No matter in what enactment, and for what purpose, the restriction on the freedom of speech is imposed, it is barred unless covered by Sub-clause 2. There can be no more direct infringement of the right of free speech than the prosecution for the making of a certain speech. The enactment of the Act is as direct an infringement of the constitutional guarantee of free speech as is possible.

There is absolutely nothing in the decision of the case of *A. K. Gopalan*, (B), that would suggest that the impugned Act does not contravene Article 19(1)(a). The Preventive Detention Act, 1950, does not contravene that provision, but it does not follow that the Special Powers Act also does not. There are important distinctions between the two Acts, one is preventive and does not directly refer to speech or expression, whereas the other is punitive and directly prohibits on pain of penalty the making of certain speeches. Undoubtedly the Word "act" in Section 3, Preventive Detention Act, includes making a speech, and since it makes a person liable to be detained so that he might not make a prejudicial speech, it can be argued that it infringes the guarantee of free speech.

Preventive detention for reasons connected with the security of the State or the maintenance of public order is permissible, vide 7th Schedule, List III, Entry 3. If a Preventive Detention Act directly infringes the guarantee of free speech, but was enacted for either of the above objects, it would be saved by Clause (2) of Article 19. A. K. Gopalan, therefore, could not, and did not, challenge the validity of Preventive Detention Act on the ground that it directly infringed his freedom of speech by detaining him so that he could not speak in a certain manner. The Supreme Court upheld it but not on the ground that taking action (such as of detention) against a person in order to prevent him from making a certain speech does not directly infringes his right of free speech.

Moreover, punishing a person for making a speech may not be same as taking action in order to prevent his doing so; the Supreme Court did not express any opinion on this matter and I would not hazard any. The decision in *A. K. Gopalan's case (B)* is, therefore, no authority for saying that Section 3, Special Powers Act, is not inconsistent with Article 19(1)(a). The reasons for which the Preventive Detention Act was upheld do not apply in the present case.

I have already pointed out that the contention of A. K. Gopalan was that he was deprived of his freedom of speech not by any provision of the Preventive Detention Act, but by being detained in exercise of the powers conferred by it. The reply was that if the detention resulted in his being deprived of the freedom of speech, it was an indirect or incidental effect; the Preventive Detention Act by itself did not cause that deprivation of the freedoms guaranteed by Article 19(1)(a). If any deprivation of the freedoms flows from the detention, the Constitution itself permits it through Schedule 7, List III, Entry 3, and none can make a complaint about it. The applicant's complaint on the other hand, is that the Act itself prohibits his making certain speeches. He complains about his arrest because of its being the result of the operation of the impugned Act and not because of any consequences arising out of the arrest.

In *A. K. Gopalan's case (B)* the detention was the cause and the deprivation of the freedom the result and cause of grievance. In the instant case, the impugned Act is the cause of the deprivation of the freedom and grievance of the applicant and the arrest is merely the effect, and, for the purposes of the application, of no consequence at all. I repeat that the impugned

Act could have been challenged even if the punishment provided under Section 3 were mere admonition and the offender were not liable to be arrested. This disposes of the second question.

14. The learned Advocate General contended that the impugned Act imposes the restrictions on the exercise of the right of free speech in the interests of the security of the State as well as of public order. I did not understand him to argue that it is a law in relation to incitement to an offence. Undoubtedly he vehemently argued that the freedom of speech does not permit an incitement to break a law. This argument must be rejected. Article 19(2) does not in so many words save a law in relation to incitement to break a law. "Incitement to break a law" is not same as "incitement to an offence", because every breach of a law does not amount to an offence. I have shown that non-payment of the irrigation dues is not an offence under the Northern India Canal and Drainage Act; I doubt if it is even a breach of any provision in the Act. That Act imposes only a evil liability and provides the means for getting the liability discharged. If a cultivator does not pay the irrigation dues, he commits no greater breach of law than is committed by a person who does not fulfil a contract made by him.

15. I do not consider that the impugned provision in the Special Powers Act imposes the restrictions in the interests of the security of the State. The security of the State is not affected merely by an incitement to cultivators not to pay the irrigation dues. If the irrigation dues are not paid, the State would lose some income; but that can hardly be said to affect the security of the State. The security of the State depends upon factors other than its consolidated funds. Undoubtedly money has to be spent in providing for the security of the State, but the words "in the interests of the security of the State cannot be understood to mean "in the interests of the consolidated fund of the State". The non-payment of irrigation dues itself does not affect the security of the State, incitement to the non-payment still less affects it. Incitement to the non-payment not only does not always result in the

non-payment but also is not contemplated by the Northern India Canal and Drainage Act itself to deprive the Government of the dues because the Government have been conferred ample powers to realise them forcibly. In AIR 1950 SC 124 (J), Patanjali Sastri J. stated at p. 128:

> "The differentiation is also noticeable in Entry 3 of List III (Concurrent List) of the Seventh Schedule, which refers to the 'security of a State' and "maintenance of public order" as distinct subjects of legislation. The Constitution thus requires a line to be drawn in the field of public order or tranquillity marking off, may be, roughly, the boundary between those serious and aggravated forms of public disorder which are calculated to endanger the security of the State and the relatively minor breaches of the peace of a purely local significance, treating for this purpose differences in degree as if they were differences in kind."

This means that the security of the State is endangered only by a serious and aggravated form of public disorder as distinguished from minor breaches of the peace which endanger only public order. Incitement to non-payment of irrigation dues is not such a serious and aggravated form of public disorder as is likely to endanger the security of the State.

16. "Public order" is not defined anywhere. Chapter VIII of the Indian Penal Code bears the heading "Offences Against The Public Tranquillity" and contains Sections 141 to 160 which punish offences of unlawful assembly and affray. Stephen divides all offences against public tranquillity of the State under two heads, one of those offences in which a normal tranquillity of a civilized society is disturbed either by actual force or at least by the show and threat of it and the other of those in which no actual force is either employed or displayed but in which steps are taken tending to cause it; see *History of the Criminal Law of England* by Stephen, Vol. II, page 243.

Under the first head come the offences of treason, unlawful assemblies, levying of war and rebellions and under the second head come formation of secret societies, seditious conspiracies and libel. In his *Commentaries on the Laws of England*, 21st Edn. 4th Volume, he includes in crimes against public order the offences of treason, official secrets, counterfeit coins, unlawful meetings, affray, forcible criminal trespass, sedition and defamation. See also *Stephen's Digest of the Criminal Law*, Part II, dealing with offences against public order; in that part are included offences of treason, mutiny, disclosure of official secrets, unlawful assembly, affray, conspiracy and libel. If any inference is to be drawn from this inclusion of certain offences in the class of offences against public order, it is that the non-payment of Government dues and its incitement are not offences against public order and that a prohibition of the incitement to the non-payment has nothing to do with the maintenance of public order.

List II of the Seventh Schedule of the Constitution includes "public order" in entry 1 and prevention of animal diseases and cattle trespass, irrigation and canals, protection of wild animals and birds, weights and measures, inns, theatres, betting and gambling, land revenue, taxes, affray and duty etc. in other entries. If public order covered every offence, there was no necessity of making separate provisions for many of the matters mentioned above. If the collection of land revenue, taxes and irrigation dues had any direct connection with the maintenance of public order, no separate provision would have been made for land revenue, etc.

In list II of the Seventh Schedule of the Government of India Act, 1935, entry I was "public order, preventive detention for reasons connected with the maintenance of public order". in *Basudeva* vs. Rex, AIR 1949 All 513 (FB)(Q), it was held by a Full Bench of this Court that the U.P. Prevention of Black-Marketing (Temporary Powers) Act (22 of 1948) was 'ultra vires' the State Legislature because preventive detention for the purpose of preventing black-marketing is not preventive detention for reasons connected with the maintenance of public order. In other words, the offence of black-marketing was held to be not an offence against public order. It was observed by Wall Ullah, A. C. J., at p. 523 that:

> "the expression 'for reasons connected with' must mean a real and genuine connection and not the fanciful, or highly problematic, connection between the maintenance of public order on the one hand and the subject of legislation, viz., black-marketing,..."

The decision was confirmed by the Federal Court in *Rex* vs. *Basudeva,* AIR 1950(FC) 67(R). Patanjali Sastri J., observing at p. 69, that:

> "The connection contemplated must, in our view, be real and proximate, not far-fetched or problematical."

Under the Bihar Maintenance of Public Order Act (5 of 1947) a person can be detained with a view to preventing him from acting in any manner prejudicial to the maintenance of the public order. In *Lalu Gope* vs. *The King,* AIR 1949 Pat 299(S), it was decided that committing thefts in running goods trains was not acting prejudicially to the maintenance of public order. The words "for reasons connected with the maintenance of public order" in List II of the Seventh Schedule of the Government of India Act, 1935, entry I, were considered by the Federal Court in *Machindar Shivaji* vs. *The King,* AIR 1950 FC 129(T), where the question was about the validity of the C. P. and Berar Safety Act of 1948 made on the authority of that entry.

Patanjali Sastry J. observed that the question before them was whether the Act was made "with a view to prevent only such act or acts as are likely to endanger the public peace." Thus impliedly he interpreted "maintenance public order" as maintenance of public peace. An offence or a breach of law which has no effect at all on the public peace or tranquillity cannot be taken to be an offence endangering public order. A law punishing such an offence cannot be taken to be a law in the interests of maintenance of public order.

The Madras Government imposed a ban upon the entry

into, or the circulation in, the State of Madras of a certain newspaper published in Bombay in exercise of the powers conferred by the Madras Maintenance of Public Order Act, 1949. The Act was passed by the State on the authority of entry 1 of List III of the Seventh Schedule of the Government of India Act, 1935. The words "public order" in that entry were interpreted by the Supreme Court in the case of *Romesh Thapar* vs. *State of Madras (J)*, at p. 127, in the following words:

> "Now 'public order' is an expression of wide connotation and signifies that state of tranquillity which prevails among the members of a political society as a result of the internal regulations enforced by the Government which they have established."

Sri S.C. Khare referred us to *Brij Bhusan* vs. *State of Delhi*, AIR 1950 SC 129(U), but we find that it is of no assistance to us. It was held in that case that a provision in an enactment requiring pre-censorship was not within the provision of the unamended Clause (2) of Article 19 which did not use the words "maintenance of public order."

17. The words "in the interests of public order" mean "for maintenance of public order". The interests of public order lie only if it is maintained. A restriction can be imposed in the interest of public order, if in the event of its not being imposed disturbance of public order is apprehended. It is not necessary that the apprehension be immediate or present or that the disturbance of public order be substantial. Whatever be the nature of gravity of the disturbance of public order, if there is an apprehension of it, a restriction can be imposed in order to remove the apprehension. All that is required is that the State must apprehend disturbance if no restriction is imposed.

The precise question before us is whether the State feared that public order might be disturbed, if the right of a person to instigate a class of persons not to pay the dues recoverable by the State as arrears of land revenue were not restricted. There might have been in 1932 an apprehension of a serious disturbance of public order if the right of free speech were not restricted; but it does not necessarily follow that the fear existed in January 1950 and the necessity for imposition of the restriction continued. There was no constitutional guarantee in 1932 as it exists now and the validity of the Act could not have been challenged prior to 1932 on the ground on which it is challenged before us. By virtue of Article 13, as soon as the Constitution was enforced, the question arose whether the Act continued to be in force or had become void.

The Act will be held to be continuing in force after the Constitution only if the restriction imposed by Section 3 of it was at that time in the interests of public order. The bare fact that it was in the interests of public order in 1932 would not suffice to keep it alive after the Constitution. Therefore, in January 1950 it must have been apprehended by the State that public order would be disturbed if the right to instigate the non-payment of certain dues were not restricted, before it could be held to remain in force. If it was not in the interests of public order to impose any restriction then, the Act automatically became void, and could not be revived subsequently on the recurrence of the apprehension. It will be irrelevant, therefore, to consider the conditions prevailing in 1954 and the fact that a political party has embarked upon an agitation against the payment of certain Government dues. We know that conditions were peaceful in January 1950 and there was no apprehension of disturbance of public order if the right to instigate the non-payment of certain Government dues was not restricted.

The Act was not in force in the Farrukhabad district in January 1950; it was enforced in that district in 1954. Still it was a law in force within the meaning of Article 13; see the definition in Sub-clause (3)(b). In considering Article 13, the Court is merely concerned with the provision that is impugned, and not with the question in what areas it was in force. Even if it was not enforced in any area, it could become void. If Section 3 was not enforced anywhere in January 1950, it only shows that there was no necessity for it, i.e., that restricting the right to instigate the non-payment was not in the interests of public order then.

18. The words "for reasons connected with the maintenance of public order" were considered by the Federal Court in *Rex* vs. *Basudeva (R)*. Black-marketing in essential commodities may at times lead to a disturbance of public order, but so also may the rash driving of a car or the sale of adulterated food-stuff. But, observed Patanjali Sastry J. at p. 69,

> "Activities such as these are so remote in the chain of relation to the maintenance of public order that preventive detention on account of them cannot, in our opinion; fall within the purview of Entry I of List II of the Government of India Act, 1935."

The act apprehended must be connected with public order in such a manner that if it is allowed to be done public order might be disturbed; unless there is such a connection, the restriction on the apprehended act cannot be said to be in the interests of public order. The learned Advocate General contended that the words "in the interests of" are more comprehensive than the words "for reasons connected with", and that the decisions interpreting the words "for reasons connected with public order" cannot aid us in interpreting the words "in the interests of public order". I do not think that the latter words convey an idea materially different from the former words. No interest can exist without some connection and it seems to me that if a restriction cannot be said to be for reasons connected with the maintenance of public order, it cannot also be said to be in the interests of public order. The Constitution never contemplated that a freedom granted by it could be infringed on the ground of a remote or problematical contingency; otherwise all freedoms could be liable to be infringed on one excuse or another and the granting of them would be in name only.

19. *Schenek* vs. *United States*, (1918) 249 US 47(V), the

Supreme Court laid down the following test of liability for speech:

> "The question in every case is whether the words used are used in such circumstances and are of such nature as to create a clear and present danger that they will bring about the substantive, evils that Congress has right to prevent."

The test was approved in the case of *Terminiello*, (1948) 93 Law Ed 1131 at p, 1135(M) where Douglas J. observed:

> "There is no room under our Constitution for a more restrictive view. For the alternative would lead to standardization of ideas either by legislatures, Courts, or dominant political or community groups."

In (1941) 86 Law Ed. 192 at p. 203(F), it was stated as:

> "a working principle that the substantive evil must be extremely serious and the degree of imminence extremely high before utterance can be punished."

The necessity for the test arose in these cases because the Legislature had not appraised a particular kind of situation and found a specific danger sufficiently imminent to justify a restriction on a particular kind of utterance; see (1941) 86 Law Ed. 192 at p. 202(P). In (1924) 69 Law Ed. 1138 at p. 1148(L), it was stated that the test

> "was manifestly intended, as shown by the context, to apply only in cases of this class, and has no application to those like the present, where the legislative body itself has previously determined the danger of a substantive evil arising from utterances of a specified character."

In *American Communications Asso*. vs. *Douds (N)*, it was made clear that the words "clear and present danger" do not supply a mechanical test in every case without regard to context. In the instant case the State legislature thought that certain utterances were likely to endanger public order and, therefore, prohibited them. The question that is presented before us is not whether the prohibition fulfils the test of clear and present danger, but whether it is in the interests of public order. The duty of the Court, before which legislative abridgment of the rights is asserted, was stated in the following words by Roberts J. in *Schneider* vs. *Irvington*, (1939) 84 Law Ed. 155, at p. 165 (W)

> "The Courts should be astute to examine the effect of the challenged legislation. Mere legislative preferences or beliefs respecting matters of public convenience may well support regulation directed at other personal activities, but be insufficient to justify such as diminishes the exercise of rights so vital to the maintenance of democratic institutions. And so, as cases arise, the delicate and difficult task falls upon the courts to weigh the circumstances and to appraise the substantiality of the reasons advanced in support of the regulation of the free enjoyment of the rights."

Sir Alfred Denning L.J. in the *Hamlyn Lecture on Freedom of Mind and Conscience, Freedom Under the Law, 1949*, stated at p. 35 that:

> "Every one in the land should be free to think his own thoughts to have his own opinions, and to give voice to them, in public or in private, so long as he does not speak ill of his neighbour; and free also to criticise the Government or any party or group of people, so long as he does not incite anyone to violence."

Even if political agitation, by the passions it arouses or the convictions it engenders, may in fact stimulate men to the violation of law and though it would be a folly to disregard the casual relation between the detestation of existing policies and forcible resistance of the authority which puts them in execution,

> "yet to assimilate agitation, legitimate as such, with direct

> incitement to violent resistance, is to disregard the tolerance of all methods of political agitation which in normal times is a safeguard of free government. The distinction is not a scholastic subterfuge, but a hard bought acquisition in the fight for freedom." (Per Judge Hand in *Masses Pub. Co. v. Patten*. (1917) 244 Fed 535 at p. 540 (X), quoted in *Selected Essays on Constitutional Law*, Vol. 2, page 1050).

Section 3 of the Act does not punish incitement to violence or to resistance by force the recovery of government dues; it punishes incitement to non payment of Government dues, in other words, political agitation against certain Government dues. The applicant told us that when he advocated non-payment of irrigation dues he did not expect any substantial response from the cultivators and that he still advocated the non-payment in order to exert pressure upon Government and to make them change their policy.

> "It is only through free debate and free exchange of ideas that government remains responsive to the will of the people and peaceful change is effected.......... Accordingly a function of free speech under our system of government is to invite dispute. It may indeed best serve its high purpose when it induces a condition of unrest, creates dissatisfaction with conditions as they are, even stirs people to anger." (Per Douglas J. in *Terminiello* vs. *Chicago (M)*, at p. 1134 of Law Ed.).

Holmes and Brandeis JJ. thought that the (greater danger to a democracy lies in the suppression of public discussion and that ideas and doctrines thought harmful or dangerous are best fought with words; see *American Communications Asso*. vs. *Douds (N)*, at p. 395. Finally, I find that maintenance of public order or preservation of public peace was not at all the object for the enactment of the Act. It itself does not purport to have been enacted in the interests of public order; its avowed object was to deal with agitation against payment of certain liabilities.

20. In conclusion I find it difficult to accept the learned Advocate General's contention that Section 3 of the Act imposes restriction on the right of free speech in the interests of public order. Disturbance of public order is not a natural and probable consequence of the instigation to non-payment of dues realisable as arrears of land revenue.

21. The question whether a restriction on the right guaranteed by Article 19(1)(a) is reasonable or not cannot arise when the restriction is not found to be in the interests of public order, etc., or in relation to libel, etc. The restriction under consideration is a prohibition of instigating a class of persons not to pay certain dues realisable as arrears of land revenue. Though it is stated in the preamble of the Act that it was enacted to deal with illegal refusal to pay certain dues, the restriction is on instigation of non-payment of all sums recoverable as land revenue regardless of whether they are legally due or not. A sum may be recoverable as arrears of land revenue even though it is not legally due. Therefore, it cannot be contended that the words "recoverable as arrears of land revenue" mean legally recoverable as such. It may appear unreasonable to prohibit instigation of nonpayment of sums which are illegally demanded from a class of persons. But, if the prohibition is found to be in the interests of public order, it justifies itself. If it is not found to be in the interests of public order, it would fall on that ground alone. No other flaw is discernible in the restriction.

Other objections to the restriction are really on the ground of its being not in the interests of public order and have already been dealt with. A restriction must not be arbitrary or excessive; see *Chintaman Rao* vs. *State of Madhya Pradesh (K)*, If an utterance is likely to disturb the public order, the ordinary remedy is to prohibit it and the prohibition cannot be said to be arbitrary or of an excessive nature. The Act is of a permanent nature, though it might have been enacted to meet a certain emergency. It might not have been in force in every district of the State at the time of its enactment, but it has been in force in a number of districts now. However, these matters have absolutely no relevancy to the question whether the restriction is reasonable or not.

22. I have come to the conclusion that on 26-1-1950 the impugned provision was not in the interest of public order. If it was, nothing has happened since then to make it not in the interest of public order in 1954.

23. I have treated irrigation dues as dues recoverable as arrears of land revenue. They may also be treated as rates due to Government, but it will make no difference to what I have stated above.

24. The application should be allowed.

M.L. Chaturvedi, J.

25. This is a petition for the issue of a writ of 'Habeas Corpus' filed under Article 226 of the Constitution.

26. The petitioner, Dr. Rammanohar Lohia, is the General Secretary of the Praja Socialist Party of India. The Party is, at the present time, advocating the non-payment of irrigation dues which were enhanced a year or two ago under the orders of the Government of the State of Uttar Pradesh. The agitation is against the payment of the enhanced dues only. On 4-7-1954, the petitioner addressed one meeting at Kaimganj in the district of Farrukhabad at 4 p.m., and another at Farrukhabad at 8-30 p.m. In both these meetings, he severely criticised the enhancement of the irrigation dues and also exhorted the audience not to pay the enhanced dues. The Station Officer, Kaimganj, decided to prosecute the petitioner under Section 3, U.P. Special Powers Act, 1932, and he sent a 'chit' to the Station Officer, in Charge police station Kotwali, Farrukhabad, asking the latter to arrest the petitioner for having committed offences under the said section. The Station Officer of Kotwali, Farrukhabad, also decided to prosecute the petitioner under the same section, and the petitioner was arrested at Railway Road, in Farrukhabad, at the house of one Lalla Babu, where the petitioner had been invited to dine. The arrest was made by the Station Officer of Kotwali, Farrukhabad, and he told the petitioner that he was being arrested under Section 3, U.P.

Special Powers Act, which will hereafter be called as the impugned section.

Immediately after the arrest of the petitioner, the City Magistrate of Farrukhabad, Sri A. H. Drummond, accompanied by the Sub-Divisional Magistrate and the Station Officer, Kaimganj, arrived at the place where the petitioner was arrested. The Station Officer of Kotwali, Farrukhabad, in his affidavit, states that he produced the petitioner before the City Magistrate as soon as he arrived on the spot, and the City Magistrate granted a remand of two days. The petitioner was then taken to the district jail of Farrukhabad and lodged there. It is then stated that two cases for making two speeches are pending before Sri P.R. Gupta, Judicial Officer; Fatehgarh, and they were taken up in the Central Jail, Fatehgarh, by the said Officer on 6-7-1954, the petitioner having, in the meantime, been transferred to the Central Jail from the District Jail. The petitioner then applied for time to move the High Court at Allahabad for the transfer of the cases, and the cases were adjourned to 19-7-1954. The present petition was made in this Court on 9-7-1954.

27. The contention of the learned counsel for the petitioner is that Section 3 of the impugned Act is inconsistent with the provisions of Article 19(1)(a) of the Constitution and has, therefore, become void since the date of the coming into force of the Constitution. The argument of the learned counsel is that Section 3 of the impugned Act directly interferes with the freedom of speech guaranteed to the petitioner under Article 19(1)(a) of the Constitution, and the restrictions placed by Section 3 of the impugned Act on this freedom are not justified by the provisions of Article 19(2) of the Constitution, inasmuch as the actions made punishable by the section do not interfere with public order or the security of the State, nor do they amount to an incitement to commit any offence.

It is further urged that, in any case, the restrictions placed by the section are unreasonable. Section 3 of the impugned Act is not thus saved by the provisions of Clause (2) of Article

19 of the Constitution. Another point was also urged at the time of the arguments, though it was not taken in the petition, and that point was that the petitioner's detention was illegal under Article 22, as he was not produced before any Magistrate within a period of 24 hours of his arrest. The learned Advocate General of U.P., who appeared for the State Government, controverted the above points raised by the petitioner's counsel, and further urged that this case was fully covered by the decision of their Lordships of the Supreme Court in the case of AIR 1950 SC 27(B).

28. These are the points that arise for consideration in this petition, but before proceeding to deal with them, a short history of the Act and the relevant provisions contained in Section 3, may be mentioned. The Act was passed in 1932 during the period of the British regime when the non-cooperation movement was in progress. Initially, the Act was to remain in force for one year, but its life was extended from time to time till in the year 1940 the U.P. Legislature deleted Sub-section (3) of Section 1 of the Act, which limited the duration of the Act, with the result that the Act became a permanent enactment as a result of the deletion of the said Sub-section. This was done by Section 2 of U.P. Act 12 of 1940. Only Sections 1 and 2 of the Act were to remain in force all the time, but the remaining sections were to come into force only when the State Government, by notifications in the official Gazette, extended all or any of the remaining provisions to any district or to any part of a district in the Uttar Pradesh.

In April 1954, the State Government applied the provisions of this Act to the districts of Mainpuri and Mirzapur, and in June 1954, it applied them, by means of a notification, to 31 other districts including the district of Farrukhabad. The relevant provisions of the Act, therefore, partake of the nature of an emergency measure to be applied only, and for the period that the State Government thought fit to apply them. Section 2 of the impugned Act donned the word "liability" as meaning

> "land revenue or any sum recoverable as arrears of land revenue or any tax, rate, cess or other due or amount payable to Government or to any local authority, or rent of agricultural land or anything recoverable as arrears of or along with such rent."

The other important section is Section 3, the validity of which is to be determined in this case. It may be quoted in full.

> "3. **'Punishment for instigation to the non-payment of a liability'**: Whoever, by words either spoken or written, or by signs or by visible representations, or otherwise, instigates, expressly or by implication, any person or class of persons not to pay or to defer payment of any liability, and whoever does any act, with intent or knowing it to be likely that any words, signs or visible representations containing such instigation shall thereby be communicated directly or indirectly to any person or class of persons, in any manner whatsoever, shall be punishable with imprisonment which may extend to six months, or with fine, extending to Rs. 250/-, or with both".

Section 4 of the Act permits a person to whom an arrear of liability is due to apply in writing to the Collector to realise it, and the Collector is bound to realise it if he was satisfied that the amount was due. The realisation is to be made as an arrear of land revenue in accordance with the law applicable to the recovery of such arrears. Section 6 provides for punishment for participation in a mock funeral ceremony, and Section 7 gives certain powers to control suspected persons; but we have nothing to do with either Section 6 or Section 7 or the following sections, excepting Section 11, which makes offences under this Act cognizable offences.

29. Rates for supplying water are determined under the rules framed under the provisions of Part V of the Northern India Canal and Drainage Act, 8 of 1873, and Section 45 of this Act provides that any sum, lawfully due under this Part

and certified by the Divisional Canal Officer to be so due, shall be recovered by the Collector from the person liable for the same, as if it were an arrear of land revenue. It is not necessary to refer to any other provision of this Act, because no question has been raised as to the legality or the fixation of the actual rates or their enhancement.

30. I propose first to consider the point raised by the learned Advocate General, which is to the effect that this case is covered by the decision in *Gopalan's case (B)*, already mentioned. The learned Advocate General's argument is that the decision in *Gopalan's case (B)*, is that if a person is deprived of his liberty by being confined to jail under some provision of law, then the validity of that provision is not to be considered with reference to the provisions of Article 19 of the Constitution at all, and the only relevant provisions in such cases are those mentioned in Articles 20, 21 and 22 of the Constitution. He says that when a citizen is" confined to jail under a statute, it necessarily follows that he loses the rights guaranteed to him under Article 19. I am not prepared to accept the broad proposition advocated by the learned Advocate General.

31. As I understand the decision in *Gopalan's case (B)*, it is to the effect that the validity of an enactment is to be judged with respect to the provisions of Article 19, if the legislation directly attempts to control a citizen's freedom of speech. But if the freedoms, enumerated in Article 19, are restricted indirectly as a result of the operation of legislation, authorising punitive or preventive detention, then the validity of the legislation is not to be judged with reference to Article 19 but with reference to the Articles dealing with the subject of detention. If the legislation, permitting detention, is in conformity with Articles 20 to 22, the mere fact, that it indirectly affects the freedoms under Article 19, will not make it a void legislation. So that the crucial point to be determined is what is the exact action which the impugned legislation hits at. If it is the curtailment of any of the freedoms guaranteed under Article 19, then it has to be judged with reference to the

provisions of that Article, but, on the other hand, if those freedoms are affected as an indirect result of a legislation, authorising punitive or preventive detention, then the provisions of Art. 19 are not to be taken into consideration. So that it is not every legislation, which permits punitive or preventive detention, which is immune from a consideration as to its validity by reference to the freedoms guaranteed under Article 19. What has to be seen in every case is the actual action which the statute prohibits. In my opinion the law, as laid down in *Gopalan's case (B)* is not that if a legislation directly interferes with freedom of speech and is not saved by the provisions of Clause (2) of Article 19, then it should be held to be invalid, if it merely provides for the imposition of a fine by way of punishment; but that it would be valid if it provides for imprisonment instead of fine.

32. In *Gopalan's case (B)* their Lordships were considering the validity of certain provisions of the Preventive Detention Act, 4 of 1950. Section 3 of that Act provides that the Central or the State Government may make an order directing the detention of a person, if satisfied that it was necessary to do so in order to prevent him from acting in any manner prejudicial to the defence of India, the relations of India with foreign powers, or the security of India, or the security of the State, or the maintenance of public order or the maintenance of supplies or services essential to the community. Their Lordships upheld the validity of this section, even though Clause (2) of Article 19, as it then stood, did not permit the placing of restrictions on freedom of speech for purposes merely of the maintenance of 'public order'. Their Lordships held that the section did not directly purport to curtail the freedoms guaranteed under Article 19 of the Constitution, but was concerned with the subject of preventive detention, and it did not matter that as a result of detention the freedoms guaranteed under Article 19 were also interfered with.

33. *Gopalan's case (B)* was considered in a subsequent case by the Supreme Court reported in AIR 1951 SC 270(C), where

an argument appears to have been made to the effect that the decision in *Gopalan's case (B)* was to some extent affected by the later decisions of the same Court in the cases of AIR 1950 SC 129(U), and AIR 1950 SC 124(J). Their Lordships unhesitatingly repelled this contention and observed,

> "Although personal liberty has a content sufficiently comprehensive to include the freedoms enumerated in Art. 19(1), and its deprivation would result in the extinction of those freedoms, the Constitution has treated these civil liberties "as distinct fundamental rights and made separate provisions in Article 19 and Articles 21 and 22 as to the limitations and conditions subject to which alone they could be taken away or abridged."

They then quoted a portion of the decision in *Gopalan's case(B)* where it was said,

> "So read, it clearly means that the legislation to be examined must be directly in respect of one of the rights mentioned in the sub-clauses (of Article 19). If there is a legislation directly attempting to control a citizen's freedom of speech or expression, or his right to assemble peaceably and without arms, etc. the question whether that legislation is saved by the relevant saving clause of Article 19 will arise. If, however, the legislation is not directly in respect of any of these subjects, but as a result of the operation of other legislation, for instance, for punitive or preventive detention, his right under any of these sub-clauses is abridged, the question of the application of Article 19 does not arise. The true approach is only to consider the directness of the legislation and not what will be the result of the detention otherwise valid, on the mode of the detenu's life."

The cases relied upon by the petitioner's counsel in that case were distinguished on the ground that the legislations held to be invalid were legislations which authorised the imposition of a ban on the circulation of a newspaper or pre-censorship on the publication of a journal.

34. A similar question of the invalidity of certain provisions of Abducted Persons (Recovery and Restoration) Act, 1949, came up for decision before a Full Bench of the East Punjab High Court in the case of *Ajaib Singh, Lehna Singh* vs. *State of Punjab*, AIR 1952 Punj 309(FB)(Y), and the learned Judges held that the relevant provisions of the said Act were valid as the freedoms guaranteed in Sub-clauses (d), (e), (f) and (g) of Clause (i) of Article 19 could be interfered with totally as the arrest and confinement were according to the procedure established by law, but they allowed the petition on a different ground. This case went up in appeal to the Supreme Court and their Lordships upheld the decision,—('Vide *State of Punjab* vs. *Ajaib Singh*, AIR 1953 SC 10(Z)), though they did not agree with the interpretation put by the Punjab High Court on Article 22 of the Constitution, with which we are not concerned in this case. While considering the point that the Act was inconsistent with the provisions of Article 19(1)(d) and (e) and Article 21, their Lordships of the Supreme Court held that the matter was concluded by the majority decision in *Gopalan's case (B)* and the High Court had correctly negatived the contention.

35. These were all cases where the main purpose of the impugned Acts was the detention of the petitioners, which incidentally deprived the petitioners of the freedoms enumerated in Article 19 also.

36. I now proceed to consider whether the actual act which the impugned section, namely, Section 3, U. P. Special Powers Act, prohibits is the freedom of speech guaranteed under Article 19(1)(a) of the Constitution, or it is the stopping of every sort of instigation to the people not to pay the dues recoverable by the Government as arrears of land revenue. I have already quoted the provisions of the impugned section in full. What it actually prohibits is instigation to any person not to pay or to defer payment of any liability as defined in Section 2. The prohibition extends to instigation, expressly or by implication,

by words either spoken or written, or by signs or by visible representations or otherwise. It also makes punishable any act done with the intent or knowing it to be likely that any such instigation, referred to before, shall be communicated to any person or class of persons in any manner whatsoever. The punishment provided is an imprisonment up to six months or a fine of Rs. 250/- or both.

The clear object in framing the statute is that there should be no instigation by any means by any person to another not to pay the dues recoverable by the Government as arrears of land revenue. Not only written and spoken words have been made punishable but also signs and visible representations, and even other activities as also every act, which is likely to communicate the words, signs or visible representations to any other person. The object of the statute is to make instigations of every kind punishable, as the Government does not want interference in the recovery of its legal dues. The direct activity made punishable by this Act in my opinion, is not the curtailment of any freedom of speech; and the validity of the Act, therefore, should not be judged with reference to Article 19 but with reference to the provisions of Article 22 of the Constitution.

37. The provisions of the Preventive Detention Act of 1950 hit at every sort of activities prejudicial to defence of India, security of India, security of the State, or the maintenance of public order, or the maintenance of supplies. The making of speeches is also an act, and though Section 3 does not specifically permit detention with a view to preventing a speech, yet there is no doubt that the making of a speech is also an activity, and the apprehension that a speech would be made justifies the order of detention. Indeed, it is generally the speeches, more than positive acts, which are apprehended to bring about the undesirable results, and numerous detentions have been made simply because it was apprehended that prejudicial speeches would be delivered. The only difference between Section 3, Preventive Detention Act, and Section 3, Special Powers Act,

is that the impugned section clearly mentions the making of a speech, whereas Section 3, Preventive Detention Act, includes it within the ambit of the expression "acting in any manner prejudicial to".

I do not think the decision in *Gopalan's case (B)* would have been different if in Section 3(1)(a), Preventive Detention Act, the word "speaking" had also been added before or after the word "acting". The Preventive Detention Act is designed as much against improper speech as the impugned section and the mere omission of the word "speaking", in my opinion, does not materially alter the position. The subject of Section 3, Preventive Detention Act, was preventive detention, whereas the subject of the impugned section is punitive detention, and what the impugned section makes punishable is all manner of instigation; and if the expression "word spoken or written" had not been used in this section, the making of a speech would still have been an instigation and punishable by the section.

38. In view of what I have stated above, I have come to the conclusion that the present case is governed by the decision in *Gopalan's case (B)*, and the validity of the impugned section is not to be considered with reference to the provisions of Article 19 of the Constitution. The decision of this point is sufficient for disposing of this petition, but, as the matter is not free from doubt, I consider it desirable to deal with the other points also that arose in the case.

39. I now come to the question that assuming that Article 19 of the Constitution applies to the case, whether the impugned section is a permissible piece of legislation and in accordance with the provision of Article 19, Clause 2. The clause was amended by Section 3 of the Constitution (First Amendment) Act of 1951. The amended clause now reads as follows:

> "(2)—Nothing in Sub-clause (a) of Clause (1) shall affect the operation of any existing law, or prevent the State from making any law, in so far as such law imposes reasonable

> restrictions on the exercise of the right conferred by the said sub-clause in the interests of the security of the State, friendly relations with foreign States, public order, decency or morality, or in relation to contempt of Court, defamation or incitement to an offence."

The learned Advocate General justified the impugned section as imposing a reasonable restriction in the interest of security of the State and public order. So that the only points that arise for consideration on this question are (1) whether the impugned section imposes reasonable restrictions, (2) whether they are in the interest of the security of the state, and (3) whether they are in the interest of public order. The impugned legislation can only be upheld if the answer to the first point, as well as to one or both of the other two, is in favour of the respondent. I propose to deal with points (2) and (3) first.

40. The contention of the learned Advocate General was that this Act did not prohibit the making of speeches in general, or even a criticism of the taxes imposed by the Government or the laws promulgated by it. He said that the criticism could be as strong as the speaker liked and in any language he chose, and that it was permissible to preach that a particular piece of legislation or a particular tax was unjust and wholly improper. The impugned section does not prohibit any of these things, but what it does prohibit is the instigation to others not to pay their legal dues. He said that instigation like this is an instigation which has to be checked in the interest of the security of the State as well as of public order. His argument was that if taxes are not paid, the Government could not go on and there was bound to be a chaos in the State. Taxes form part "of the consolidated fund" of the State, and the security of the State depended on the maintenance of an adequate consolidated fund. So that it was in the interest of the security of the State itself that an instigation not to pay the just dues has to be stopped.

I do not agree with the Advocate General on this point.

There is a very limited number of taxes, the complete non-payment of which can result in undermining the financial security of a State. The number of taxes and of other Government dues is very large and it cannot be said that the non-payment of each one of these taxes or dues wil' result in financial unstability of the State. As argued by the petitioner, Dr. Rammanohar Lohia, no movement of non-payment of taxes in general is ever likely to succeed, because the people, who pay most of those taxes, are not likely to be influenced by such a propaganda. An instigation not to pay a major tax or even the land revenue of the agricultural lands is also not likely to succeed to such an extent as to jeopardize the security of the State. As regards its financial condition instigations like these cannot be said to have as their natural consequence the effect of undermining the security of a State, nor can it be said to be its likely result. The possibility of the undermining of a State as a result of an instigation not to pay taxes is so remote that I do not think that the suppression of an activity like this can be said to be in the interest of the security of the State. If Clause (2) of Article 19 had not been amended, I do not think the impugned section could be said to be valid as a reasonable restriction to avoid undermining the security of the State. But the amended clause has now brought in the consideration of public order also and has justified the placing of restrictions on the freedom of speech in the interest of public order. I have come to the conclusion that the impugned section can be said to have been enacted "in the interest of" public order.

41. The learned counsel for the petitioner argued that the impugned section made a mere instigation punishable, even though there may be no question of the commission of any act of violence or of breach of peace. A simple exhortation to persons not to pay Government ues has been made punishable, though there may be no question on any breach of peace resulting from this instigation. His contention was that "public order" merely meant the absence of breach of peace or acts of violence. The learned Advocate General, however, contended

that "public order" was not merely the absence of breach of peace and acts of violence, but had a positive aspect as well. According to him, "public order" signified ordered society based on proper regulation and attempting to undermine ordered society was disturbing "public order". The expression "public order" is of a wide import. But no definition of the word appears to have been attempted, though instances of what acts amount to disturbance of public order are to be found in a number of cases.

The learned counsel for the petitioner drew our attention to same passages in the *Stephen's Commentaries on the Laws of England*, Vol. IV, page 126, *Stephen's Digest of the Criminal Law*, part II, and *Blackstone's Commentaries*, Vol. IV, Ch. XI, where offences against public order are mentioned; and he wanted to draw an inference that the expression "public order" was confined to acts which would amount to offences described as offences against public order in these different books. The inference drawn by the learned counsel however, does not appear to be justified, because these books were dealing with offences against public order and were not attempting to give any definition of the expression "public order" itself. They enumerated the acts, which were offences against public order, and dealt with those particular acts. The inference that everything, that fell outside the ambit of those acts, was not public order, does not appear to be justified. He also referred to the Defence of India Act, Section 2, and to the Defence of India Rules, Rules 26 and 29, but here again no definition of the expression "public order" was meant to be given, and provision was sought to be made for certain activities which were considered to be prejudicial to the State.

42. I may now come to the cases cited by the learned counsel for the petitioner. The first case cited by him was the case of AIR 1949 All 513(FB)(A), in this case the validity of the U.P. Prevention of Black-Marketing (Temporary Powers) Act, 22 of 1949, was challenged, and the matter was referred to a Full Bench of this Court for decision. Section 3 of the above Act

permitted the detention of a person up to a period of six months about whom the Provincial Government was satisfied that he habitually indulged in black-marketing. "Black-marketing" was defined to include disposing of or otherwise dealing in essential commodities with a view to making gain in a manner which may, directly or indirectly, defeat or tend to defeat the provisions of the U.P. Control of Supplies (Temporary Powers) Act of 1947, or the Essential Supplies (Temporary Powers) Act of 1946, or of any Order made under any of these two Acts.

The Constitution had not come into force on the date of the decision of this case, and the attack on the legality of the legislation was based on the absence of the legislative competence of the State Government to pass such a legislation. The learned Judges held that the Provincial Legislature was competent to enact the laws dealing with preventive detention for reasons connected with the maintenance of public order, and also to enact the laws concerning production, supply and distribution of goods. But they held that this last power of enacting laws for production, supply and distribution of goods did not also imply a power to direct detention as a preventive measure. They then considered whether this preventive detention could be said to be connected with the maintenance of public order, and they came to the conclusion that it was not so connected. They accordingly held that the preventive detention of a person indulging in black-marketing was not within the competence of the State Legislature.

Mr. Justice Waliullah was of the opinion that, even if there was some distant connection between black-marketing and public disorder, it could not be said that the detention was for reasons connected with the maintenance of public order. The expression "for reasons connected with", according to the learned Judge, meant "a real and genuine connection" between the maintenance of public order on the one hand and the subject of legislation, namely, black-marketing, on the other. Mr. Justice Wanchoo was also substantially of the same view, and he held,

> "The connection, to my mind, which is envisaged in item 1 of List II must be direct and clear as between cause and effect and not remote and doubtful like the one urged".

According to the learned Judge, "public order" implies absence of violence and an orderly state of affairs in which citizens can peacefully pursue their normal vocations in life. This case went up in appeal to the Federal Court and the Federal Court upheld the decision of this Court, vide AIR 1950 F. C. 67(R). The learned Judges of the Federal Court held,

> "It is true that black-marketing in essential commodities may at times lead to a disturbance of public order, but so may, for example, the rash driving of an automobile or the sale of adulterated food-stuffs. Activities such as these are so remote in the chain of relation to the maintenance of public order that preventive detention on account of them cannot, in our opinion, fall within the purview of Entry 1 of List II".

43. The case of *Dilbagh Singh* vs. *Emperor*, AIR 1944 Lah 373(Z1), does not appear to be very much in point, as the decision in that case was that the detention under Rule 129 of the Defence of India Rules, with the object that the police may have greater facilities for investigating into suspected offence, could not be said to be permissible under Rule 129 of the Defence of India Rules.

44. The case of AIR 1949 Pat 299(S), is an authority for the proposition that a habitual thief could not be detained under the Bihar Maintenance of Public Order Act, 1947, because it could not be said that his actions were prejudicial to public safety and maintenance of public order. Habitual commission of theft, according to the learned Judges, did not disturb public order.

45. In the case of *State* vs. *Ahmed Ali*, AIR 1951 All 459(Z2), it has been held by a learned single Judge of this Court that the spread of disaffection against a party Government could not

be said to be a ground for inferring that the public order would not be maintained. It is the right of every citizen in a democratic Government to spread disaffection against a particular party Government; but the disaffection should not be so spread as to result in violence or to resort to other illegitimate course. I respectfully agree with the decision in this case, but the point that arises in the present case is very much different from the point that arose in the reported case.

46. The two cases of the Supreme Court cited on this point are the cases of AIR 1950 SC 124(J), and AIR 1950 SC 129(U). These cases were decided before the amendment of Clause (2) of Article 19 of the Constitution, and the question as to what is the meaning of the expression "public order" did not directly arise in those cases for decision. But their Lordships have made certain observations which afford some guidance. "Public Order" has been described as

> "an expression of wide connotation signifying that state of tranquillity prevailing among the members of a political society as a result of the internal regulations enforced by the Government which they have instituted."

The expression "public safety" has been defined as ordinarily meaning security of the public or their freedom from danger, but the meaning of the expression must vary according to the context. I am not concerned here with the meaning of the expression "public safety".

47. In the second case *Brij Bhushan's case (U)* it has been observed,

> "I think that "public order" may well be paraphrased in the context as public tranquillity and the words "public safety" and "public order" may be read as equivalent to security of the State and public tranquillity."

Here their Lordships were discussing the meaning of the expression "public order" with reference to context as used in the Act impugned before them, namely, the East Punjab. Public

Safety Act of 1949. Applying the meaning of the expression "public order" as expressed in the case of *Romesh Thapar (J)*, I think that an exhortation to the members of the public not to obey the laws in general or any particular law is likely to disturb the state of tranquillity prevailing among the members of the public, and the preaching of disobedience of a law or laws if meant to disturb that public tranquillity, of course, while referring to the law or laws, I mean those laws, which have been duly promulgated and are valid laws not inconsistent in any manner with the provisions of our Constitution. The criticism of a law or laws is one thing, because that may be with a view to have the laws changed and it is the very essence of democracy that every member of the public should have the right to propagate his views and to make all legitimate attempts to change a law or laws, which he considers improper or working a hardship on the public or any class of public. But exhortation to disobey duly promulgated and valid laws has a tendency of disturbing the state of tranquillity prevailing among the members of the public as a result of the regulations or laws enforced by the Government. The same is the position with respect to an exhortation not to pay taxes duly imposed or other legal dues recoverable by the State. That, to my mind, is the position keeping in view the meaning and significance of the expression "public order", as laid down in *Romesh Thapar's case (J)*, and the provisions of the impugned section would be justified as having been enacted "in the interest of" public order.

48. In the present case, however, the position is still clear. What the impugned section makes punishable is an instigation not to pay the legal dues of the Government, which means the disobedience of the laws which have made those dues recoverable by the Government by the exercise of certain coercive process. This sort of instigation, in the circumstances at present prevailing in the country, is likely to lead even to breaches of peace and violence. The majority of persons to whom exhortation is made are likely to be uneducated people, who can easily be misled to take the law into their own hands

and to resist the realisation of the legal dues by the public servants. This, in the ordinary course of things, is likely to lead to riots and breaches of public peace. An exhortation, therefore, in my opinion, to the members of the public to disobey the duly promulgated and valid laws, specially where those laws happen to authorise the public servants to realise the dues by coercive processes, is an act which can be classed as one subversive of public order.

Laws relating to property, including money, which lay down the process by which the property is to be seized, or the money realised, are in the very nature of things likely to be looked upon as good or bad according to the angle of vision from which they are seen, and there has always been difference of opinion as regards the reasonableness or otherwise of such laws. An exhortation to the judgment-debtors in general to refuse to obey the decrees passed by the Courts would, to my mind, lead to public disorder, and the same is the position with respect to the recovery of legal dues by the officers of the Government. This has, in the past, led to riots and disturbances of public peace on a larger or small scale and, in my opinion, the natural result of such an exhortation is to disturb public tranquillity and help in creating riots. So applying even the narrower definition to the expression "public order", namely, the maintenance of public peace and tranquillity, I think that the making of an instigation in this respect is really in the interest of public order, and the legislation is justified under the amended provisions of Clause (2) of Article 19 of the Constitution.

49. I now propose to consider the question whether the restriction imposed on the freedom of speech on a citizen by the impugned section is a reasonable one or not. The learned counsel for the petitioner argued that the possibility of the commission of riots and breaches of peace, as a result of the instigation not to pay the enhanced irrigation rates, is a very remote possibility and not a natural consequence of the instigation. As I have already stated, I do not agree with this

contention of the learned counsel. The public dues are recovered by the Officers of the Government by having recourse to coercive processes and, if the members of the public acting upon the instigation decide not to pay the dues, the occurrence of riots is the natural and likely consequence of the instigation.

In support of his argument, the learned counsel for the petitioner referred to a number of American cases in which the well known rule of "clear and present danger" was held to be the rule by which the validity of a legislation was to be judged. He referred to six cases, namely, (1924) 69 Law Ed 1138(L); (1930) 75 Law Ed 1117(H); (1936) 81 Law Ed 1066(G); (1939) 84 Law Ed 1093(I); (1941) 86 Law Ed 192(P); (1948) 93 Law Ed 1131(M).

50. The law in America as regards the freedom of speech, as also on many other points, is different from the law laid down by our Constitution. The First and the Fourteenth Amendments of the American Constitution do not impose any restrictions on the freedom of speech, and the Courts, therefore, had to make their own rules as regards the reasonableness or the existence of that freedom, and as regards the limitations which could be imposed by the State in the exercise of its police powers. In our Constitution, the position is very different. The freedoms, as enumerated in Article 19(1), are made subject to the succeeding clauses of the same Article, and when judging the constitutionality of an Act the Courts in India have to judge those Acts according to the provisions of the Constitution itself. The observations made in some of these cases themselves do not really support the wide proposition urged by the learned counsel, namely, that the acts, of disorder must be "immediate and necessary consequence" of the freedom sought to be curtailed. Whether the consequence of a particular act or speech is likely to disturb the public order is a matter which in the first instance, has to be left to the discretion of the Legislature, and there is a presumption that the restrictions imposed by the Legislature are reasonable ones because it is the members of the Legislature, who are the representatives of the people and

who are expected to know better their reactions to particular actions or speeches. The issue of reasonableness is certainly justiciable and cases have happened in which Courts have held that the restrictions were not reasonable. But, as I have already said, there is a presumption in favour of the validity of a legislation on this point, and a restriction imposed by a legislation should be held by the Courts to be unreasonable only if, in spite of the presumption in favour of the legislation, the Court comes to the conclusion that the restriction contained in it is not a reasonable one. Even the cases cited by the learned counsel for the petitioner contain observations which support this view. In the first case referred to above, it has been held at p. 1147.

> "The case is to be considered in the light of the principle that the State is primarily the judge of regulations required in the interest of public safety and welfare; and that its police statutes may only be declared unconstitutional where they are arbitrary or unreasonable attempts to exercise authority vested in the State in the public interest."

And again

> "And the immediate danger is none the less real and substantial because the effect of a given utterance cannot be accurately foreseen. The State cannot reasonably be required to measure the danger from every such utterance in the nice balance of a jeweller's scale. A single revolutionary spark may kindle a fire that, smouldering for a time, may burst into a sweeping and destructive conflagration. It cannot be said that the State is acting arbitrarily or unreasonably when, in the exercise of its judgment as to the measures necessary to protect the public peace and safety, it seeks to extinguish the spark without waiting until it has enkindled the flame or blazed into the conflagration."

I think it can safely be said that a State cannot reasonably be required to postpone the adoption of measures until the utterances or instigations have led to actual disturbance of the public peace. It would be acting wisely and properly if it adopts measures which suppress the threatened danger. The quotations made above refer to acts which tend to overthrow the Government itself, but I think the principles laid down there apply equally to the cases of maintenance of public order. Some of these cases have laid down that full opportunity must be given to the citizen for political discussion, and indeed such an opportunity is essential to the security of the State. No exception can be taken to this proposition, and the State cannot be permitted to stop political discussion; but a clear instigation to disobey the laws, which legalise the recovery of certain State dues, transgresses the limit of political discussion.

51. The learned Advocate-General drew our attention to the case of '(1949) 94 Law Ed 925(N)'. In this case the Supreme Court has held that the rule of "clear and present danger" does not apply to every case, and it is the reason behind the rule that has to be seen while determining the constitutionality or otherwise of the statute than the rule itself. The American cases cited above are not very helpful, excepting that they illustrate the rule which is more or less universal that a person is held responsible for the natural consequences of his act and not those which may be far-fetched or too remote.

52. As provided by Sub-section (2) of Section 1, Section 3 and the following sections of the U.P. Special Powers Act only come into force when the State Government decides to apply those provisions to a particular area or areas. The impugned section, therefore, comes into force only when the State Government thinks that there is an emergency and the provisions really partake of the nature of an emergency legislation. The section appears to have remained inoperative from 1940 till the month of April 1954, when its provisions were made applicable to two of the districts in this State, but subsequently in June 1954 it was considered desirable to extend the provisions to 31 other districts. Of course, it has been left

to the State Government to decide as to the existence of an emergency, and the delegation of this power on the State Government cannot be said to be unconstitutional or invalid. The position, therefore, (sic) that the impugned section has been brought into force in the case of an emergency, and this is an additional reason for holding that the provisions of the statute do not create an unreasonable restriction on the freedom of speech.

53. In view of what I have stated above, I have come to the conclusion that the impugned section is a permissible piece of legislation and is protected by the provisions of Clause (2) of Article 19 of the Constitution.

54. There is one part of the section which, in my opinion, may not be protected by the provisions of Clause (2) of Article 19. The definition of the word "liability" as given in Section 2, Special Powers Act, includes rent of agricultural land or anything recoverable as arrears of or along with such rent. Section 4 provides that any person to whom an arrear of liability is due may apply in writing to the Collector to realise it, and the Collector shall, after satisfying himself that the amount claimed is due, proceed to recover it as arrears of land revenue. Section 3 makes it punishable to instigate nonpayment of an amount like this as well. It is difficult to say that the State Government should first take upon itself to recover dues of a private individual and then make an instigation not to pay it penal, on the ground that this instigation is likely to lead to breaches of peace and disorder. I very much doubt whether this portion of the impugned section is a valid piece of legislation, but the question does not arise in this case and this part is severable from the rest of the section. It does not, therefore, affect the validity of the relevant portion of Section 3.

55. I now come to the last point argued in the case, namely, that the detention of the petitioner was illegal inasmuch as the provisions of Clause (2) of Article 22 have not been followed, as the petitioner was not produced before a Magistrate within a period of 24 hours of his arrest. According to the facts stated

in the counter affidavit, filed by the Station Officer, police station Kotwali, Farrukhabad, the petitioner was first arrested at the house of Lalla Babu, and the arrest was made by the Station Officer himself as the petitioner was supposed to be guilty of the commission of a cognizable offence. Soon after his arrest, however, within a few minutes, the City Magistrate of Farrukhabad also reached the spot along with the Sub-Divisional Magistrate of Kaimganj. The petitioner was then produced by the Station Officer, Kotwali, before the City Magistrate, who granted a remand for two days. The petitioner was then sent to the district jail, and on the 6th of July the Judicial Officer went to try him in the jail. There an application was made for the adjournment of the case, and the case was adjourned to the 19th of July.

The argument of the learned counsel is that, in the circumstances of this case, it must be taken to be proved that the arrest itself was directed by the City Magistrate and, therefore the production of the petitioner before the City Magistrate was not such a production as would bring it within the meaning of the expression as used in Clause (2) of Article 22 of the Constitution. In support of this submission, the learned counsel cited a recent Division Bench decision of this Court in 'AIR 1954 All 601(A)'. What happened in this case was that the petitioners were in effect arrested by the City Magistrate and they were taken into custody under his orders and under his direct supervision. The City Magistrate then remanded the petitioners into jail custody and the order of remand was signed by him without scrutinising as to the legality and propriety of the procedure adopted by him. On these facts it was held that there was no proper production of the petitioners before a competent Magistrate within 24 hours of their arrest, and consequently the further detention in jail was illegal and unconstitutional.

This decision is binding upon us, and, assuming that it contains a correct exposition of law, I think the facts of the case before me are substantially different from the facts of the case before the Division Bench referred to above. In the instant case the facts appear to be that the petitioner was arrested without warrant by the Officer-in-charge Kotwali, and a few minutes after that the City Magistrate also reached the spot, and the Station Officer produced the petitioner before the City Magistrate who remanded the petitioner to custody. The essential difference between the two cases is that in the reported case it was the Magistrate who himself directed and supervised the arrest of the petitioners, whereas in the instant case the arrest was made by the Station Officer, authorised to arrest the petitioner, as being accused of a cognizable offence. He was then produced before the City Magistrate who granted a remand. The City Magistrate was not present at the time of the arrest and could not be said to have ordered or supervised the arrest. The decision in the Division Bench case, therefore, does not govern the instant case, and the facts proved in the case clearly show that the petitioner was produced before a Magistrate well within the time mentioned in Clause (2) of Article 22 of the Constitution.

56. After I had written my judgment, I had the benefit of reading the judgment of my learned brother Desai. Besides certain other matters, he has relied on one point which I consider it necessary to mention in my judgment as well. The view expressed by him is that the validity of the impugned section should be seen, with reference to the date on which the Constitution came into force and according to him, on that date, in any case, it cannot be said that the impugned section was necessary in the interest of public order. I do not agree with this view and I am of the opinion that the impugned section was not inconsistent with Article 19 of the Constitution, even on 26-1-1950. Though the impugned section was on the statute book, the State Government had not extended its application to any place in the State of Uttar Pradesh. It was to come into operation only if circumstances arose, which induced the State Government to apply the provisions of section to any local area in the State of Uttar Pradesh. While judging its validity

the circumstance can be taken into consideration that this provision has always been in the nature of an emergency provision. If as an emergency provision it is valid today, it should also be taken to be valid on 26-1-1950, though no such emergency may then have been in existence as it has arisen in the last few months in this State. So far, however, I agree with my brother that, if the impugned section is held to be inconsistent with Article 19 on the coming into force of the Constitution, then the legislation would continue to be void and must also be held to be void today.

57. In the first of the two points, that we have decided to refer to a third Judge for his opinion, the main question, to my mind, is whether the impugned section is to be judged with reference to Article 19(1)(a) of the Constitution or not, and whether that consideration is shut out by the decision of their Lordships of the Supreme Court in *Gopalan's case (B)*.

58. For the reasons that I have mentioned above, I am of the opinion that this petition should be dismissed.

BY THE COURT

59. Since we differ on the following points, we refer the matter to the Hon'ble the Chief Justice for obtaining a third Judge's opinion on them:

(1) Was the provision of Section 3, U.P. Special Powers Act of 1932, making it penal for a person by spoken words to instigate a class of persons not to pay dues recoverable as arrears of land revenue, inconsistent with Article 19(1)(a) of the Constitution on 26-1-1950?

(2) If so, was it in the interests of public order? (The matter was then referred to a third Judge viz., Agarwala J., who delivered the following opinion):

Agarwala, J.

60. Dr. Rammanohar Lohia was arrested for having

committed an offence under Section 3, U.P. Special Powers Act (14 of 1932), in that he delivered two speeches, one at Kaimganj on 4-7-1954 and another at Farrukhabad at 8-30 p.m. on the same date. In these speeches he is alleged to have incited the cultivators not to pay enhanced irrigation rates to Government. He made an application to this Court under Art. 226 of the Constitution for the issue of a writ of 'Habeas Corpus' on the allegation, 'inter alia', that Section 3, U.P. Special Powers Act, under which he was arrested and detained was inconsistent with the provisions of Article 19 of the Constitution and, therefore, void and inoperative. The application was heard by a Bench of two Judges of this Court. Desai, J., was of opinion that the application should be allowed while Chaturvedi, J., was of a contrary opinion. The points on which the learned Judges differed have been formulated as follows:

1. Was the provision of Section 3 of the U.P. Special Powers Act of 1932, making it penal for a person by spoken words to instigate a class of persons not to pay dues recoverable as arrears of land revenue, inconsistent with Article 19(1)(a) of the Constitution on 26-1-1950?
2. If so, was it in the interests of public order? On account of this difference of opinion the case has come to me for my opinion on the points above referred to.

61. As the facts of the case have been given in the judgments of my learned brothers, it is not necessary for me to repeat them. I shall, therefore, straightaway deal with the points of law on which my learned brothers hold different views. But before I do so I consider it necessary to make certain general observations:

62. Section 3, Special Powers Act, has created a new offence called "instigation to the nonpayment of a liability". The section is as follows:

"Section 3. '**Punishment for instigation to the non-**

> **payment of a liability**'. Whoever, by words either spoken or written, or by signs or by visible representations, or otherwise, instigates, expressly or by implication, any person or class of persons not to pay or to defer payment of any liability, and whoever does any act, with intent or knowing it to be likely that any words, signs or visible representations containing such instigation shall thereby be communicated directly or indirectly to any person or class of persons, in any manner whatsoever, shall be punishable with imprisonment which: may extend to six months, or with fine, extending to Rs. 250/-, or with both."

63. Section 2 of the Act defines 'liability'. It means,

> "land revenue or any sum recoverable as arrears of land revenue or any tax, rates, cess or other due or amount payable to Government or to any local authority or rent of agricultural land or anything recoverable as arrears of or along with such rent."

In short Section 3 makes it penal for a person to instigate another person or class of persons not to pay or defer payment of any amount payable to Government or local authority or the payment of agricultural rent to a Zemindar. It is important to remember that while instigation not to pay or defer payment of the above dues has been made an offence, the non-payment or deferring payment of such dues is not an offence at all. Thus though a person who does not make payment of a liability or defers payment thereof is not guilty of any offence, yet this Act makes a person who instigates another not to pay or defer payment of any liability guilty of a crime.

64. This Act was passed in 1932 during the British rule and was temporary, but after the Congress Government had resigned in the Provinces and the Governor's autocratic rule was introduced under Section 93, Government of India Act, 1935, it was made permanent in 1940 and since then it has continued to exist on the Statute Book. On 26-1-1950, India became a

Sovereign Republic under a new Constitution which guaranteed to the citizens of India several freedoms. One of such freedoms is the right to "freedom of speech and expression" (Article 19(1)(a)). This freedom means that every citizen of India has, subject to certain limitations, an absolute right to 'say' anything he likes, good, bad or indifferent, right or wrong, palatable or unpalatable to the Government.

65. The reason why such a wide freedom of thought and expression should be available to the citizens of modern progressive societies has been well put by Bury in his *History of Freedom of Thought*:

> "If the history of civilization has any lesson to teach, it is this: there is one supreme condition of mental and moral progress which it is completely within the power of man himself to secure, and that is perfect liberty of thought and discussion. The establishment of this liberty may be considered the most valuable achievement of modern civilization, and as a condition of social progress it should be deemed fundamental. The considerations of permanent utility on which it rests must outweigh any calculations of present advantage which from time to time might be thought to demand its violation."

66. Any law curtailing this absolute freedom would be void, because every law which contravenes the rights guaranteed by the Constitution is void as declared by Article 13. But an absolute freedom to say anything one would like to say, may lead to evils which may not be in the interests of the State as a whole. The interests of the State are, therefore, secured as against the freedom of the individual by laying down the limitations under which the freedom may be exercised. These limitations are mentioned in Clause (2) of Article 19, and are in respect of seven matters:

(a) Security of state;
(b) friendly relations with foreign States;

(c) public order;
(d) decency or morality;
(e) contempt of Court;
(f) defamation;
(g) incitement to an offence.

In the present case we are mainly concerned with "public order". If there be any law placing reasonable restrictions on the otherwise absolute right of free speech and expression, in respect of or in the interest of the above seven subjects, then such law cannot be said to be void.

67. These restrictions being in the nature of exceptions to the general rule of the absoluteness of freedom of speech and expression are to be directly construed. Moreover since the exceptions to the absolute freedom of speech and thought are specifically and expressly laid down in the Constitution, it is clear that there can be no other exceptions than those which are so specifically and expressly mentioned. If the liberty of a citizen is curtailed by any law then it must be shown that the law falls within the four corners of these exceptions and it must also be shown that the restrictions are reasonable.

68. The first question that has been referred to me is based upon the contention that Article 19(1)(a) does not apply to a punitive detention under Section 3, Special Powers Act, at all. The argument is based upon certain observations of the Supreme Court in two cases: AIR 1950 SC 27(B) and AIR 1951 SC 270(C). In *Gopalan's case (B)*, A. K. Gopalan had been detained under Section 3(1), Preventive Detention Act (4 of 1950). On behalf of Gopalan his detention was challenged, 'inter alia', upon the ground that his detention prevented him from exercising the freedom guaranteed under Article 19 of the Constitution and that therefore, the section of that Act under which he was detained was unconstitutional. This argument was rejected by the Supreme Court. Kama J., observed:

"The Article 19(1)(a) has to be read without any

> preconceived notions. So read, it clearly means that the legislation to be examined must be directly in respect of one of the rights mentioned in the sub-clauses. If there is a legislation directly attempting to control a citizen's freedom of speech or expression or his right to assemble peaceably and without arms etc., the question whether that legislation is saved by the relevant saving clause of Article 19 will arise. If, however, the, legislation is not directly in respect of any of these subjects but as a result of the operation of other legislation, for instance for punitive or preventive detention, his right under any of the sub-clauses of Article 19 is abridged, the question of the application of Article 19 does not arise. The true approach is only to consider the directness of the legislation and not what will be the result of the detention otherwise valid, on the mode of the detenu's life."

The observations of the majority of the other Judges were in a similar strain. Patanjali Sastri J. (as he then was) observed:

> "Where, as a penalty for committing a crime or otherwise, the citizen is lawfully deprived of his freedom, there could no longer be any question of his exercising or enforcing the rights referred to in Clause (1) (of Article 19). Deprivation of personal liberty in such a situation is not, in my opinion, within the purview of Article 19 at all but is dealt with by the succeeding Articles 20 and 21. In other words, Article 19 guarantees to the citizens the enjoyment of certain civil liberties 'while they are free', while Articles 20 to 22 secure to all persons—citizens and non-citizens—certain constitutional guarantees in regard to punishment and prevention of crime."

It is not necessary to quote the observations of the other learned Judges. It will be noticed that the learned Judges of the Supreme Court were meeting the argument that was advanced on behalf of Gopalan that he was deprived of the liberty guaranteed to every citizen under Article 19 as a result of the detention under the Preventive Detention Act. No question was raised in that case whether the Preventive Detention Act itself was void on the ground that it restrained the freedom of speech and expression or of other rights mentioned in Article 19 before a person was detained.

If the same argument is advanced in connection with punitive detention, namely that punitive detention is bad because by reason of that detention a person is not free to exercise the rights conferred by Article 19, then also the argument will have to be rejected. I do not read the observations of the Supreme Court to mean that if the complaint is that a person is not free to exercise the rights guaranteed to him under Article 19 and a restraint is placed upon the exercise of those rights and because of the violation of those restraints he is detained punitively, then also Article 19(1)(a) will have no application to his case.

A little reflection will show that such an argument would lead to a complete negation of the freedom guaranteed under Article 19. The easiest thing for the legislature to do would be to make a law making it an offence to exercise any of the rights mentioned in Article 19 and then to say, 'Because he is being detained for breach of the law so made, Article 19(1)(a) will have no application'. I do not think the learned Judges of the Supreme Court ever intended to lay down such a proposition. It was urged that this is exactly what they have said in the later case, AIR 1951 SC 270(C). I do not think that any such conclusion can be drawn from the observations made in that case.

69. Ram Singh was arrested by the order of the District Magistrate, Delhi, under Section 3, Preventive Detention Act, 1950, under an order reciting that he was to be detained "with a view to the maintenance of public order in Delhi." In the grounds of detention communicated to him, however, reference was made to certain speeches which were said to have been made by him or were likely to be made in future, speeches which were likely to excite disaffection between Hindus and

Muslims, and thereby to affect the maintenance of public order in Delhi.

The case at first came before the High Court of East Punjab. The argument on behalf of Ram singh was that he was being detained because he wanted to exercise his right of freedom of speech and expression. This argument was rejected by the East Punjab High Court but it was observed that there was a certain anomaly which was supposed to have arisen on account of the Supreme Court's decision in two other cases, AIR 1950 SC 129(U), AIR 1950 SC 124(J) and that this anomaly could be removed only by the Supreme Court. When the matter came before the Supreme Court, it was observed that there was no such anomaly. After quoting the observations of Kania C. J., in *Gopalan's case (B)*, Patanjali Sastri, J., observed:

> "It follows that the petitioners now before us are governed by the decision in *Gopalan's case (B)*, notwithstanding that the petitioner's right under Article 19(1)(a) is prejudiced 'as a result of his detention under the Act'."

Here, again, therefore, their Lordships were repelling the plea to the effect that the exercise of the rights guaranteed under Article 19 were being curtailed because of, or as a result of, the detention. No doubt, there is an observation in the judgment to the following effect:

> "It was decided by a majority of five to one (in Gopalan's case) that a law which authorises deprivation of personal liberty did not fall within the purview of Article 19 and its validity was not to be judged by the criteria indicated in that Article but depended on its compliance with the requirements of Articles 21 and 22, and as Section 3 satisfied those requirements, it was constitutional."

It was urged by the Advocate General on the basis of this observation in the judgment that wherever a person was deprived of his liberty by reason either of preventive detention or punitive detention, then in all those cases he cannot raise the plea that the Act under which he was detained contravened Article 19 of the Constitution. As I have already stated, this is not a conclusion that has to be drawn from what their Lordships observed in that case. They were all the time considering the question of abridgment or curtailment of the rights guaranteed under Article 19 'as a result of punitive or preventive detention'.

They were not considering the question which falls for consideration in this case before us, that where an Act directly curtails the right of freedom of speech and as a result of the violation of the provisions of which a person is punitively detained, whether in such a case he can rely upon the rights to the freedoms guaranteed to him by Article 19. In my judgment, while Article 19(1) is not contravened when curtailment of the freedom mentioned therein is brought about as a result of detention preventive or punitive under laws otherwise valid, (and it may be further said that while in the case of preventive detention, Article 19(1) is not contravened at all (as pointed out in *Brij Bhushan's case (U))),* Article 19(1) is contravened when punitive detention is effected 'as a result of the exercise of those freedoms. In the present case Dr. Lohia's complaint is not that Article 19(1)(a) has been contravened because he has been detained; his complaint is that the said Article is contravened because the impugned Act made it unlawful for him to exercise the freedom of speech and expression guaranteed to him.

70. It was then urged that Section 3, Special Powers Act, does not directly deal with the subject of freedom of speech and expression but that it deals with a certain kind of instigation, namely instigation to refuse to pay or defer payment of a liability of the kind mentioned in Section 2 of the Act. It was urged that the fact that the instigation was to be done by means of speech or other kind of expression was merely incidental and the main object of the Act was to prevent an 'act' of instigation and that just as under the Preventive Detention Act, which was held valid by the Supreme Court, a person could be detained if he was considered to be likely to do an act which threatened

the security of the State or public order, so also Section 3 of the impugned Act must be considered to be valid.

In my judgment this is not a correct reading of the effect of Section 3, Special Powers Act. There can be no doubt to my mind that the direct attack in Section 3, Special Powers Act, is on the right of freedom of speech and expression. 'To instigate' means to goad or urge forward; to set on; to provoke; to incite. How are all these actions to be done except by means of speech or some other mode of expression? No other mode has been suggested to me on behalf of the State. The object of the legislation is, therefore, clearly one to restrain a particular kind of speech or expression, namely a speech or expression which incites or provokes or urges a person, or class of persons, to do a certain thing or not to do a certain thing mentioned in the section. I think, therefore, that Section 3 of the impugned Act is a legislation directly dealing with the freedom of speech and expression and prejudicing the right guaranteed under the Constitution, and as such its validity must be considered with reference to Clause (2) of that Article. I would, therefore, answer the first question referred to me in the affirmative.

71. This leads me to consider whether the section in question is a restraint upon the right of speech and expression in the interests of 'public order'. Sub-clause (2) of Article 19 justifies reasonable restraint on the right of freedom of speech and expression on several grounds. Before my learned brothers before whom the case was argued in the first instance it was urged that the restraint imposed by Section 3, Special Powers Act, was in the interests of the 'security of the State'. Both the learned Judges were of opinion that this contention was not sound. The argument was, however, repeated before me. From the form of the second question I take it that I was not called upon to answer this argument, but I allowed the learned Advocate General to deal with it and I have no hesitation in saying that I agree with the view of my learned brothers on this point. It is not necessary for me to elaborate the reasons for this view because they have already dealt with it in detail in

their judgments. I would, therefore, proceed to consider whether the impugned section imposes a restriction on the right of freedom of speech and expression guaranteed under Article 19(1)(a) in the 'interest of public order'.

72. 'Public order' has not been defined in any statute, but we have the pronouncement of the highest authority in the land as to what it really means and connotes. In AIR 1950 SC 124(J), Patanjali Sastri, J. (as he then was) observed:

> "Now, 'public order' is an expression of wide connotation and signifies that state of tranquillity prevailing among the members of a political society as a result of the internal regulations enforced by the Government which they have instituted."

The learned Judge was dealing with the question whether 'public safety' and 'public order' were comprised within the expression 'security of the State'. It may be recalled that Clause (2) of Article 19, before its amendment by the Constitution First Amendment Act, 1951, did not protect restraints on the rights conferred under Article 19(1)(a) on the ground that they were in the interests of 'public order' though the restraints could be imposed on the ground that the 'security of the State' was threatened. His Lordship differentiated 'security of the State' from 'public order' and held that 'security of the State' referred to serious threats to public peace and tranquillity, while 'public order' under the various clauses of Article 19 referred to less serious threats to 'public peace and tranquillity'.

> "The Constitution thus requires a line to be drawn in the field of public order or tranquillity marking off, more or less roughly, the boundary between those serious and aggravated forms of public disorder which are calculated to endanger the security of the State and the relatively minor breaches of the peace of purely local significance, treating for this purpose differences in degree as if they were differences in kind."

There can be little doubt that 'Public Order' was taken by his Lordship in *Romesh Thappar's case (J)* as something intimately connected with peace and tranquillity. It was urged by the learned Advocate General that in the definition of public order, the words "as a result of the internal regulations enforced by the Government which they have instituted" every kind of regulation was intended to be included. It was urged that 'public order' need not necessarily connote a state of peace and tranquillity but that it also embraces within its scope a state of society in which the laws in force are observed. I do not think that this was what was intended to be conveyed when the expression 'internal regulations' was used. From the observations made in the case it must be held that by 'internal regulations' it was meant internal regulations relating to peace and tranquillity.

The use of the expression 'public order' in legislative enactments and by learned writers on the subject, clearly shows that the expression is used in connection with a 'state of peace and tranquillity' and that a law 'in the interests of public order' has reference to a violent disturbance of public peace and tranquillity. In the Penal Code, for instance, Chap. VIII deals with 'offences against public tranquillity' and defines the offences of 'unlawful assembly', 'rioting', 'promoting enmity between classes' and 'affray'. All these are offences which disturb or tend to disturb public peace and tranquillity. In *Stephen's History of Criminal Law of England*, Vol. 2, the learned author divides all activity against public tranquillity under two heads: one consisting of offences in which tranquillity of a civilised society is disturbed by actual force or at least by the show and threat of it, and the other in which no actual force is either employed or displayed but in which steps are taken tending to cause it. In his *Commentaries on the Laws of England*, 21st Edn., Vol. 4, the learned author includes in crimes against 'public order' the offences of treason, official secrets, counterfeit coins, unlawful meetings, affray, forcible criminal trespass, sedition and defamation.

73. It was urged that no one can have the freedom to incite disobedience of laws whether it leads to violence or not, and every such incitement must be held to be a threat to 'public order'. In this connection my attention was invited to a passage in the *Selected Essays on Constitutional Law*, Vol. 2, p. 1050, to the following effect:

> "Judge Hand places outside the limits of free speech one who counsels or advises otherwise to violate existing laws. It is true, he says, that any discussion designed to show that existing laws are mistaken in means or unjust in policy may result in their violation, but if one stops short of urging upon others that it is their duty or their interest to resist the law, he should not be held to have attempted to cause illegal conduct."

The case in which these observations were made has not been placed before me and I am unable, therefore, to say in what circumstances the learned Judge was led to make these observations. I cannot, however, imagine that incitement to the breach of every kind of law whether it involved violence or threat to public peace or not was intended by the learned Judge when he spoke of violation of existing laws.

74. It was said that in order that a democracy should run successfully, it is essential that its citizens should obey the laws duly promulgated by the State. I agree that the observance of the rules of law by all is one of the basic conditions of the successful working of a democracy. The Rule of Law in which the law is obeyed not only by the officers and servants of the State but by all its citizens is a *sine-qua-non* of all democracies as indeed of all civilized societies. No responsible person or party in a democracy would wantonly incite the people to disobedience of laws duly promulgated. But occasions may be imagined when thoroughly honest men of the highest integrity may consider it their conscientious duty to advise people to disobey an unjust law non-violently and to disobey it themselves.

75. Socrates, who was charged for "corrupting the youth", i.e., inciting the younger generation to break the laws of the land and paid with his life for his freedom of thought and speech, said at his trial:

> "Men of Athens, I honour and love you; but I shall obey God rather than you, and while I have life and strength I shall never cease from the practice and teaching of philosophy, exhorting anyone whom I meet.... For know that this is the command of God; and I believe that no greater good has ever happened in the State than my service to God.... If you think that by killing men you can prevent someone from censuring your evil lives, you are mistaken.... That is not a way of escape which is either possible or honourable; the easiest and the noblest way is not to be disabling others, but to be improving yourselves."

76. Thoreau in advising Civil Disobedience to unjust laws said:

> "Law never made men a whit more just; and by means of their respect for it, even the well disposed are daily made the agents of injustice. A common and natural result of an undue respect for law is that you may see a file of soldiers, Colonel, Captain, Corporal pirates, powder-monkeys and all marching in admirable order over hill and dale to the wars, against their wills, nay, against their common sense and consciences, which makes it very steep marching indeed, and produces a palpitation of the heart."

77. Gandhi in his written statement before the Hunter Committee (October 1919) explained the philosophy of Satyagraha thus:

> "That, law-breaker breaks the law surreptitiously and tries to avoid the penalty; not so that civil resister. He ever obeys the laws of the State to which he belongs, not out of fear of the sanctions, but because he considers them to

be good for the welfare of society. But there come occasions, generally rare when he considers certain laws to be so unjust as to render obedience to them a dishonour. He then openly and civilly breaks them and quietly suffers the penalty for their breach. And in order to register his protest against the action of the law-givers, it is open to him to withdraw his co-operation from the State by disobeying such other laws whose breach does not involve moral turpitude."

78. But though a man will be punished for his disobedience of the laws it is not necessary that the law should punish in every case those who incite such disobedience. The vital difference between actual disobedience and incitement to disobedience is that the latter is an exercise of the right of freedom of speech and expression which can be curtailed only if it falls within the ambit of Clause (2) of Article 19.

79. In my opinion our Constitution safeguards to every citizen of India the freedom to preach non-violent disobedience to civil laws, not being laws mentioned in Clause (2) of Article 19.

80. If the contention of the learned Advocate-General that an incitement to breach of every kind of laws is likely to lead to a breach of public order were true, it would hardly have been necessary for the fathers of the Constitution to single out in Clause (2) of Article 19, laws relating to seven matters only including 'incitement of offences'. Indeed the reference to "incitement to an offence" clearly shows that an incitement to a breach of every civil law is not necessarily contemplated in Clause (2).

81. In order to decide whether a particular law restraining the freedom of speech of inciting disobedience to a law is in the interest of public order or not, two things have to be remembered first, that incitement to a breach of every law does not necessarily lead to its breach and even if it leads to its breach it does hot necessarily result in public disorder; and

second that the connection between the impugned law and the threat to public peace and tranquillity must be clear and proximate and not far-fetched or problematic. The first proposition was very clearly expressed by Harold J. Laski in his *Liberty in the Modern State*:

> "It is said that ideas are explosive and dangerous. To allow them such unfettered freedom is, in fact, to invite disorder. But, to this position, there are at least two final answers. It is impossible to draw a line around dangerous ideas, and any attempt at their definition involves monstrous folly. If views, moreover, which imply possible disorder are able to disturb the foundations of the State, there is something supremely wrong with the governance of that State. For disorder is not a habit of mankind. We cling so eagerly to accustomed ways that, as even Burke insisted, popular violence is always the outcome of a deep popular sense of wrong. The common man can only be persuaded to outbreak, granted his general habits, when the Government of the State has lost its hold upon his affection; and that loss is always the reflection of a profound moral cause.... Almost always freedom of speech results in a mitigation which renders disorder unnecessary; almost always, also, prohibition of that freedom merely makes the agitation more dangerous because it drives it underground.... No Government is entitled to assume that disorder is imminent: the proof must be offered to an Independent authority. And the proof so offered must be evidence that the utterance to which it takes exception was, at the time and in the circumstances in which it was made, definitely calculated to result in a breach of the peace."

The second proposition has been laid down by the Supreme Court in AIR 1950 FC 67(R) confirming a Full Bench decision of this Court AIR 1949 All 513(FB)(Q). In that case the question was whether black-marketing in special commodities can be in respect of the maintenance of public order. The

Supreme Court observed that

> "It is true that black-marketing in essential commodities may at times lead to a disturbance of public order, but so may, for example, the rash driving of an automobile or the sale of adulterated foodstuffs. Activities such as these are so remote in the chain of relation to the maintenance of public order that preventive detention on account of them cannot fall within the purview of legislative authority. The connection between the legislation and the object of the legislation must be real and proximate, not far-fetched or problematic."

82. Instances in which disobedience of laws was considered not to constitute a threat to public order are numerous. The instance of black-marketing in essential commodities has already been quoted. In AIR 1949 Pat 299(S), it was held that the remaining at large of a habitual criminal convicted or suspected or committing thefts in running goods trains was not an act prejudicial to the maintenance of public order. In AIR 1944 Lah 373(Z1), the activity of certain contractors in making large claims and receiving payment for work which they had never done and of cheating the Government on a large scale was held not to constitute a threat to public order. In (1939) 310 US 88(I) a statute forbidding loitering or picketing at the scene of a labour dispute was considered to be in violation of the freedom of speech and expression guaranteed by the Constitution.

In *Sodhi Shamsher Singh* vs. *State of Pepsu*, AIR 1954 SC 276(Z3) a person was alleged to have published and distributed pamphlets which were couched in the most filthy and obscene language and amounted to a vitriolic attack upon the character and integrity of the Chief Justice of PEPSU who was accused of gross partiality and communal bias. It was held by the Supreme Court that the orders of detention should be held to be illegal and must be set aside as the publication or distribution of the pamphlets could not have any rational connection with the maintenance of law and order in the State or prevention of acts leading to disorder or disturbance of public tranquillity. It cannot, in my opinion, be laid down as a general proposition that an incitement to the breach of any kind of law would have a proximate and clear connection with the disturbance of public order.

83. We may now consider whether the incitement mentioned in Section 3, Special Powers Act, has a clear and proximate connection with public order. Now, Section 3 prohibits an incitement "not to pay, or to defer payment of, any liability". As mentioned already the incitement in the present case was with reference to the payment of the rates for the use of canal water. The non-payment of such rates which have been prescribed under rules made under the Northern India Canal and Drainage Act, 1873, has not been made an offence. If the payment is not made, it is recovered by the Collector as arrears of land revenue. *Prima facie*, the non-payment has no connection with public order, public order being considered in the sense which I have already discussed, namely the maintenance of public peace and tranquillity.

But it is urged by the learned Advocate-General that incitement to the non-payment of dues such as are mentioned in the Special Powers Act may be acted upon, which action would compel the Government to use coercive process for their realisation, which process would be resented by the defaulters, which resentment would lead to resistance to the coercive process, which would result in violence and, therefore, in the disturbance of public order. To my mind, there are here too many presumptions which are not warranted. Remembering what Laski said in the passage already quoted, and remembering what the Supreme Court held in the black-marketing case (*Rex* vs. *Basdeva (R)*) already noted, it may be stated that it is more than probable that barring extreme cases, the incitement to non-payment will not be obeyed, and even if it is obeyed will not lead to violence, and that in any case the connection between the incitement and public order is too far-fetched and problematic rather than clear and proximate. That a widespread agitation for non-payment of taxes and other dues, mentioned in the Special Powers Act, may sometimes lead to a disturbance of public order, may be admitted. But what may happen in extreme cases is not the true test of the validity or constitutionality of a piece of legislation. The question is whether the impugned legislation covers acts which are innocent in themselves or which have no proximate connection with the disturbance of public order. If the impugned legislation covers such acts, the legislation would be bad even though it also covers acts which in extreme cases may lead to disturbance of public order unless the two kinds of acts can be separated.

Let us suppose that the instigator were to clearly say that the payment of the liability may be refused or deferred, but that there should, be no resistance to the coercive process of recovery or the enforcement of the liability. To my mind, such instigation cannot reasonably be said to threaten public order. The impugned section does cover such cases. Again, it can hardly be said that if one individual instigates another individual not to pay certain dues or to deter payment of a certain liability when there is no general campaign of non-payment and there is no incitement to a general disobedience of laws, there will be a threat to public order. Such instigation is also covered by the provisions of the impugned section, and therefore the section is unconstitutional because as it stands, it is not possible to make it applicable to those extreme cases alone in which there may be a threat to public peace and tranquillity. It may be that in the present case, Dr. Lohia delivered the speeches to which objection has been taken, in connection with a widespread agitation carried on by the party of which he is the General Secretary and in that case his action might be legitimately considered to be a threat to public peace and tranquillity. But that is immaterial. The validity of an enactment is to be judged with reference to the activities it prohibits or restrains and not with reference to the actions of the accused,

84. But it was urged that though these actions may be

covered by the impugned section, the Act was never intended to be applied to such cases and in this connection reference was made to the provisions of Section 1 of the Act. Section 1 gives a discretion to the State Government to extend the other provisions of the Act by notification in the official gazette to any district or to any part of a district in the Uttar Pradesh. It was urged that this discretion shows that the Act was not intended to be applied to individual cases when there was no general campaign of non-payment of liabilities. What the intention of the Legislature was can be judged only by what is stated in the Act itself or in the statement of objects and reasons. It does not appear from the Act itself or from the statement of objects and reasons that the Act was intended to be applied only to such extreme cases. A similar argument was advanced before the Supreme Court in *Romesh Thappar's case (J)*, but it was repelled by the majority of the Judges, and Patanjali Sastri J. (as he then was) delivering the judgment of the majority observed:

> "It was said that an enactment which provided for drastic remedies like preventive detention and ban on newspapers must be taken to relate to matters affecting the security of the State rather than trivial offences like rash driving or an affray. But whatever ends the impugned Act may have been intended to subserve, and whatever aims its framers may have had in view, its application and scope cannot, in the absence of limiting words in the Statute itself, be restricted to those aggravated forms of prejudicial activity which are calculated to endanger the security of the State. Nor is there any guarantee that those authorised to exercise the powers under the Act will in using them discriminate between those who act prejudicially to the security of the State and those who do not."

We have to substitute the words 'public order' in place of 'security of the State' to make these observations fully applicable to the case in hand. To the same effect were the observations of Mahajan J. (as he then was) in AIR 1951 SC 118(K). Observed his Lordship:

> "The law cannot be held valid because the language employed is wide enough to cover restrictions both within and without the limits of constitutionally permissible legislative action affecting the right."

85. But it was urged that in a case of this kind you must have regard to the opinion of the Legislature and when the Legislature thinks that an activity attempted to be prohibited by it is calculated to endanger public order, that opinion must be respected by the Courts. Undoubtedly, the Courts lean in favour of the validity of a legislative enactment and would strain every nerve, if that were legally possible, to hold that that enactment was valid rather than that it was invalid. But this principle can be applied only when the Courts are in a position to judge that this was indeed the intention of the Legislature. In the present case it is impossible to say that in enacting the Special Powers Act the Legislature considered that the activity which it sought to prevent was not in the interests of public order.

The U.P. Special Powers Act (14 of 1932) was enacted when the Government of India Act, 1919 was in force. The sphere of legislative activity of the local Legislatures was not carved out under that Act as was done under the Government of India Act, 1935, and the local Legislature could make laws subject to the confirmation of the Governor-General on any subject relating to 'peace' and 'good Government'. These terms include the whole legislative field including matters not connected with public order. When the Act was made permanent in 1940 by the Governor in exercise of his powers under Section 93, Government of India Act, 1935, it was nowhere stated that the Governor considered the instigation to defer payment of liabilities or the refusal to payment of liabilities as a threat to public order. The matter covered by the enactment clearly falls under the various entries in List 2 of the Seventh Schedule of the Government of India Act, 1935. Entry 39 dealing with land revenue, Entries 40 to 54 dealing with taxes, rates etc., Entry 13 dealing with local authority, and Entries 20 and 21 dealing with agricultural rent would cover the entire legislation. It is, therefore, difficult to say that the Governor considered the Act to be in the interests of public order.

A feeble argument was addressed on the basis of the Act being adapted by the President by the Adaptation of Laws Order, 1950, under Article 372 of the Constitution. Article 372 continues in force the existing laws but it clearly provides that such continuance shall be subject to the other provisions of the Constitution. The mere fact that the impugned Act has been adapted by the President does not, therefore, mean that we are not to consider its validity with reference to the other provisions of the Constitution. The only adaptation that was made in the Act was a formal one; instead of 'the Provincial Government' the words 'State Government' were substituted. This was done simply to bring the language of the Act in conformity with the terminology of the Constitution. A formal adaptation like this could hardly be said to involve a recognition by the President that he considered the Act to be otherwise valid or that the adaptation made by him showed that he considered that the prohibition contained in Section 3 of the Act was in the interests of public order. I do not, therefore, consider that in the present case there is before us the opinion of the Legislature as regards the Act being in the interests of public order.

86. On behalf of the petitioner it was urged that a clear and present danger test should be applied to cases like the present as has been the practice of the American Courts. In the view that I have expressed above it is not necessary for me to enter into any detailed discussion of this question. I have expressed my view on the point in delivering the judgment of a Bench of this Court in connection with a contempt case (see*Lakhan Singh* vs. *Balbir Singh*, AIR 1953 All 342(Z4)).

87. Lastly, the learned Advocate-General urged that the impugned legislation was in the interests of morality. This was

not urged before the Bench and the questions referred to me do not involve a consideration of the point. I, therefore, refrain from entering into a discussion of the matter beyond saying that in my judgment there can be no question of the impugned legislation having any proximate connection with morality, Instances in which great men of all ages have considered certain laws to be unjust are not wanting. The prohibition contained in Section 3 applies to payment of certain liabilities. These liabilities may or may not be considered to be just. If they are not considered to be just, though wrongly not so considered I cannot say that those who think like this and instigate people not to make these payments considered by them to be unjust are in any manner acting against morality. Morality and law are different conceptions. They cannot be equated. In my opinion the answer to the second question must be in the negative.

88. My answers to the questions referred to me, therefore, are:

Question No. 1: The provision of Section 3, U.P. Special Powers Act, 1932, making it penal for a person by spoken words to instigate a class of persons not to pay dues recoverable as arrears of land revenue, was inconsistent with Article 19(1)(a) of the Constitution on 26-1-1950.

Question No. 2: The restrictions imposed by Section 3, U.P. Special Powers Act, 1932, were not in the interests of public order.

89. Let these answers be returned to the Judges making the reference.

ORDER

M.L. Chaturvedi, J.

90. We differed on two points of law in this petition and referred them to a third Judge. The third Judge has now given his opinion and he has answered both the questions in favour

of the petitioner. The result is that this petition must be allowed. We consequently, allow the petition, hold that the petitioner's detention is illegal and we release him forthwith. The petitioner shall be entitled to receive from the respondents a sum of Rs. 500/- as costs of this petition.

91. We certify that the case involves substantial questions of law as to the interpretation of the Constitution.

2. THE SUPERINTENDENT, CENTRAL PRISON, FATEHGARH vs. RAM MANOHAR LOHIA

DATE OF JUDGMENT
21/01/1960

BENCH : Sinha, Bhuvneshwar P.(Cj)
Gajendragadkar, P.B.
Subbarao, K., Gupta
K.C. Das, Shah, J.C.
BENCH : Subbarao, K.
BENCH : Subbarao, K.
Sinha, Bhuvneshwar P.(cj)
Gajendragadkar, P.b.
Gupta, K.c. Das
Shah, J.c.

Citation: 1960 AIR 633 1960 SCR (2) 821
Citator Info : APL 1962 SC 1106 (8), APL 1962 SC 1166 (15), R 1963 SC 812 (10), MV 1966 SC 740 (49,66), RF 1967 SC 1110 (16), RF 1971 SC2486 (14), RF 1973 SC 1091 (6), R 1974 SC 911 (2,4), R 1987 SC 998 (4), RF 1989 SC 371 (9),

ACT: Fundamental Right—Infringement of-Enactment imposing restrictions on freedom of speech-Constitutional validity—Test-"In the interest of Public order". Meaning of Doctrine of severability-Applicability—Constitution of India, Arts. 19(1) (a), 19(2)U.P. Special Powers Act, 1932 (U.P. XIV Of 1932) s. 3.

HEADNOTE

Section 3 of the U.P. Special Powers Act, 1932 (XIV of 1932), provided as follows:

> "Whoever, by word, either spoken or written, or by signs or by visible representations,or otherwise, instigates, expressly or by implication, any person or class of persons

not to pay or to defer payment of any liability, and whoever does any act, with intent or knowing it to be likely that any words, signs or visible representations containing such instigation shall thereby be communicated directly or indirectly to any person or class of persons, in any manner whatsoever, shall be punishable with imprisonment which may extend to six months, or with fine, extending to Rs. 250, or with both."

The appellant, who was prosecuted under the section for delivering speeches instigating cultivators not to pay enhanced irrigation rates to the Government, applied to the High Court for a writ of *Habeas Corpus* on the ground, amongst others, that the said section was inconsistent with Art. 19(1) (a) of the Constitution and as such void.The High Court decided in favour of the appellant and he was released. The State appealed to this Court and the question for determination was whether the impugned section embodied reasonable restrictions in the interests of public order and was thus protected by Art. 19(2) of the Constitution.

Held, that even though in a comprehensive sense all the grounds specified in Art. 19(2) of the Constitution on which any reasonable restrictions on the right to freedom of speech must be based can be brought under the general head "public order", that expression, inserted into the Article by the Constitution (First Amendment) Act, 1951, must be demarcated from the other grounds and ordinarily read in an exclusive sense to mean public peace, safety and tranquility in contradistinction to national upheavals, such as revolution, civil strife and war, affecting the security of the State.
Romesh Thappar vs. *The State of Madras* (1950) S.C.R. 594, *Brij Bhushan* vs.*The State of Delhi*. (1950) S.C.R. 605, *The State of Bihar* vs. *Shailabala Devi*. (1952) S.C.R. 654 and *Cantewell* vs. *Connecticut*. (1940) 310 U.S. 296, discussed.

It is well settled by decisions of this Court that in a restriction in order to be reasonable must have a reasonable relation to the object the Legislation has in view and must not go beyond it. Restrictions, therefore, meant to be in the interest of public order which have no proximate relationship or nexus with it but can be only remotely or hypothetically connected with it, cannot be reasonable within the meaning of Art. 19(2) of the Constitution.
Rex vs. *Basudeva*, A.I.R.(1950) F.C. 67, applied.
Ramji Lal Modi vs. *The State of U.P.* (1957) S.C.R. 860 and *Virendra* vs. *The State of Punjab*, (1958) S.C.R. 308, explained.

So judged, it cannot be said that the acts prohibited under the wide and sweeping provisions of s. 3 of the Act can have any proximate or even foreseeable connection with public order sought to be protected by it, and, consequently, that section, being violative of the right to freedom of speech guaranteed by Art. 19(1) (a) of the Constitution, must be struck down as unconstitutional.

It would be incorrect to argue that since instigation by a single individual not to pay taxes might ultimately lead to a revolution resulting in distruction of public order, that instigation must have a proximate connection with public order. No fundamental rights can be restricted on such hypothetical and imaginary consideration.

Nor is it possible to accept the argument that in a democratic set up there can be no scope for agitational approach or that any instigation to break a bad law must by itself constitute a breach of public order, for to do so without obvious limitations would be to destroy the right to freedom of speech on which democracy is founded.

It is not possible to apply the doctrine of severability relating to fundamental rights as enunciated by this Court to the provisions of the impugned section, since it is not possible

to precisely determine whether the various categories of instigation mentioned therein fall within or without the constitutionally permissible limits of legislation and separate the valid parts from the invalid.
R.M.D. Chamarbaugwalla vs. *The Union of India* (1957) S.C.R.93o, explained and distinguished.
Romesh Thappar vs. *The State of Madras* (1950) S.C.R. 594 and *Chintaman Rao* vs. *The State o Madhya Pradesh.* (1950) S.C.R. 759, referred to.

JUDGMENT
CRIMINAL APPELLATE JURISDICTION: Criminal Appeal No. 76 of 1956.

Appeal from the judgment and order dated August 27, 1954, of the Allahabad High Court in Criminal Misc. Writ No. 20 of 1954.

K. L. Misra, Advocate-General for the State of Uttar Pradesh. G. Q. Mathur and C. P. Lal, for the appellants. N. S. Bindra, for the respondent.1960. January 21. The Judgment of the Court was delivered by SUBBA RAO J.—This appeal raises the question of interpretation of the words " in the interest of public order " in Art. 19(2) of the Constitution.

The facts are not in dispute and they lie in a small compass. The respondent, Dr. Rammanohar Lohia, is the General Secretary of the Socialist Party of India. The U. P. Government enhanced the irrigation rates for water supplied from canals to cultivators. The party to which the respondent belongs resolved to start an agitation against the said enhancement for the alleged reason that it placed an unbearable burden upon the cultivators. Pursuant to the policy of his party, the respondent visited Farrukhabad and addressed two public meetings wherein he made speeches instigating the audience not to pay enhanced irrigation rates to the Government. On July 4, 1954, at 10 p.m. he was arrested and produced before the City Magistrate, Farrukhabad, who remanded him for two days. After investigation, the Station Officer, Kaimganj, filed a charge-sheet against the respondent before Sri P. R. Gupta, a Judicial Officer at Farrukhabad. On July 6, 1954, the Magistrate went to the jail to try the case against the respondent, but the latter took objection to the trial being held in the jail premises. When the Magistrate insisted upon proceeding with the trial, the respondent obtained an adjournment on the ground that he would like to move the High Court for transfer of the case from the file of the said Magistrate. Thereafter the respondent filed a petition before the High Court for a writ of*Habeas Corpus* on the ground, among others, that s. 3 of the U. P. Special Powers Act (Act No. XIV of 1932), 1932, (hereinafter called the Act) was void under the Constitution.

In the first instance the petition came up for disposal before a division bench of the High Court at Allahabad consisting of Desai and Chaturvedi, Elaborate arguments were addressed before them covering a wide field. The learned Judges delivered differing judgments expressing their views on the main points raised before them. They referred the matter to the Chief Justice for obtaining the opinion of a third Judge on the following two points: "(i) Was the' provision of s. 3 of the U. P. Special Powers Act of 1932 making it penal for a person by spoken words to instigate class of persons not to pay dues recoverable as arrears of land revenue, inconsistent with Art. 19(1)(a) of the Constitution on the 26th of January, 1950 ?" and "(ii) if so, was it in the interests of public order ?". The petition was placed before Agarwala, J., as a third Judge, who agreeing with Desai, J., gave the following answers to the questions referred to him :

> Question No. (i). "The provision of section's of the U. P. Special Powers Act, 1932, making it penal for a person by spoken words to instigate a class of persons not to pay dues recoverable as arrears of land revenue, was inconsistent with Article 19(1)(a) of the Constitution on the 26th January, 1950."

> Question No. (ii). " The restrictions imposed by section 3 of the U. P. Special Powers Act, 1932, were not in the interests of public order."

In the usual course the matter was placed before the two learned Judges who first heard the case and they, on the basis of the majority view, allowed the petition and directed the respondent to be released.. The State has preferred the present appeal against the said order of the High Court.

The learned Advocate General, appearing for the appellant. stated before us that he did not propose to canvass the correctness of the majority view on one of the important points raised in the case, namely, that the effect of the passing of the Act did not *ipso facto* deprive a citizen of his freedom of speech guaranteed. under Art. 19(1) (a) of the Constitution and its validity should be tested by the provisions of Art. 19(2) thereof. He did not. concede the validity of the finding in this regard but assumed its correctness for the purpose of this case. Nothing further, therefore, need be mentioned on this point.

The gist of the argument of the learned Advocate General may be stated thus: The legislature can make laws placing reasonable restrictions on the rights of a citizen to freedom of speech and expression in the interests of public order among other grounds. The words "in the interests of public order" are wider in connotation than the words "for the maintenance of public order". Laws are rules made by the legislature for the governance of the people in the State which they are bound to obey, and they are enacted to keep public peace and order. The avowed object of s. 3 of the Act was to prevent persons from instigating others to break the laws imposing a liability upon a person or class of persons to pay taxes and other dues to the State, any authority or to any land-owner. The impugned section was enacted in the interests of public order and therefore the section was protected by Art. 19(2) of the Constitution. The learned Advocate General pointed out that the object of the State in preferring this appeal was to obtain the decision of this Court on the question of constitutional validity of s. 3 of the Act and not to pursue the matter against Dr. Lohia.

The respondent was not present at the time the appeal was heard and was not represented by an advocate. As the question raised was an important one, we requested Mr. N. S. Bindra to assist the Court, and he kindly agreed to do so. He supported the majority view of the High Court. We record our thanks for his assistance.

At the outset it would not be out of place to notice briefly the history of the Act. The Act was originally passed in the year 1932 during the British rule. In an attempt to offset the campaign of non-payment of taxes and other forms of agitation resorted to by the Congress Party, originally it was put on the statute book for one year; but in 1940 when the State was under the "Governor's rule", the Act was made permanent. Under the Act, ss. 1 and 2 came into effect immediately on the passing of the Act and S. 1(2) enabled the Government by notification to extend all or any of the remaining sections to any district or to any part of a district in the United Provinces. After the Constitution, the Act was not repealed but was allowed to continue, with necessary adaptations, in the statue book. Between April and June, 1954, the State Government extended the provisions of the Act to 33 districts including Farrukhabad district. Now let us look at the provisions of the Act to ascertain its scope and field of operation. The preamble discloses that it was enacted in 1932 to make provision against and to take powers to deal with instigation to the illegal refusal of the payment of certain liablities and s. 2 defines " liablity " to mean "land revenue or any sum recoverable as arrears of land revenue or any tax, rate, cess or other dues or amount payable to Government or to any local authority, or rent of agricultural land or anything recoverable as arrears of or along with such rent". Section 3 prescribes the punishment for instigation to the non-payment of a liability. As the argument centres round this section, it will be convenient to read the same:

Section 3: Whoever, by word, either spoken or written, or by signs or by visible representations, or otherwise, instigates, expressly or by implication, any person or class of persons not to pay or to defer payment of any liability, and whoever does any act, with intent or knowing it to be likely that any words, signs or visible representations con. taining such instigation shall thereby be communicated directly or indirectly to any person or class of persons, in any manner whatsoever, shall be punishable with imprisonment which may extend to six months, or with fine, extending to Rs. 250, or with both."

Section 4 says that any person to whom an arrear of liability is due may apply to the Collector to realize it and the Collector is authorized to realize the same as an arrear of land revenue. The impugned section may be dissected into the following components (i) whoever by word, either spoken or written, or by signs or by visible representations or otherwise, (ii) instigates, (iii) expressly or by implication, (iv) any person or class of persons, (v) not to pay any liability, (vi) to defer payment of any liability, (vii) does an act with intent that any words etc. shall be communicated to any person or class of persons, (viii) with the knowledge that it is likely that such words etc. shall be communicated to any person or class of persons, (ix) such communication may be made directly, or indirectly and (x) shall be punished with imprisonment or with fine or with both. Under this section a wide net has been cast to catch in a variety of acts of instigation ranging from friendly advice to a systematic propaganda not to pay or to defer payment of liability to Government, any authority or to any person to whom rent is payable in respect of agricultural land. The meaning of this section, read along with ss. 2 and 4, can be ascertained more clearly by illustration than by definition. (1) A instigates B not to pay any liability to Government, any authority or to any land owner; (2) A instigates B to defer payment of any liability - to Government, any authority or landlord; (3) A instigates a class of persons to do the same; (4) A may do any one of the foregoing things not only by word, but also by signs, visible representations or otherwise; (5) A may do any one of the things bona fide either to get the claim decided in a Court of law or to gain time to get the law changed; (6) A may instigate B not to pay any amount due to Government or to any authority, but the said amount can be recovered by the authority concerned as arrears of land revenue; (7) A may tell C with intention or with knowledge that the said instigation may be communicated to B so that he may not pay; (8) any statement by A to C may imply such instigation. In its wide amplitude the section takes in the innocent and the guilty persons, bona fide and mala fide advice, individuals and class, abstention from payment and deferment of payment, expressed or implied instigation, indirect or direct instigation, liability due not only to Government but to any authority or landholder. In short, no person, whether legal adviser or a friend or a well-wisher of a person instigated can escape the tentacles of this section, though in fact the rent due has been collected through coercive process or otherwise.

We shall now proceed to consider the constitutional validity of this section. The material portions of the relevant provisions of the Constitution may now be read: Article 19: " (1) All citizens shall have the right-

(a) to freedom of speech and expression;

(2) Nothing in sub-clause (a) of clause (1) shall affect the operation of any existing law, or prevent the State from making any law, in so far as such law imposes reasonable restrictions on the exercise of the right conferred by the said sub-clause in the interests of the security of the State, friendly relations with foreign States, public order, decency or morality or in relation to contempt of court, defamation or incitement to an offence."

Clause (2) of Art. 19 was amended by the Constitution (First Amendment) Act, 1951. By this amendment several new grounds of restrictions upon the freedom of speech have been introduced, such as friendly relations with foreign States, public order and incitement to an offence. It is self evident and common place that freedom of speech is one of the bulwarks of a democratic form of Government. It is equally obvious that freedom of speech can only thrive in an orderly society. Clause (2) of Art. 19, therefore, does not affect the operation of any existing law or prevent the State from making any law in so far as such law imposes reasonable restrictions on the exercise of the right of freedom of speech in the interest of public order, among others. To sustain the existing law or a new law made by the State under cl. (2) of Art. 19, so far as it is relevant to the present enquiry, two conditions should be complied with, viz., (i) the restrictions imposed must be reasonable; and (ii) they should be in the interests of public order. Before we consider the scope of the word,-, of limitation,"reasonable restrictions" and "in the interests of ", it is necessary to ascertain the true meaning of the expression public order "in the said clause. The expression "public order" has a very wide connotation. Order is the basic need in any organised society. It implies the orderly state of society or community in which citizens can peacefully pursue their normal activities of life. In the words of an eminent Judge of the Supreme Court of America "the essential rights are subject to the, elementary need for order without which the guarantee of those rights would be a mockery". The expression has not been define in the Constitution, but it occurs in List II of its Seventh Schedule and is also inserted by the Constitution (First Amendment) Act, 1951 in el. (2) of Art.

19. The sense in which it is used in Art. 19 can only be appreciates by ascertaining how the Article was construed before it was inserted therein and what was the defect to remedy which the Parliament inserted the same by the said amendment. The impact of cl. (2) of Art. 19 on Art. 19(1)(a) before the said

amendment was subject to judicial scrutiny by this Court in *Romesh Thappar* vs. *The State of Madras*(1). There the Government of Madras, in exercise of their powers under s. 9(1-A) of the Madras Maintenance of Public Order Act, 1949, purported to issue an order whereby they imposed a ban upon the entry and circulation of the journal called "Cross -.Roads" in that State. The petitioner therein contended that the said order contravened his fundamental right to freedom of speech and expression. At the time when that order was issued the (expression "public order" was not in Art. 19(2) of the Constitution; but the words "the security of the State" were there. In considering whether the impugned Act was made in the interests of security of the State, Patanjali Sastri, J., as he then was, after citing the observation of Stephen in his*Criminal Law of England*, states:

> "Though all these offences thus involve disturbances of public tranquillity and are in theory offences against public order, the difference between them being only a difference of degree, yet for the purpose of gurading the punishment to be inflicted in respect of them they may be classified into different minor categories as has been done by the Indian Penal Code. Similarly, the Constitution, in formulating the varying criteria for permissible legislation imposing restrictions on the fundamental rights enumerated in article 19 (1), has placed in a distinct category those offences against public order which aim at undermining the security of the State or overthrowing it, and made their prevention the sole justification for legislative abridgement of freedom of speech and expression, that is to say, nothing less than endangering the foundations of the State or threatening its overthrow could justify curtailment of the rights to freedom of speech and expression..."

The learned Judge continued to state:

" The Constitution thus requires a line to be drawn in the

> field of public order or tranquillity marking off, may be, roughly, the boundary between those serious and aggravated forms of public disorder which are calculated to endanger the security of the State and the relatively minor breaches of the peace of a purely local significance, treating for this purpose differences in degree as if they were differences in kind. "

The learned Judge proceeded further to state:

> "We, are therefore of opinion that unless a law restricting freedom of speech and expression is directed solely against the undermining of the security of the State or the overthrow of it, such law cannot fall within the reservation under clause (2) of article 19, although the restrictions which it seeks to impose may have been conceived generally in the interests of public order."

This decision establishes two propositions, viz., (i) maintenance of public order is equated with maintenance of public tranquillity; and (ii) the offences against public order are divided into two categories, viz., (a) major offences affecting the security of the State, and (b) minor offences involving breach of purely local significance. This Court in *Brij Bhushan* vs. *The state of Delhi* (1) followed the earlier decision in the context of s. 7 (1) (c) of the East Punjab Public Safety Act, 1949. Fazl Ali, J., in his dissenting judgment gave the expression " public order " a wider meaning than that given by the majority view. The learned Judge observed at p. 612 thus:

> "When we approach the matter in this way, we find that while' public disorder' is wide enough to cover a small riot or an affray and other cases where peace is disturbed by, or affects, a small group or persons, 'public unsafety (or insecurity of the State), will usually be connected with serious internal disorders and such disturbances of public tranquillity as jeopardize the security of the State."

This observation also indicates that "public order" is equated with public peace and safety. Presumably in an attempt to get over the effect of these two decisions, the expression "public order" was inserted in Art. 19 (2) of the Constitution by the Constitution (First Amendment) Act, 1951, with a view to bring in offences involving breach of purely local significance within the scope of permissible restrictions under cl. (2) of Art. 19. After the said amendment, this Court explained the scope of *Romesh Thappar's* case (1) in *The State of Bihar* vs. *shailabala Devi* (). That case was concerned with the constitutional validity of s. 4 (1) (a) of the Indian Press (Emergency Powers) Act, 1931. It deals with the words or signs or visible representations which incite to or encourage, or tend to incite to or encourage the commission of any offence of murder or any cognizable offence involving violence. Mahajan, J., as he then was, observed at p. 660. The deduction that a person would be free to incite to murder or other cognizable offence through the press with impunity drawn from our decision in Romesh Thappar's case could easily have been avoided as it was avoided by Shearer J., who in very emphatic terms said as follows:

> "I have read and re-read the judgments of the Supreme Court, and I can find nothing in them myself which bear directly on the point at issue, and leads me to think that, in their opinion, a restriction of this kind is no longer permissiblc."

The validity of that section came up for consideration after the Constitution (First Amendment) Act, 1951, which was expressly made retrospective, and therefore the said section clearly fell within the ambit of the words "in the interest of public order". That apart the observations of Mahajan, J., as he then was, indicate that even without the amendment that section would have been good inasmuch as it aimed to prevent incitement to murder.

The words "public order" were also understood in America and England as offences against public safety or public peace.

The Supreme Court of America observed in *Cantewell* vs. *Connecticut* (1) thus:

> "The offence known as breach of the peace embraces a great variety of conduct destroying or menacing public order and tranquillity. It includes not only violent acts and words likely to produce violence in others. No one would have the hardihood to suggest that the principle of freedom of speech sanctions incitement to riot. When clear and present -danger of riot, disorder, interference with traffic upon the public streets, or other immediate threat to public safety, peace, or order appears, the power of the State to prevent or punish is obvious."

The American decisions sanctioned a variety of restrictions on the freedom of speech in the interests of public order.

They cover the entire gamut of restrictions that can be imposed under different heads in Art. 19(2) of our Constitution. The following summary of some of the cases of the Supreme Court of America given in a well-known book on Constitutional Law illustrates the range of categories of cases covering that expression.

> "In the interests of public order, the State may prohibit and punish the causing of 'loud and raucousnoise' in streets and public places by means of sound amplifying instruments, regulate the hours and place of public discussion, and the use of the public streets for the purpose of exercising freedom of speech; provide for the expulsion of hecklers from meetings and assemblies, punish utterances tending to incite an immediate breach of the peace or riot as distinguished from utterances causing mere 'public inconvenience, annoyance or unrest'."

In England also Acts like Public Order Act, 1936, Theatres Act, 1843 were passed: the former making it an offence to use threatening, abusive or insulting words or behaviour in any public place or at any public meeting with intent to provoke a breach of the peace or whereby a breach of the peace is likely to be caused, and the latter was enacted to authorise the Lord Chamberlain to prohibit any stage play whenever he thought its public performance would militate against good manners, decorum and the preservation of the public peace. The reason underlying all the decisions is that if the freedom of speech was not restricted in the manner the relevant Acts did, public safety and tranquillity in the State would be affected.

But in India under Art. 19(2) this wide concept of "public order" is split up under different heads. It enables the imposition of reasonable restrictions on the exercise of the right to freedom of speech and expression in the interests of the security of the State, friendly relations with foreign States, public order, decency or morality, or in relation to contempt of court, defamation or incitement to an offence. All the grounds mentioned therein can be brought under the general head "public order" in its most comprehensive sense. But the juxtaposition of the different grounds indicates that, though sometimes they tend to overlap, they must be ordinarily intended to exclude each other. "Public order" is therefore something which is demarcated from the others. In that limited sense, particularly in view of, the history of the amendment, it can be pustulated that"public order ".is synonymous with public peace, safety and tranquillity. The next question is what do the words "interest of public order" mean ? The learned Advocate General contends that the phrase "in the interest of public order" is of a wider connotation than the words "for the maintenance of public order" and, therefore, any breach of law which may have the tendency, however remote, to disturb the public order would be covered by the said phrase. Support is sought to be drawn for this wide proposition from the judgment of this Court in *Ramji Lal Modi* vs. *The State of U.P.* (1). It is not necessary to state the facts of that case, as reliance is placed only on the observations of Das, C.J., at p. 865, which read:

"It will be noticed that the language employed in the

> amended clause is "in the interests of" and not "for the maintenance of". As one of us pointed out in *Debi Saron* vs. *The State of Bihar* (2), the expression "in the interests of" makes the ambit of protection very wide. A law may not have been designed to directly maintain public order and yet it may have been enacted in the interests of public order."

The learned Chief Justice again in *Virendra* vs. *The State of Punjab* (3) observed, at p. 317, much to the same effect:

> "As has been explained by this Court in Ramji Lal Modi v. The State of U.P. (1), the words "in the interests of" are words of great amplitude and are much wider than the words "for the maintenance of." The expression "in the interests of" makes the ambit of the protection very wide, for a law may not have been designed to directly maintain the public order or to directly protect the general public against any particular evil and yet it may have been enacted "in the interests of" the public order or the general public as the case may be."

We do not understand the observations of the Chief Justice to mean that any remote or fanciful connection between the impugned Act and the public order. would be sufficient to sustain its validity. The learned Chief Justice was only making a distinction between an Act which expressly and directly purported to maintain public order and one which did not expressly state the said purpose but left it to be implied therefrom; and between an Act that directly maintained public order and that indirectly brought about the same result. The distinction does not ignore the necessity for intimate connection between the Act and the public order sought to be maintained by the Act. Apart from the said phrase, another limitation in the clause, namely, that the restrictions shall be reasonable, brings about the same result. The word "reasonable" has been defined by this Court in more than one decision. It has been held that in order to be reasonable, "restrictions must have reasonable relation to the object which the legislation seeks to achieve and must not go in excess of that object". The restriction made "in the interests of public order" must also have reasonable relation to the object to be achieved, i.e., the public order. If the restriction has no proximate relationship to the achievement of public order, it cannot be said that the restriction is a reasonable restriction within the meaning of the said clause. A full bench decision of the Federal Court in *Rex* vs. *Basudeva* (1) contains some observations which give considerable assistance to construe the words. In that case, the appellant was detained in pursuance of the order made by the Government of U.P. under the U.P. Prevention of Black-Marketing (Temporary Powers) Act, 1947. The question was whether the preventive detention provided for in s. 3(1) (i) of the said Act was preventive detention for reasons connected with the maintenance of public order. The argument in that case ran on the same lines as in the present case. The learned Advocate General there urged that habitual black-marketing in essential commodities was bound sooner or later to cause a dislocation of the machinery of controlled distribution which, in turn, might lead to breaches of the peace and that, therefore, detention with a view to prevent such black marketing was covered by the (1) A.I.R. (1950) F.C. 67 entry. Answering that argument, Patanjali Sastri, J.,as he then was, pointed out, at p. 69:

> "Activities such as these are so remote in the chain of relation to the maintenance of public order that preventive detention on account of them cannot, in our opinion, fall within the purview of Entry I of List II...........The connection contemplated must, in our view, be real and proximate., not far-fetched or problematical." The decision, in our view, lays down the correct test. The limitation imposed in the interests of public order to be a reasonable restriction, should be one which has a proximate connection or nexus with public order, but not one far-fetched,

> hypothetical or problematical or too remote in the chain of its relation with the public order. We shall now test the impugned section, having regard to the aforesaid principles. Have the acts prohibited under s. 3 any proximate connection with public safety or tranquility ? We have already analysed the provisions of s. 3 of the Act. In an attempt to indicate its wide sweep, we pointed out that any instigation by word or visible representation not to pay or defer payment of any exaction or even contractual dues to Government, authority or a landowner is made an offence. Even innocuous speeches are prohibited by threat of punishment. There is no proximate or even forseeable connection between such instigation and the public order sought to be protected under this section. We cannot accept the argument of the learned Advocate General that instigation of a single individual not to pay tax or dues is a spark which may in the long run ignite a revolutionary movement destroying public order. We can only say that fundamental rights cannot be controlled on such hypothetical and imaginary considerations. It is said that in a democratic set up there is no scope for agitational approach and that if a law is bad the only course is to get it modified by democratic process and that any instigation to break the law is in itself a disturbance of, the public order. If this argument without obvious limitations be accepted, it would destroy the right to freedom of speech which is the very foundation of democratic way of life. Unless there is a proximate connection between the instigation and the public order, the restriction, in our view, is neither reasonable nor is it in the interest of public order. In this view, we must strike down s. 3 of the Act as infringing the fundamental right guaranteed under Art. 19(1)(a) of the Constitution.

The learned Advocate General then contended that the section is severable and that if so severed, the section may be made to function within the limited field that stands the test of Art.

19(2) of the Constitution. He asks us to read the section as follows :

> "Whoever, by word, either spoken or written, or by signs or by visible representations, or otherwise, instigates, expressly or by implication, any class of persons not to pay or to defer payment of any liability, and whoever does any act, with intent or knowing it to be likely that any words, signs or visible representations containing such instigation shall thereby be communicated directly or indirectly to any class of persons, in any manner whatsoever, shall be punishable with imprisonment which may extend to six months, or with fine, extending to Rs. 250, or with both."
> By so doing he argues that instigation of a class of persons only is made liable and thereby the section is rid of the vice of unconstitutionality.

The doctrine of severability vis-a-vis the fundamental rights is sought to be supported on the basis of the wording of Art. 13(1) of the Constitution. Under that Article laws, in so far as they are inconsistent with the provisions of Part III, are void only to the extent of such inconsistency. But this implies that consistent and inconsistent parts of a law are severable. This doctrine in its relation to fundamental rights was considered by this Court in three decisions. In *Romesh Thapper's* case (1) such an. argument has been repelled by this Court. Patanjali Sastri, J., as he then was, stat@d the legal position thus at p. 603: (1) [1950) S.C.R. 594, 600, 601 602.

> "Where a law purports to authorise the imposition of restrictions on a fundamental right in language wide enough to cover restrictions both within and without the limits of constitutionally permissible legislative action affecting such right,it is not possible to uphold it even so far as it may be applied within the constitutional limits, as it is not severable. So long as the possibility of its being applied for purposes not sanctioned by the Constitution cannot be ruled out, it

must be held to be wholly unconstitutional and void."

In *Chintaman Rao* vs. *The State of Madhya Pradesh* the same principle is again restated. Mahajan, J., as he then was observed at p. 765:

> "The law even to the extent that it could be said to authorize the imposition of restrictions in regard to agricultural labour cannot be held valid because the language employed is wide enough to cover restrictions both within and without the limits of constitutionally permissible legislative action affecting the right. So long as the possibility of' its being applied for purposes not sanctioned by the Constitution cannot be ruled out, it must be held to be wholly void."

The wide reach of this principle appears to have been circumscribed to some extent in a later decision of this Court in *R. M. D. Chamarbaugwalla* vs. *The Union of India* (2). In that case the constitutionality of ss. 4 and 5 of the Prize Competitions Act (42 of 1955) was challenged on the ground that prize competition' as defined in s. 2(d) of the Act included not merely competitions that were of a gambling nature but also those in which success depended to a substantial degree on skill. This Court, having regard to the history of the legislation, the declared object thereof and the wording of the statute, came to the conclusion that the competitions which were sought to be controlled and regulated by the Act were only those competitions in which success did not depend to any substantial degree on skill. That conclusion was sufficient to reject the contention raised in that case; but even on the assumption that prize competition as defined in s. 2(d) of the Act included those in which success depended to substantial degree on skill as well as those in which it did not so depend, this Court elaborately considered the doctrine of severability and laid down as many as seven rules of construction. On the application of the said rules it was held that the impugned provisions were severable in their application to competitions in which success did not depend to any substantial degree on skill.

The foregoing discussion yields the following results: (1) "Public order" is synonymous with public safety and tranquillity: it is the absence of disorder involving breaches of local significance in contradistinction to national upheavals, such as revolution, civil strife, war, affecting the security of the State; (2) there must be proximate and reasonable nexus between the speech and the public order; (3) s. 3, as it now stands, does not establish in most of the cases comprehended by it any such nexus; (4) there is a conflict of decision on the question of severability in the context of an offending provision the language whereof is wide enough to cover restrictions both within and without the limits of constitutionally permissible legislation; one view is that it cannot be split up if there is possibility of its being applied for purposes not sanctioned by the Constitution and the other view is that such a provision is valid if it is severable in its application to an object which is clearly demarcated from other object or objects falling outside the limits of constitutionally permissible legislation; and (5) the provisions of the section are so inextricably mixed up that it is not possible to apply the doctrine of severability so as to enable us to affirm the validity of a part of it and reject the rest.

It is not necessary in this case to express our preference for one or other of the foregoing decisions. Assuming that the summary of the rules of construction given in the last of the cases cited supra are correct and exhaustive, we are not satisfied that in the instant case the impugned section with the omissions suggested by the learned Advocate General could, wholly or to any extent, be salvaged. The words of the section with the suggested omissions continue to suffer from the same vice they are subjected to without the said omissions. The suggested omissions from the section only exclude individuals from the operation of the section and confine it to a class of persons and in other respects it is not freed from the defects already pointed out by us. In *R. M. D. Chamarbaugwalla's* case (1) the difference between two classes of competitions, namely, those that are of gambling nature and those in which success depends on skill, is clear-cut and has long been recognized in legislative practice. But in the present case it is not even possible to predicate with some kind of precision the different categories of instigation falling within or without the field of constitutional prohibitions. The constitutional validity of a section cannot be made to depend upon such an uncertain factor. Whether the principle of the first two decisions is applied or that of the third is invoked, the constitutional validity of the section cannot be sustained. We, therefore, hold that s. 3 of the Act is void as infringing Art. 19(1)(a) of the Constitution. The, entire section therefore must be struck down as invalid. If so, the prosecution of the respondent under that section is void.

The learned Advocate General made an impassioned appeal to persuade us to express our view that though the present section is void on the ground that it is an unreasonable restriction on the fundamental right, in the interests of public order the State could legitimately re-draft it in a way that it would conform to the provisions of Art. 19(2) of the Constitution. It is not this Court's province to express or give advice or make general observations on situations that are not presented to it in a particular case. It is always open to the State to make such reasonable restrictions which are permissible under Art. 19(2) of the Constitution.

In the result, the appeal is dismissed.

Appeal dismissed.

3. RAMMANOHAR LOHIA AND OTHERS vs. V.S. SUNDARAM

Bench: B N C

Equivalent citations: 1955 CriLJ 1603

ORDER
26/4/1955

Brij Narain J.C.

1. This is an application by Dr. Rammonohar Lohia and six others for a writ of *Habeas Corpus*. The petitioners alleged that they were wrongfully and illegally arrested on 11-4-1955 at about 5-30 p.m. in the Tikendrajit Park, Imphal when Dr. Ram Monohar Lohia was delivering a speech on the ground that the holding of public meetings was prohibited by an order on the analogy of Section 144, Criminal P.C., dated 17-12-1954, passed i by the District Magistrate, Manipur, within a radius of two miles from the Court of the District Magistrate, Manipur and this order was subsequently substituted by another order dated 21-12-1954 by which the area was increased to 4 miles and both those orders were proclaimed without being published in the Manipur Gazette, from police van.

On 15-2-1955 the Chief Commissioner, Manipur, published the Notification No. HP/83/54 whereby this order analogous to Section 144, Criminal P.C. was extended for another period of 3 months within the radius of 4 miles from the Court of the District Magistrate, Manipur.

According to the petitioners the people of Manipur, after the illegal abolition of the Manipur State Legislative Assembly, have been exercising their right under Article 19 of the Constitution of India in assembling peaceably and in giving expression and making speeches on the subject, but the executive Government have denied them their above-mentioned fundamental rights and arrested various persons under various sections of the Indian Penal Code. Accordingly they formed a reception committee of which S. Nabakumar Singh was elected the Secretary for inviting the petitioners for holding a public meeting on the 11th instant in the Tikendrajit Park, Imphal to discuss whether the Legislative Assembly and the Council of Ministers were rightly abolished and whether those should be reinstated. S. Nabakumar Singh applied to the District Magistrate, Manipur on 7-4-1955 for holding the said public meeting but the District Magistrate wanted a guarantee illegally that there would be no disorder, but as no such guarantee could possibly be given as the petitioners could not become responsible for any action of other people present, the District Magistrate refused permission—on 11-4-1955. The petitioners held a meeting in, exercise of their fundamental right under Article 19 of the Constitution, and when even though there was nobody else except 3 or 4 persons who also hurriedly left the place at the sight of the Inspector General of Police and the District Magistrate coming near them, the District Magistrate told the petitioners that as there was an order Under Section 144, Criminal P.C., prohibiting assemblage of 5 or more persons within a radius of 4 miles from the office of the District Magistrate, Manipur, in which lay the place of their meeting, the entire meeting was unlawful and he ordered them to disperse. No time was given to them to disperse and the petitioners were arrested Under Sections 143, 145 and 188, IPC.

The petitioners were produced before the Additional District Magistrate, Manipur, 3 hours later, and the latter ordered that the petitioners might go on bail of Rs. 1000/- each otherwise they would be remanded to jail 'bajat' (custody) till 25-4-1955 without assigning any reason for such remand. Inside the jail also the petitioners have alleged, by their affidavit dated 20-4-1955, that they have been physically tortured by the jail warders by being pushed and dragged and some of the petitioners were even thrown down on the floor. It has further been alleged that some in the petitioners have been kept for a day in a single cell being locked up day and night quite contrary to law.

2. On behalf of the opposite parties Shri V.S. Sundaram, District Magistrate, has in his affidavit contended that the present application is misconceived and is not maintainable as there is no scope for interference under Article 226 of the Constitution in this matter. It has been contended that the Constitution of the Manipur State Act ceased to have any force after the integration of the Manipur State with the Union Government, and the Manipur State Legislative Assembly and the Council of Ministers were lawfully abolished. Further contention on behalf of the opposite parties is 'that though the Code of Criminal Procedure has not been expressly extended to this State but the provisions of the Code are strictly followed in the administration, of criminal justice by all Courts including the highest Court of the State, and thus judicial recognition is given to the applicability of the Code subject to any specific provision of the Manipur State Courts Act, 1947, and so the order on the analogy of Section 144, Criminal P.C. could legally be promulgated by the District Magistrate, Manipur, as was done in this case.

The District Magistrate apprehended breach of public peace and disturbance of public tranquillity, and he was satisfied that a speedy remedy was necessary to maintain public order, and so the order, mentioned above were duly promulgated and were brought to the knowledge of the general public and the present petitioners fully knew about these orders before 11-4-1955. The permission to hold the meeting on 11-4-1955 on the Polo Ground (Tikendrajit Park) was not granted as it was apprehended that such a meeting which was to be addressed by Dr. Rammanohar Lohia, petitioner No. 1, a prominent leader of the P.S. Party, would result in the disturbance of public peace and order. On 11-4-1955 according to the opposite parties, Dr. Rammanohar Lohia petitioner No. 1 with 11 others including the remaining petitioners assembled in the Polo Ground and a big crowd also gathered there.

On receipt of this information the District Magistrate along with the Inspector General of Police went to the spot and found

Dr. Rammanohar Lohia making a speech advocating movement which occasioned breach of peace in the past. The District Magistrate interrupted him and gave him his identity, informed him of the existence of the order Under Section 144, Criminal P.C. and also showed him the order. Dr. Rammanohar Lohia answered back that the said order was illegal and was about to continue his speech whereupon the District Magistrate declared this assembly unlawful and commanded it to disperse. At this 5 persons dispersed but Dr. Lohia and six other persons refused to disperse and persisted in holding the meeting, and so they were placed under arrest under Sections 143, 145 and 188, IPC. As these petitioners are going to be tried for these substantive offences in due process of law by the Additional District Magistrate, it is contended that the present petitioners are not entitled to maintain the present Writ petition.

3. On behalf of the State the judicial record of G, R. Case No. 213 of 1955 relating to the case against the petitioners under Sections 143, 145 and 188, IPC was also produced before me and I think the F. I. R. deserves to be taken into consideration. It is as follows:

O. C. Imphal P. S.

Today at about 5-30 p.m. the following 7 persons held a public meeting in the Tikendrajit Park, about a mile North-West of Imphal P.S. Within about 50′ from the place where they were holding the meeting, there was nobody else except 2/3 persons who also hurriedly left the place at the sight of the I.G.P. Anil D.M., Manipur, coming near them. The D.M. told the seven persons, who were together and one of whom, Dr. Lohia, was delivering a speech addressing the public gathering near the main road at a distance of about 50′ only from him, that as there was order Under Section 144, Criminal P.C., prohibiting assemblage of five or more persons within a radius of four miles from the office of the D.M., Manipur, in which lay the place of their meeting, the meeting was unlawful and ordered them to disperse. They refused to disperse. Dr. Lohia said to the officers that he was doing his business and that they also might do their own. They were, therefore, arrested. No force was used, against them. The names of the seven persons are given below:

1. Dr. Rammanohar Lohia
2. Laisram Achow Singh of Wangkhei
3. Aribam Tomba Surendra Sarma of Bamon Leikai
4. Oinam Budhi Singh of Pisum Oinam Leikai
5. Thongam Kanhai Singh of Waikhom Leikai
6. Thokchom Chandrasekhor Singh of Thokchom Leikai
7. Irengbam Bijoy Singh of Uripok Tourangbam Leikai

So, please register a case under Section 143/145/188, I.P.C.

The following Police Officers who were also on duty with me at the place will prove the case:

1. Sri M. Kalachand Singh, City Inspector.
2. Sri Kunjakishore Singh, Town S. I.
3. Sri Ibochouba Singh, S. I. of Police and others.

11-4-55.

Sd/-
L. Gopal Singh.
Deputy Superintendent of Police (1)
Manipur.

4. Shri Sougaijam Nabakumar Singh submitted the following application to the District Magistrate, Manipur on 7-4-1955:

To
The District Magistrate, Manipur.

Re: Permission for holding a public meeting at Polo-ground on 11-4-55.

Dear Sir,

I would be very glad if you would kindly permit us to hold a public meeting at Imphal Polo-ground at 2 p.m. 6 p.m. on 11-4-55 by using a mike. The meeting is to be addressed by the Praja Socialist leader, Dr. Rammanohar Lohia regarding the present Satyagraha movement for Legislative Answerably in Manipur.

I would also request you to permit us to use mike, on that day for publicity purpose for the said meeting within the prohibited area under Section 144, Criminal P.C.

Thanking you in anticipation.

Yours faithfully,
Sd/-
Sougaijam Nabakumar Singh
7-4-55.

5. The facts which are clearly established from the documents referred to above are that Shri S. Nabakumar Singh applied for permission on 7-4-1955 for holding a meeting regarding the present Satyagraha movement for Legislative Assembly in Manipur and this permission was not granted on the ground that a guarantee was not given to the effect that there would be no disorder at this meeting. It further appears from these documents that within about 50′ from the place where Dr. Lohia was making a speech there were only 2 or 3 persons who also hurriedly left the place at the sight of the Inspector General of Police and the District Magistrate coming near them and so only 7 persons were left at that spot. It has not been specified in the F.I.R. that any appreciable number of persons were present near the main road and so it can be safely inferred that an appreciable number of persons had not gathered there and the people going on the road might be stopping there for a very short interval just to see what was going on there. The meeting which was being addressed by Dr. Lohia thus appears to have been attended to only by the 7 petitioners.

6. The order under which the present petitioners have been arrested purports to be on the 'analogy' of Section 144, Criminal P.C, which runs as follows:

> 144. (1) In cases where, in the opinion of a District Magistrate, a Chief Presidency Magistrate, Sub-Divisional

Magistrate, or of any other Magistrate (not being a Magistrate of the third class) specially empowered by the State Government or the Chief Presidency Magistrate or the District Magistrate to act under this section, there is sufficient ground for proceeding under this section and immediate prevention or speedy remedy is desirable:

Such Magistrate may, by a written order stating the material facts of the case and served in manner provided by Section 134, direct any person to abstain from a certain act or to take certain order with certain property in his possession or under his management, if such Magistrate considers that such direction is likely to prevent, or tends to prevent, obstruction, annoyance or injury, or risk of obstruction, annoyance or injury, to any person lawfully employed, or danger to human life, health or safety, or a disturbance of the public tranquillity, or a riot, or an affray.

2. An order under this section may, in case of emergency or in cases where the circumstances do not admit of the serving in due time of a notice upon the person against whom the order is directed, be passed ex-parte.
3. An order under this section may be directed to a particular individual, or to the public generally when frequenting or visiting a particular place.
4. Any Magistrate may, either on his own motion or on the application of any person aggrieved, rescind or alter any order made under this section by himself or any Magistrate subordinate to him, or by his predecessor-in-office.
5. Where such an application is received, the Magistrate shall afford the applicant an early opportunity of appearing before him either in person or by pleader and showing cause against the order; and, if the Magistrate rejects the application wholly or in part, he shall record in writing his reasons far so doing.
6. No order under this section shall remain in force for

> more than two months from the making thereof; unless, in cases of danger to human life, health or safety, or a likelihood of a riot or an "affray, the State Government by notification in the Official Gazette, otherwise directs.

7. There is no doubt that Magistrates are empowered under Section 144(3), Criminal P.C., to temporarily override private rights for the preservation of the public tranquillity as the preservation of public peace is a paramount function of the Government. The main question which, therefore, arises for determination in this connection would be whether there was any apprehension of breach of public peace, if one man were to address a gathering of 7 persons only and whether any restriction could legally be imposed even under Section 144, Criminal P, C, on fundamental rights allowed to the citizens of Indian Union under Article 19(1)(a) and (b) under such circumstances. It has not been alleged in this case that the present petitioners had assembled there with arms or that they were in any way rowdy at the time of their arrest. There is no doubt that ordinarily the question whether there exists sufficient ground for apprehension of the breach of peace, is to be decided by the Magistrate who promulgates order under Section 144, Criminal P.C. But it is settled law that where there is no apprehension of a breach of peace, a Magistrate should not restrain the liberty of private individuals by means of an order under this section, vide *Thaldn Aung Bala* v.s *District Magistrate, Rangoon* AIR 1939 Rang 181 (A), in which it has been laid down that Section 144 deals with urgent eases of nuisance and apprehended danger of breach of public peace and where such danger is apprehended and if in consequence thereof an immediate prevention is necessary, the Magistrate specially empowered in that behalf may issue instructions to individuals or the public in general to abstain from certain acts. The power thus conferred on the magistrates is an extraordinary power which enables them to suspend the lawful rights for the public peace and safety. But the Magistrates should bear in mind that

every citizen has a right to ventilate his grievances either in the public or in private and ask for redress, and this right cannot be curtailed so long as it is exercised in a lawful manner; and it is illegal assumption of power to issue an order under Section 144, Criminal P.C. on a pretended apprehension of danger of the breach of public peace: vide *Francis Duke Coleridge Summer* vs. *Jogendra Kumar* AIR 1933 Cal 348(B); *Abdul* vs. *Lucky Narain Mundul*, 5 Cal 132(C); *Tlafizuddin* vs. *C. Laborde* AIR 1928 All 14(D) and *Sundaram Chetti* vs. *The Queen*, 6 Mad 203(FB)(E).

8. In, *In re Srikanta Iyer* AIR 1937 Mad 31.1(F), it was held that where interference with right to speak is expected, opponents should be prohibited from interfering under Section 144, Criminal P.C. and not the other persons from speaking;, vide also *Mt. Jasoda Lekhraj* vs. *Emperor* AIR 1939 Sind-167(G).

9. I have already mentioned above that the application dated 7-4-1955 referred to above shows that the speeches which were to be delivered in this meeting were regarding the Satyagraha movement for Legislative Assembly in Manipur. If the movement itself is not illegal the speeches for strengthening the movement in a non-violent manner, and given before a very limited number of persons cannot possibly be deemed to be disturbing public tranquillity. It has not been disputed before us during the course of arguments that during the time of His Highness the Maharaja Churachand Singh in the year 1938 there was an agitation for creation of Legislative Assembly. After the death of His Highness Maharaja Churachand Singh, the present Maharaja agreed to have a Legislative Assembly and the Manipur State Constitution Act, 1947 was then enacted. The provisions of this Act, if examined in detail, would go to show that His-Highness Maharaja Bodhchandra Singh (the present Maharaja) agreed to the creation of Legislative Assembly as would appear from the following sections:

> (3) **Government of the State by His Highness the Maharaja:** The territories for the time being and hereafter vested in the Maharajah are governed by and in tile name

of the Maharajah. All rights, authority and jurisdiction which appertain or are incidental to the Government of such territories arc exercisable by the Maharajah subject to the provision of this Act.

10. This means that the Maharajah agreed to become a constitutional Ruler.

8. **The Maharajah's Prerogatives:** (a) All family matters which are the Maharajah's sole concern as head of the Ruling family, all matters which are his sole concern as the Defender of Faith and all matters connected with Titles, Honours and Palace Ceremonies shall be deemed to fall within the Maharajah's personal Prerogative and in such matters the Maharajah shall exercise full discretion subject to the provisions of the Constitution and Laws of the State. 'The Maharajah's Prerogative shall not, however, be taken to comprise any matter wherein the legitimate interests of the State Administration or a civil right sustainable in a court of law is involved.' It will be within the prerogative of the Maharajah to remit punishment and pardon offenders subject to the provisions of the Manipur State Courts Act provided that this prerogative shall not prejudice the right of any individual to compensation."
9. (b) The Maharajah means His Highness the Maharajah of Manipur the Constitutional Head of the State.
10. Council of Ministers: (a) Subject to the provisions of this Act and subject also to the provisions of the Rules for the Administration of the Manipur State the Executive Authority of the State is delegated to and shall vest in the Council of Ministers.

    (b) Where under this Act or the Rules for the Administration of the State, it is requisite that the approval of the Maharajah shall be taken to any measure, the Chief Minister shall seek the approval of the Maharajah in person or in writing and shall obtain the Maharajah's orders thereon. Should in any case the Maharajah's approval be withheld, the Maharajah shall be pleased to inform the Chief Minister in person or in writing and to communicate his reasons for withholding such approval in writing to the Council.

17. There shall be constituted a State Assembly. The Assembly shall be elected for a period of three years and shall comprise Representatives freely elected by the people on an adult franchise and on the principle of Joint Electorate....

11. Under this section even the depressed classes and the poorest hill men were allowed to exercise their right of franchise along with the members of the highest classes, and no separate seats were allotted for the backward classes for which only members of those classes might be eligible for voting.

27. When the Council or the Assembly consider that a law should be enacted, the Council shall cause a bill to be drafted, which shall be laid" before the Assembly and a reasonable time shall be given for consideration thereof. The Council shall then cause to be made such alterations or amendments as may be deemed necessary in the light of the advice tendered by the Assembly and the Chief Minister shall submit the Bill in its final form for the assent of the Maharajah.

30. Where the Assent of the Maharaja to any Bill is withheld, the Council may cause the selfsame Bill to be introduced in the next session of the Assembly and if passed without amendment by a 75 per cent majority of the Assembly, the Bill shall be certified over the Seal of the Council and shall become Law.

A perusal of these sections makes it quite clear that the Manipur State Constitution Act, 1947 is sufficiently democratic and the power under this Act rests with the people, as in cases where 75 per cent majority of the Assembly agreed to pass a Bill the Maharajah's assent was waived. Thus the Maharajah was given three powers under this Constitution, viz., (1)

Prerogatives on personal matters, (2) approval or disapproval of executive order, and (3) giving assent to Legislative matters.

12. The Manipur State merged with the Dominion of India on 15-10-1949 and Article 1 of Manipur Merger Agreement given in Appendix XXXII of the White Paper on Indian States shows that by this agreement under Article 1 His Highness the Maharajah of Manipur ceded to the Dominion Government full and exclusive authority, jurisdiction and powers for and in relation to the governance of the State and agreed to transfer the Administration of the State to the Dominion Government on the fifteenth day of October 1949 (hereinafter referred to as "the said day").

13. As from the said day the Dominion Government was to be competent to exercise the said powers, authority and jurisdiction in such manner and through such agency as it may think lit.

14. This agreement thus makes it clear that His Highness the Maharajah ceded to the Dominion Government authority, jurisdiction and powers in relation to the governance of the Manipur State enjoyed by him on 15-10-1949. In accordance with the Manipur State Constitution Act, 1947 the Dominion Government is competent to exercise the powers of governance, authority and jurisdiction in such manner and through such agency as it might think fit. The question which now arises is whether the Dominion Government ever thought it proper to take a retrogressive step to annul the Manipur State Constitution Act, 1947. The Central Government passed the Manipur Administration Order, 1949 'Under Sections 3 and 4 of the Extra Provincial Jurisdiction Act, 1947 (Act XLVII of 1947) and of all other powers enabling it in this behalf on 15-10-1949 and para. 5 of this order clearly lays down that all laws in force in Manipur or any part thereof immediately before the commencement of this Order shall continue in force until repealed or amended by a competent legislature or authority.

Provided that all powers exercisable under the said laws by His Highness the Maharajah or the Government of the State shall be exercisable by the Chief Commissioner, who shall be appointed by the Central Government at the head of the administration of the Manipur State. Under paragraph 7, however, it has been laid down that as from 15-10-1949, 'the Ministers' in Manipur State shall cease to function and 'the Legislature' of the State shall stand 'dissolved'. It has been contended by learned advocate for the petitioners that paragraph 7 of the Manipur Administration Order, 1949, is ultra vires and void as the Manipur State Constitution Act, 1947, was not repealed by the Central Government and so this paragraph which is inconsistent with para. 5 and all other provisions of the Manipur State Constitution Act, 1947, cannot be deemed to be operative.

15. The Central Government got all the powers which were exercised by the Maharajah at the time of merger by the agreement of the merger and the Chief Commissioner was to exercise those powers later on under the Manipur Administration Order, 1949, but the rights of the people enjoyed under the Manipur State Constitution Act, 1947, were never suppressed nor do they appear to have been, at any time attempted to be suppressed as the Manipur State Constitution Act, 1947, was never repealed. Its provisions, therefore, so far as they are not inconsistent with the provisions of the Indian Constitution will continue to remain in force under Article 372 of the Constitution of India. The Manipur State Administration Order, 1949, was passed in exercise of the powers conferred by Sections 3 and 4 of the Extra Provincial Jurisdiction Act, 1947 and these sections lay down that it shall be lawful for the Central Government to exercise extra provincial jurisdiction in such manner as it thinks fit and any such jurisdiction may be delegated to any officer or authority in such manner and to such extent as the Central Government may think fit. Under Section 4 any order under Sub-section (1) may provide for determining the law of procedure to be observed, whether by applying with or without modifications all or any of the provisions of any enactment in force in any province or

otherwise. Under the Manipur Administration Order, 1949, the Manipur State Constitution Act, 1947, had been kept intact under para. 5 but under Clause (7) the existing Legislature was dissolved and the Ministers then functioning ceased to function. The abolition of the Legislative Assembly and the Council of Ministers is not a mere matter of procedure and as no action was taken by the President for a period of three years nor by the Parliament under Article 239 and Article 245(1) of the Constitution of India, the Manipur State Constitution Act 1947 cannot be deemed to have been repealed, Even if para. 7 of the Manipur Administration Order, 1949 be deemed to mean that the Legislative Assembly and the Council of Ministers were temporarily disbanded, requests for their restoration would not be deemed to be illegal or tend to create disorder. The argument that the restoration of the Legislative Assembly is inter-linked with the report of the States Re-organisation Commission, has not been established to have any force as no document has been produced which might show that this matter has been referred to the Commission.

16. It has been argued that even in a case of conquest, the ancient laws of the conquered, remain in force so long as the conqueror does not change or alter them, vide *Halsbury's Laws of England* 1933 edition, volume 11, page 239, para. 456, "in conquered or ceded countries which at the time of their acquisition, had already laws of their own, the Crown has power to alter and change those laws, but until this is actually done the ancient laws of the countries remain in force;" vide also 'Edgar Sammut v. Strickland'. AIR 1939 PC 39(H); *Freeman* vs. *Fairlie*, 1 Moo Ind App 305(I) and *Campbell* vs. *Hall* (1774) 20 State Tr 239 at p. 325(J); as well as *Forbes* vs. Cochvane, (1824) 2 B and C 448(K); *Anand Balkrishna Behare* vs. *Police Lashkar*. 1949 Madh BLR 160 CL) and *Barm* vs. *Parsram* AIR 1954 Madh B 78(M).

17. Article 51 of the Constitution of India lays down a Directive principle of State Policy as follows:

51. The State shall endeavour to

(a) promote international peace and security;
(b) maintain just and honourable relation between nations;
(c) foster respect for international law and treaty obligations in dealings of organised peoples with one another; and
(d) encouragement of international disputes by arbitration.

18. The Central Government have not repealed the Manipur State Constitution Act, 1947, and if it was intended to remove the Ministers who were working in October 1949 from the Legislature which was functioning at that time, para. 7 of the Manipur Administration Order would not be void, but it would only mean that the personnel then functioning would cease to function. I think para. 7 cannot be interpreted to mean that the Manipur State Constitution Act, 1947 or any particular section thereof was ever sought to be repealed by this paragraph, and so it could not properly be urged on the basis of this paragraph that the requests for electing fresh Legislature and for appointment of fresh Ministers under the Manipur State Constitution Act, 1947 which has not been repealed uptil now, were in any way illegal or against the maintenance of public peace. Even if meetings are held and people peacefully request the Government for enforcing the provisions of Manipur State Constitution Act, 1947, such meetings would not be against the spirit of the Constitution, or even against the provisions of Section 144, Cr.P.C. as they would not tend to disturb public tranquillity in any manner. In the present case, as has already been pointed out, there were only 7 persons present in the meeting and the number of persons going on the road does not appear to be appreciable, and so it cannot be said that there was any apprehension of the breach of peace or danger to public tranquillity on this occasion.

19. If the people of Manipur in spite of making repeated requests could not get any satisfactory answer they could, in exercise of their fundamental right conferred under Article 19

of the Constitution of India, give expression to their ideas in peaceful assemblies where they could collect together without arms and so an order under Section 144, Criminal P.C. restricting the fundamental right under Cls. (a) and (b) of Article 19(1) of the Constitution of India was not justified in this case.

20. It has been contended by the learned Government Advocate that no question of infringement of fundamental rights arises in this case, for the petitioners are being prosecuted under specific Sections 143, 145 and 188, IPC and as they can agitate during the course of their trial that order Under Section 144, Criminal P.C. was not justified and their assembly was not unlawful, the present petition should be dismissed, and reliance has been placed on *Mool Chand* vs. *Emperor* AIR 1948 All 281(N) and *Prabha Sharma* vs. *State of Madhya Bharat*, AIR 1955 Madh B 20(O).

21. The Indian Constitution has taken care to enumerate and classify the rights of individual in specific terms and also to delimit the restriction which may for reasons specifically stated be imposed by State Authority. They are broadly classified under the following 7 heads:

1. Right to equality (Articles 14-18)
2. Right to freedom (Articles 19-22)
3. Right against exploitation (Articles 23-24)
4. Right to freedom of religion (Articles 25-28)
5. Cultural and educational rights (Articles 29 and 30)
6. Right to property (Article 31)
7. Right to constitutional remedy (Articles 32-35).

22. Article 246 of the Constitution of India which defines the scope of the legislative powers of the Parliament and the State Legislatures is itself subject to the provisions contained in Part III (Fundamental Rights). Article 13 of the Constitution runs as follows:

13. (1) All laws in force in the territory of India immediately before the commencement of this Constitution, in so far as they are inconsistent with the provisions of this

Part, shall, to the extent of such inconsistency, be void.

2. ...

23. This provision makes it clear that if any order Under Section 144, Criminal P.C., be made inconsistent with this part, it shall be void.

24. Article 19 of the Constitution of India runs as follows:

19. (1) All citizens shall have the right

(a) to freedom of speech and expression;

(b) to assemble peaceably and without anus;

(c) to form associations and unions;

(d) to move freely throughout the territory of India;

(e) to reside and settle in any part of the territory of India;

(f) to acquire, hold and dispose of property; and

(g) to practise any profession, or to carry on any occupation, trade or business.

2. Nothing in Sub-clause (a) of Clause (1) shall affect the operation of any existing law in so far as it relates to, or prevent the State from making any law relating to libel, slander, defamation, contempt of Court or any matter which offends against decency or morality or which undermines the security of, or tends to overthrow, the State.

3. Nothing in Sub-clause (b) of the said clause shall effect the operation of any existing law in so far as it imposes, or prevent the State from making any law imposing, in the interests of public order, reasonable restrictions on the exercise of the right conferred by the said sub-clause.

25. A careful reading of Articles 13 and 19 of the Constitution of India makes it clear that Fundamental Rights granted under (a) and (b) of Sub-clause (1) of Article 19 cannot be circumvented or restricted except to the extent provided in sub-cls. (2) and (3) of Article 19, These sub-clauses make it

clear that the fundamental rights can be restricted only by an existing law. Article 366(10) of the Constitution of India defines existing law as follows:

> 366. (10) "existing law" means any law, Ordinance, order, bye-law, rule or regulation passed or made before the commencement of this Constitution by any Legislature, authority or person having power to make such law, Ordinance, order, bye-law, rule or regulation;

Restriction on the fundamental rights of the present petitioners has been made on the analogy of Section 144, Criminal P.C. Section 1, Sub-section (2) of the Criminal Procedure Code clearly lays down that it extends to the whole of India except the State of Kashmir and Jammu and Manipur, which means that the Criminal Procedure Code is not the "existing law" in Manipur State as contemplated in sub-cls. (2) and (3) of Article 19 of the Constitution of India. The Merged States (Laws) Act, 1949 which came into force on 1-1-1950 enforced the Code of Criminal Procedure Act 5 of 1898 in all the Part C States vide schedule appended to this Act (S. 3 of the Act). Part C States (Laws) Act, 1950 came into force on 16-4-1950 and it was laid down in Section 3 that the Acts and the Ordinances specified in the schedule to the Merged States (Laws) Act 1949 were extended to the States of "Tripura" and "Vindhya Pradesh", but so far as the Part C State of Manipur which came in to existence on 23-1-1950, the Acts and Ordinances referred in Sub-section (1) of Section (3), other than those specified in schedule were extended. In this schedule a number of Acts including the Code of Criminal Procedure, Code of Civil Procedure, the Transfer of Property Act, the Legal Practitioners Act, the Suits Valuation Act, the Indian Succession Act and others were not extended to Manipur. It is thus clear that the. Code of Criminal Procedure cannot be said to be the "existing law" of Manipur State within the meaning of sub-cls. 2 and 3 of Article 19 of the Constitution of India, and so no provision of this Code can curtail the fundamental rights of the citizens within the Manipur State.

26. It has been contended that even though the Code of Criminal Procedure is not specifically enforced it has always been valid in spirit in this State as was laid down in *Sagolsem Indramani Singh* vs. *State of Manipur*, (S) AIR 1955 Manipur 9(P). Reliance has also been placed on the judgment of the Hon'ble Supreme Court in *Pangam bam Kalenjoy Singh* vs. *State of Manipur*, Criminal Appeal No. 72 of 1951(Q), in which an observation to the following effect has been made:

> Though the Code of Criminal Procedure has not been applied to Manipur, the trial has been substantially in accordance with the procedure laid down by that Code. But as there is no appellate Tribunal in that State for a case of this kind, we have heard the appeal as Court of ordinary appeal and have gone into evidence.

27. The procedure in civil and criminal Courts in Manipur is regulated by the Manipur State Courts Act, 1947 as amended by the Parliament in 1950, but this Act does not give detailed provisions regarding procedure, generally both the parties agree to follow the procedure laid down in the Code of Criminal Procedure in criminal cases. But where the provisions of the Code of Criminal Procedure are at variance with the provisions of the Manipur State Courts Act, the latter prevails. In the two cases on which reliance has been placed by the prosecution there was no question of curtailment of citizen's liberty under any penal provision of the Code of Criminal Procedure and as the parties acquiesced to the detailed procedure laid down in Act 5 of 1898, that procedure was followed and where one of the parties did not comply with a specific provision regarding sanction, it was held that that provision was binding on that party. These cases are not and can never be any authority for the proposition that the Code of Criminal Procedure is the "existing law" of Manipur and the liberty of all citizens can be curtailed under any of its penal provisions like Section 144, Cr.P.C.

28. The District Magistrate of Manipur realised this difficulty and so in the order dated 17-12-1954 the words "order on the analogy" of Section 144, Cr.P.C. were used. A perusal

of Sub-clause (2) and (3) of Article 19 of the Constitution makes it clear that such analogous order can never be deemed to be the "existing law" either under those clauses or under Article 366(10) of the Constitution of India and so such order must be deemed to be void under Article 13(1) of the Constitution of India.

29. The Writ of *Habeas Corpus* is a prerogative process for securing liberty of the subject by affording an effective means of immediate release from unlawful detention whether in prison or in private custody. The full name of writ is *Habeas corpus* ad subjiciendum' which means that you have the body to submit or answer. Under Section 491, Cr.P.C. it was laid down in *C.P. Matthen* vs. *District Magistrate Trivandrum* AIR 1939 PC 213(R), that the High Court could not issue a common law writ of *Habeas Corpus* in any cases covered by Section 491, but by the coming into force of the Indian Constitution a vital difference has taken place in regard to this matter and has rendered the above decision of the Privy Council almost of only academic interest now. Under both the Articles 226 and 32 powers have been conferred to issue writs in the nature of *Habeas Corpus* untrammelled by any statutory provision and a writ in the nature of common law writ of Habeas Corpus may be issued now by the High Courts, vide *Chitaley's Constitution of India,* Volume II, page 1659. In view of the wider powers of the High Courts under Article 226, the provisions of Section 491, Cr.P.C. can be treated as practically superseded by Article 226 of the Constitution of India, vide *In re Kunjan Nadar,* (S) AIR 1955 Trav-C 74(S).

30. Whether the detention is lawful or not is a matter depending upon provisions of law that may be applicable to a particular case as construed by the Court in each case. It may be mentioned in this connection that Article 21 of the Constitution guarantees to every person as a fundamental right that he shall not be deprived of his personal liberty except according to the procedure established by law. And under Article 22 of the Constitution further safeguards are guaranteed as

fundamental rights to all persons in the matter of their personal liberty. Any law passed either by the Parliament or by any of the State Legislature which is inconsistent with these provisions, will be ultra vires. The Court to which an application for*Habeas Corpus* is made has the power to examine the validity of any law under which a person is detained, In the matter of*Omritolall Dey*, 1 Cal 78(T), in which a person was arrested in execution of decree under the warrant of Presidency Small Cause Court in Calcutta. At the time of the arrest,, the person was entitled to privilege from arrest. He applied for *Habeas Corpus*. It was contended that the High Court could not go behind the Commitment of the Presidency Small Cause Court. This contention was rejected. The writ of Habeas Corpus is a writ of right against which no privilege of person and place can avail, vide *Chitaley's Constitution of India*, Volume 11 page 1660.

31. The contention that the present petition should be dismissed because the present petitioners can raise all the points urged in this Court, before the Additional District Magistrate, has thus no force as the order under Section 144, Cr.P.C. in so far as it was intended to prohibit a meeting of 7 persons only at a stage when the agitation is said to have practically fizzled out, and when there could be absolutely no danger to public tranquillity by such meeting, is, ultra vires and not legally enforceable.

32. The provisions under Article 13 of the Constitution in fact provide for "judicial review" with a view to bring all legislations in India in conformity with the Constitution as was observed by Hon'ble Shri Patanjali Shastry C. J,, in *The State of Madras* vs. *V. G. Row*:

> We think it right to point out, what is sometimes overlooked that our Constitution contains express provision for judicial review of legislation as to its conformity with the Constitution, unlike in America where the Supreme Court has assumed extensive powers of reviewing legislative acts under cover of the widely interpreted "due process" clause in the Fifth and Fourteenth Amendments. If, then, the

> Courts in this country face up to such important and none too easy task, it is not out of any desire to tilt at legislative authority in a crusader's spirit, but in discharge of a duty plainly laid upon them by the Constitution. This is especially true as regards the "fundamental rights", as to which this Court has been assigned the role of a sentinel on the *qui vive*. While the Court naturally attaches straight weight to the legislative judgment, it cannot assert its own duty to determine finally the constitutionality of an impugned statute. We have ventured on these obvious remarks because at appears to have been suggested in some quarters that the Courts in the new set up are out to seek clashes with the legislatures in the country.

33. A number of minor points were also raised on behalf of the petitioners and the order under Section 144, Cr.P.C. was sought to be challenged on the ground that it was vague and it was not duly promulgated and that it was malicious as the motive not assuming authority was really to restrict freedom of a speech and not to secure public tranquillity. There is no doubt that an order under Section 144, Cr.P.C. is a judicial order and not merely administrative order vide, *D.V. Belvi* vs. *Emperor* AIR 1931 Bom 325(V) and *Motilal Gangadhar* vs. *Emperor* AIR 1931 Bom 513(W).

But in this case the order passed by the learned District Magistrate is quite specific and the fact that the boundaries in which the order was to remain in force were not given, will not make the order invalid when it is otherwise definite vide *Sorab Shavaksha Batliwala* vs. *Emperor* AIR 1935 Bom 33(X). The rulings reported in *Gulam Mohammad* vs. *Bhuban Mohan Moitra*, 2 Cal WN 422(Y); *Vasant B. Kale* vs. *Emperor* AIR 1934 Bom 375(Z); *Ashutosh Roy* vs. *Haris Chandra* AIR 1925 Cal 625(Zl); *Satish Chandra Roy* vs. *Emperor*, 11 Cal WN 79(Z2) and *Sat Narain* vs. *Emperor* AIR 1939 All 746(Z3), in which it is laid down that the area within which the order under Section 144, Cr.P.C. should remain operative must be limited and definite to a particular place, cannot go to establish that the order in question in this case is invalid because in the later rulings it has been held that such a place can be a entire district, vide *Abdul Karim* vs. *Emperor* AIR 1937 Lah 80(Z4), in which it was held that the mere fact that the order related to such a large district of Lahore would not make the order illegal vide also*Abu Husain* vs. *Emperor* AIR 1940 Cal 358(25).

33a. The argument that the order in question (Under Section 144, Cr.P.C.) could not be issued to the general public, also does not appear to be of any force. It is settled law that order under Section 144(3), Cr.P.C. cannot be issued to the general public except when frequenting or visiting particular places vide AIR 1939 All 746(Z3) and *Emperor* vs. *Turab Khan*' AIR 1942 Oudh 39(Z6), but the particular place meant in the order in question has been sufficiently specified. The mere fact that the area is sufficiently large will not be of any material importance when in an earlier case referred to above orders covering the entire district of Lahore have been held to be perfectly legal.

34. It has been argued that the order under Section 144, Cr.P.C. in this case was not duly promulgated and so there can be no conviction under Section 156, IPC for violating such order, vide *Satish Chandra Mukhuti* vs. *Lokendra Lai Pa*l, 39 Cal WN 1053(Z7), but I think the order under Section 144, Cr.P.C. in question cannot be deemed to be illegal when the present petitioners had full knowledge of it and an application was presented on their behalf for permission to hold a meeting. The fact that the order under Section 144, Cr.P.C. was not affixed in public places will also not be of material consequence for the same reason vide 'In the matter of *Madan Kishoro*, AIR 1940 Pat 446(Z8).

35. Publication of the order under Section 144, Cr.P.C. by the Hon'ble Chief Commissioner of Manipur in the Manipur Gazette dated 15-2-1955 appears to be in conformity with the provisions of Section 144, Clause (6), Cr.P.C. as by means of this notification the State Government directed that the order under Section 144, Cr.P.C. issued by the District Magistrate,

Manipur would continue to remain in force for the next 3 months. The mere fact that the order had to be extended for about 5 months or more will be of no serious consequence if in the opinion of the State Government its continuance was necessary in the public interest.

36. It thus becomes clear that the order under Section 144, Cr.P.C. issued by the District Magistrate, Manipur cannot be deemed to be binding in so far as the fundamental rights of the petitioners were sought to be curtailed thereby when there was absolutely no likelihood of breach of peace or any danger to public tranquillity, if the petitioners were allowed to exercise their rights. The District Magistrate, Manipur, could not be deemed to be acting under the provisions of the Code of Criminal Procedure as the latter enactment has not been made applicable to this State. As such this order in question involves a violation of the de facto doctrine, vide *Pulin Behari* vs. *King Emperor*, 16 Cal WN 1105 at p. 1131(Z9).

37. I have already shown above that the petitioners were exercising their right of speech and assemblage without arms in a peaceful manner in order to vindicate their rights for enforcement of public rights adumbrated in the Manipur State Constitution Act, 1947, and so the assembly of 7 persons could not be deemed to be an unlawful assembly within the meaning of Section 141, IPC and the present petitioners could not legally be deemed to be members of any unlawful assembly. An assembly to be unlawful must be of 5 or more persons if the common object of the persons composing of that assembly is

First: To overawe by criminal force, or show of criminal force, the Central or any Provincial Government or Legislature, or any public servant in the exercise of the lawful power of such public servant; or

Second: To resist the execution of any law, or of any legal process, or

Third: To commit any mischief or criminal trespass, or other offence, or

Fourth: By means of criminal force, or show of criminal force, to any person to take or obtain possession of any property or to deprive any person of the enjoyment of a right of way, or of the use of water or other incorporeal right of which he is in possession or enjoyment, or to enforce any right or supposed right, or

Fifth: By means of criminal force, or show of criminal force, to compel any person to do what he is not legally bound to do, or to omit to do what he is legally entitled to do.

38. The present petitioners numbering seven were trying to get the provisions of law (Manipur State Constitution Act 1947) acted upon and they were not using any criminal force and so their assembly could not possibly be deemed to be an unlawful assembly; and their rights to freedom of speech and rights of assemblage could not legally be curtailed as was done in this case. As the order under Section 144, Cr.P.C. issued in this case was not a legal and valid order no prosecution under Section 188, IPC could legally ensue for disobedience of this order.

39. The result is that the present petition must be allowed and the petitioners are set at liberty and the commitment order under Sections 143, 145 and 188, IPC against them is quashed. As the petitioners raised a number of pleas which were found to be without force, it is ordered that the parties will bear their own costs.

4. DR. RAMMANOHAR LOHIA VS. STATE OF BIHAR AND OTHERS

DATE OF JUDGMENT
07/09/1965

BENCH : SARKAR, A.K.
BENCH : SARKAR, A.K.
HIDAYATULLAH, M.
DAYAL, RAGHUBAR
MUDHOLKAR, J.R.
BACHAWAT, R.S.

Citation: 1966 AIR 740 1966 SCR (1) 709
Citator Info: F 1967 SC 908 (6), R 1970 SC 814 (7), R 1970 SC 852 (8), F 1970 SC 1228 (3, 4), RF 1971 SC 530 (233, 237), RF 1971 SC 2486 (8, 15), RF 1972 SC 655 (8), R 1972 SC 739 (12), R 1972 SC 1256 (8, 27), R 1972 SC 1656 (5), R 1972 SC 1749 (7), RF 1972 SC 1924 (15), R 1972 SC 2259 (6), R 1973 SC 295 (7), F 1973 SC 844 (1), F 1973 SC 1062 (4), RF 1973 SC 1091 (2), R 1974 SC 156 (4), R 1974 SC 255 (7), RF 1974 SC 1336 (12), F 1975 SC 134 (6), R 1975 SC 953 (9), RF 1975 SC 1215 (5), F 1976 SC 780 (5), E 1976 SC 1207 (33, 116, 123, 144, 361, 363, 473) D 1977 SC 1027 (23), R 1980 SC 494 (10), RF 1980 SC 898 (42), R 1981 SC 2166 (21, 22), RF 1982 SC 1315 (11, 20, 36), RF 1985 SC 18 (6, 15), F 1985 SC 1416 (126), RF 1986 SC 872 (119), R 1987 SC 998 (5, 6), R 1987 SC 1748 (11), R 1987 SC 2332 (15), RF 1988 SC 208 (8), RF 1989 SC 364 (12), R 1989 SC 764 (13), RF 1990 SC 496 (9), RF 1990 SC 1086 (18), RF 1992 SC 687 (8), RF 1992 SC 979 (7)

ACT: Defence of India Rules, 1962, r. 30(1)(b)—"Public order" and "law and order", difference between—Scope of rule. Constitution of India, 1950, Art. 359(1)—President's Order suspending rights under Arts. 21 and 22—Right to move Supreme Court under Art. 32—Effect on.

HEAD-NOTE

Rule 30(1)(b) of the Defence of India Rules, 1962, provided that a State Government might, if it was satisfied with respect to a person that with a view to preventing him from acting in a manner prejudicial, inter alia to "public safety and maintenance of public order" it is necessary to do so, order him to be detained. A District Magistrate to whom the power of the Government of the State of Bihar had been delegated under S. 40(2) of the Defence of India Act, 1962, ordered the detention of the petitioner under the rule. The order stated that the District Magistrate was satisfied, that with a view to prevent the petitioner from acting in any manner prejudicial to the "public safety and the maintenance of law and order," it was necessary to detain him. Prior to the making of the order the District Magistrate had, however, recorded a note stating that having read the report of the Police Superintendent that the petitioner's being at large was prejudicial to "public safety and maintenance of public order", he was satisfied that the petitioner should be detained under the rule. The petitioner moved this Court under Art. 32 of the Constitution for a writ of Habeas Corpus directing his release from detention, contending that:

(i) though an order of detention to prevent acts prejudicial to public order may be justifiable an order to prevent acts prejudicial to law and order would not be justified by the rule;

(ii) the order mentioned a notification which did not contain the necessary delegation;

(iii) the District Magistrate acted beyond his jurisdiction by considering the danger not only in his district but in the entire State; and

(iv) all the conditions mentioned in the rule must be cumulatively applied before the order of detention could be made. The respondent-State raised a preliminary objection, that the President of India had made an Order under Art. 359(1) that the right of a person to move any court for the enforcement of the rights conferred by Arts. 21 and 22 shall remain suspended for the period during which the proclamation of emergency under Art. 352 was in force, if such person had been deprived of any such rights under the Defence of India Act or any rule made thereunder, and that therefore, this Court was prevented from entertaining the petition.

HELD: (Per Full Court): (i) The petition was maintainable. Per Sarkar, J.: The order of the President does not form a bar to all applications for release from detention under the Act or the Rules. Where a person was detained in violation of the mandatory provisions of the Defence of India Act his right to move the Court was not suspended. Since the petitioner contended that the order of detention was not justified by the Act or Rules and was therefore against the provisions of the Act, the petitioner was entitled to be heard. [716 G; 717 A-B]

Per Hidayatullah and Bachawat, JJ.: The net result of the President's Order is to stop all claims to enforce rights arising from laws other than the Defence of India Act and the Rules, and the provisions of Art. 22 at variance with the Defence of India Act and the Rules are of no avail. But the deprivation must be in good faith under the Defence of India Act or any rule or order made thereunder. The President's Order does not say that even if a person is proceeded against in breach of the Defence of India Act or the Rules or mala fide he cannot move the Court to complain that the Act and the Rules under colour of which some action was taken, do not warrant it. It follows, therefore, that this Court acting under Art. 32 on a petition for the issue of a writ of Habeas Corpus must not allow breaches of the Defence of India Act or the Rules to go unquestioned, as Art. 359 and the President's Order were not intended to condone an illegitimate enforcement of the Defence of India Act. [731 B, E, F; 733 B-C].

Per Raghubar Dayal, J.: This Court can investigate whether the District Magistrate exercised the power under r. 30 honestly and bona fide, or not, that is, whether he ordered detention on being satisfied as required by r. 30. [748 H].

Per Mudholkar, J.: Before an entry into the portals of this Court could be denied to a detenu, he must be shown an order under r. 30(1) of the Defence of India Rules made by a competent authority stating that it was satisfied that the detenu was likely to indulge in activities which would be prejudicial to one or more of the matters referred to in the rule. If the detenu contends that the order, though it purports to be under r. 30(1), was not competently made, this Court has the duty to enquire into the matter. Upon an examination of the order, if the Court finds that it was not competently made or was ambiguous, it must exercise its power under Art. 32, entertain the petition thereunder and make an appropriate order. [755 H; 756 A-B] *Makhan Singh* vs. *State of Punjab*, [1964] 4 S.C.R. 797 followed.

(ii) Per Sarkar, Hidayatullah, Mudholkar and Bachawat JJ.: The petitioner should be set at liberty.

Per Sarkar J.: The order detaining the petitioner would not be in terms of the rule unless it could be said that the expression "law and order" means the same thing as "Public order". What was meant by maintenance of public order was the prevention of disorder of a grave nature, a disorder which the authorities thought was necessary to prevent in view of the emergent situation created by external aggression; whereas, the expression "maintenance of law and order" may mean prevention of disorder of comparatively lesser gravity and of local significance only. [718 B, D, E] Courts are only entitled to look at the face of the order, because the satisfaction which justifies the order under the rule is the subjective satisfaction of the detaining authority. If on its face an order of detention is in terms of the rule, ordinarily, a court is bound to stay its hands and uphold the order. When an order is on the face of it not in terms of the rule, a court cannot enter into an investigation whether the order of detention was: in fact in terms of the rule. So the State cannot be heard to say of prove that an order was in fact made to prevent acts prejudicial to public order though the order does not say so. It is not a case where the order is only evidence of the detention having been made under the rule. The order is conclusive as to the state of the mind of the person who made it and no evidence is admissible to prove that state of mind. Extraneous evidence such as the note made by the District Magistrate was not admissible to prove that the rule had been complied with. [718 G-H; 718 B-D 720 G; 722 B-C] is not taking too technical a view, but is a matter of substance. If a man can be deprived of his liberty under a rule by the simple process of the making of an order, he can only be so deprived if the order is in terms of the rule. If for the purpose of justifying the detention such compliance by itself is enough, a non-compliance must have a contrary effect. A more reference in the detention order to the rule is not sufficient to show that by "law and order" what was meant was "public order". [719 F-G: 720 A-C] The order no doubt mentions another ground of detention, namely, prevention of acts prejudicial to public safety, and in so far as it did so, it was clearly within the rule. But the order has notwithstanding this to be held illegal, though it mentioned a ground on which a legal order of detention could have been based, because, it could not be said in what manner and to what extent the valid and invalid grounds operated on the mind of the authority concerned and contributed to the creation of subjective satisfaction. [722 E; G-11] *Sh. Shibban Lal Saksena* vd. *State of U.P.* [1954] S.C.R. 418, followed.

Per Hidayatullah and Bachawat, JJ.: The satisfaction of the detaining authority cannot be subjected to objective tests and courts are not to exercise appellate powers over such authorities and an order proper on its face, passed by a competent authority in good faith, would be a complete answer to a petition for a *writ of Habeas Corpus*. But when from the order itself circumstances appear which raise a doubt whether the officer concerned had not misconceived his own powers, there is need to pause and enquire. The enquiry then is, not with a view to investigate the sufficiency of the materials but into the officer's notions of his power. If the order passed by him showed that he thought his powers were more extensive than they actually were, the order might fail to be a good order. No doubt, what matters is the substance; but the form discloses the approach of the detaining authority to the serious question and the error in the form raises the enquiry about the substance. When the liberty of the citizen is put within the reach of authority and the scrutiny by courts is barred, the action must comply not only with the substantive requirements of law but also with those forms which alone can indicate that the substance has been committed with. [739 H; 740 B-C, E; 741 C; F] The District Magistrate acted to "maintain law and order" and his order could not be read differently even if there was an affidavit the other way. If he thought in terms of "public order" he should have said so in his order, or explained how the error arose. A mere reference to his earlier note was not sufficient and the two expressions cannot be reconciled by raising an air of similitude between them. The contravention of law always affects order but before it can be said to affect public order, it must affect the community or the public at large. One has to imagine three concentric circles, the largest representing "law and order", the next representing "public order" and the smallest representing "security of State". An act may affect "law and order" but not "public order", just as an act may affect "public order" but not "security of the State". Therefore, by using the expression "maintenance of law and order" the District Magistrate was widening his own field of action and was adding a clause to the Defence of India Rules. [740 E-F, H; 746 B-E; 747 D, E] The order on its face shows two reasons, but it was not certain that the District Magistrate was influenced by one consideration and not both, because, it was not open to the Court to enquire into the material on which the District Magistrate acted, or to examine the reason, to see whether his action fell within the other topic, namely, public safety. [746 F-G]

Per Mudholkar J.: The use of the expression "maintenance of law and order" in the impugned order makes it ambiguous on its face and therefore the order must be held to be had. No doubt the order also refers to public safety. But then the questions arise: What is it that weighed with the District

Magistrate, the apprehension regarding public safety or an apprehension regarding maintenance of law and order? Was the apprehension entertained by the District Magistrate that the petitioner, if left at large, was likely to do something which will imperil the maintenance of public order generally, or was it that he apprehended that the petitioner's activities may cause disturbances in a particular locality? His order, which was the only material which could be considered, gave no indication on those questions. The expression "law and order" does not find any place in the rule and is not synonymous with "public order". "Law and order" is a comprehensive expression in which would be included not merely public order but matters such as public peace, tranquillity, orderliness in a locality or a local area and perhaps other matters. [756 H; 757 A, C, D, F]

Per Raghubar Dayal J. (dissenting): The District Magistrate made the impugned order on his being satisfied that it was necessary to do so with a view to prevent the petitioner from acting in a manner prejudicial to public safety and maintenance of public order. The impugned order was therefore valid and consequently, the petitioner could not move this Court for the enforcement of his rights under Arts. 21 and 22 in view of the President's Order under Art. 359(1). [755 B-C]

The detaining authority is free to establish that any defect in the detention order is of form only and not of substance it being satisfied of the necessity to detain the person for a purpose mentioned in r. 30, though the purpose has been inaccurately stated in the detention order. The existence of satisfaction does not depend on what is stated in the order and can be established by the District Magistrate by his affidavit. His omission to refer to "maintenance of public order" does not mean that he was not so satisfied, especially when his note refers to the petitioner being at large to be prejudicial to public safety and the maintenance of public order. The petitioner's affidavit and rejoinder show that the District Magistrate was satisfied of the necessity of detaining the petitioner to prevent him from acting in a manner prejudicial to the public order, because of the setting of events that happened on that date. "Maintenance of law and order" may be an expression of wider import than "public order", but in the context in which it was used in the detention order and in view of its use generally, it should be construed to mean maintenance of law and order in regard to maintenance of public tranquillity. [749 C-D; 750 C-D; 751 C, F-G] *Sodhi Shamsher Singh* vs. *State of Pepsu*, A.I.R. 1954 S.C. 276, referred to.

Even if the expression "maintenance of law and order" in the impugned order be not construed as referring to "maintenance of public order" the impugned order cannot be said to be invalid in view of its being made with a double objective, that is, with the object of preventing the petitioner from acting prejudicially to the public safety and the maintenance of law and order. His satisfaction with respect to any of the purposes mentioned in r. 30(1) which would justify his ordering the detention of a person is sufficient for the validity of the order. There is no room for considering that be might not have passed the order merely with one object in view, the object being to prevent him from acting prejudicially to public safety. It is not a case where his satisfaction was based on two grounds, one of which is irrelevant or non-existent. There does not appear to be any reason why the District Magistrate would not have passed the order of detention against the petitioner on the satisfaction that it was necessary to prevent him from acting prejudicially to public safety. [752 H; 753 B-D; 754 A-D]

(iii) Per Sarkar, Hidayatullah, Raghubar Dayal and Bachawat, JJ. The delegation was valid.

Per Sarkar J.: In spite of the mistake in the order as to the Notification delegating the power, evidence could be given to show that the delegation had in fact been made, because, the mistake did not vitiate the order. To admit such evidence would not be going behind the face of the order, because, what is necessary to appear on the face of the order is the satisfaction of the Authority of the necessity for detention for any of the reasons mentioned in r. 30(1)(b), and not his authority to make the order. [721 D, F-G]

Per Hidayatullah, Raghubar Dayal and Bachawat JJ.: There was only a clerical error in mentioning the wrong notification and being a venial fault did not vitiate the order of detention. Also, S. 40(2) does not require the imposition of any conditions but only permits it. [737 F; 738 A; 741 G; 748 D]

(iv) Per Hidayatullah, Raghubar Dayal and Bachawat, JJ.: There was nothing wrong in the District Magistrate taking a broad view of the petitioner's activities so as to weigh the possible harm if he was not detained. Such a viewing of the activities of a person before passing the order against him does not necessarily spell out extra-territoriality, but is really designed to assess properly the potentiality of danger which is the main object of the rule to prevent. [737 G-H; 748 D]

(v) Per Hidayatullah, Raghubar Dayal, Mudhlkar and Bachawat, JJ. It is not necessary that the appropriate authority should entertain an apprehension that the person to be detained is likely to participate in every one of the activities referred to in the rule. [739 F; 748 D; 756 F]

JUDGMENT

ORIGINAL JURISDICTION: Writ Petition No. 79 of 1965. Petition under Art. 32 of the Constitution of India for enforcement of Fundamental Rights.

The petitioner appeared in person.

A.V. Viswanatha Sastri and S.P. Varma, for the respondents.

Sarkar J., Hidayatullah J. (on behalf of himself and Bachawat J.) and Mudholkar J. delivered separate concurring Judgments. Raghubar Dayal J. delivered a dissenting opinion.

Sarkar, J. Dr. Rammanohar Lohia, a member of the Lok

Sabha, has moved the Court under Art. 32 of the Constitution for a writ of Habeas Corpus directing his release from detention under an order passed by the District Magistrate of Patna. The order was purported to have been made under r. 30(1)(b) of the Defence of India Rules, 1962.

Dr. Lohia, who argued his case in person, based his claim to be released on a number of grounds. I do not propose to deal with all these grounds for I have come to the conclusion that he is entitled to be released on one of them and to the discussion of that ground alone I will confine my judgment. With regard to his, other grounds I will content myself only with the observation that as at present advised, I have not been impressed by them.

The order of detention runs thus: "Whereas I, J.N. Sahu, District Magistrate, Patna, am satisfied that with a view to preventing him from acting in any manner prejudicial to the public safety and the maintenance of law and order, it is necessary to make an order that he be detained. Now, therefore, in exercise of the powers conferred by clause (b) of sub-rule (1) of rule 30 of the Defence of India Rules, 1962 read with Notification No. 180/COW I hereby direct that Dr. Rammanohar Lohia be arrested and detained in the Contra Jail Hazaribagh, until further orders." Now the point made by Dr. Lohia is that this order is not in terms of the rule under which it purports to have been made and, therefore, furnishes no legal justification for detention. The reason why it is said that the order is not in terms of the rule is that the rule does not justify the detention of a person to prevent him from acting in a manner prejudicial to the maintenance of law and order while the order directs detention for such purpose. It is admitted that the rule provides for an order of detention being made to prevent act prejudicial to the maintenance of public order, but it is said that public order and law and order are not the same thing, and, therefore, though an order of detention to prevent acts prejudicial to public order might be justifiable, a similar order to prevent acts prejudicial to law and order would not be justified by the rule. It seems to me that this contention is well founded. Before proceeding to state my reasons for this view, I have to dispose of an argument in bar advanced by the respondent State. That argument is that the petitioner has, in view of a certain order of the President to which I will presently refer, no right to move the Court under Art. 32 for his release. It is said that we cannot, therefore, hear Dr. Lohia's application at all. To appreciate this contention, certain facts have to be stated and I proceed to do so at once.

Article 352 of the Constitution gives the President of India a power to declare by Proclamation that a grave emergency exists whereby the security of India is threatened *inter alia* by external aggression. On October 26, 1962, the President issued a Proclamation under this article that such an emergency existed. This presumably was done in view of China's attack on the north eastern frontiers of India in September 1962. On the same day as the Proclamation was made, the President passed the Defence of India Ordinance and rules were then made thereunder on November 5, 1962. The Ordinance was later, on December 12, 1962, replaced by the Defence of India Act, 1962 which however continued in force the rules made under the Ordinance. On November 3, 1962, the President made an order under Art. 359(1) which he was entitled to do, declaring "that the right of any person to move any court for the enforcement of the rights conferred by Article 21 and Article 22 of the Constitution shall remain suspended for the period during which the Proclamation ... is in force, if such person has been deprived of any such rights under the Defence of India Ordinance, 1962 or any rule or order made thereunder." There is no doubt that the reference in this Order to the "Defence of India Ordinance, 1962" must, after that Ordinance was replaced by the Act, as earlier stated, be understood as a reference to the Act: see *Mohan Chowdhury* vs. *The Chief Commissioner*, Tripura, (1964) 3SCR 442 (1). I should now state that the Proclamation is still in force. It is not in dispute that the present petition has been made for the enforcement of Dr. Lohia's right to personal liberty under Arts. 21 and 22. These articles in substance—and it should suffice for the present purpose to say no more—give people a certain personal liberty. It is said by the respondent State that the President's Order under Art. 359(1) altogether prevents us from entertaining Dr. Lohia's petition and, therefore, it should be thrown out at once. This would no doubt, subject to certain exceptions to which a reference is not necessary for the purposes of the present judgment, be correct if the Order of November 3, 1962 took away all rights to personal liberty under Arts. 21 and 22. But this, the Order does not do. It deprives a person of his right to move a court for the enforcement of a right to such personal liberty only when he has been deprived of it by the Defence of India Act—it is not necessary to refer to the Ordinance any more as it has been replaced by the Act—or any rule or order made thereunder. If he has not been so deprived, the Order does not take away his right to move a court. Thus if a person is detained under the Preventive Detention Act, 1950, his right to move the Court for enforcement of his rights under Arts. 21 and 22 remains intact. That is not a case in which his right to do so can be said to have been taken away by the President's Order. This Court has in fact heard applications under Art. 32 challenging a detention under that Act: see *Rameshwar Shaw* vs. *District Magistrate of Burdwan* (1). If any person says, as Dr. Lohia does, that he has been deprived of his personal liberty by an order not made under the Act or the Rules there is nothing in the President's Order under Art. 359(1) to deprive him of his right to move the Court under Art. 32. The Court must examine his contention and decide whether he has been detained under the Act or the Rules and can only throw out his petition when it finds that he was so detained, but not before then. If it finds that he was not so detained, it must proceed to hear his petition on its merits. The right under Art. 32 is one of the fundamental rights that the Constitution has guaranteed to all persons and it cannot be taken away except by the methods as provided in the Constitution, one of which is by an order made under Art. 359.

The contention that an order under that article has not taken away the constitutional right to personal liberty must be examined.

Mr. Verma said that *Smith* vs. *East Elloe Rural District Council* (1) supported the contention of the respondent State. I do not think so. That case turned on an entirely different statute. That statute provided a method of challenging a certain order by which property was compulsorily purchased and stated that it could not be questioned in any other way at all. It was there held that an action to set aside the order even on the ground of having been made mala fide, did not lie as under the provision no action was maintainable for the purpose. That case is of no assistance in deciding the question in what circumstance a right to move the court has been taken away by the entirely different provisions that we have to consider. Here only a right to move a court in certain circumstances has been taken away and the question is, has the court been moved on the present occasion in one of those circumstances? The President's Order does not bar an enquiry into that question. Apart from the fact that the reasoning on which the English case is based, has no application here, we have clear observations in judgments of this Court which show that the Order of the President does not form a bar to all applications for release from detention under the Act or the Rules. I will refer only to one of them. In *Makhan Singh* vs. *The State of Punjab* (3) it was said, "If in challenging the validity of his detention order, the detenu is pleading any right outside the rights specified in the Order, his right to move any court in that behalf is not suspended" and by way of illustration of this proposition, a case where a person was detained in violation of the mandatory provisions of the Defence of India Act was mentioned. That is the present case as the petitioner contends that the order of detention is not justified by the Act or Rules and hence is against its provisions. The petitioner is entitled to be heard and the present contention of the respondent State must be held to be ill founded and must fail. I now proceed to consider the merits of Dr. Lohia's contention that the Order detaining him had not been made under the Defence of India Rules. I here pause to observe that if it was not so made, there is no other justification for his detention; none is indeed advanced. He would then be entitled to his release.

I have already stated that the Proclamation of Emergency was made as the security of India was threatened by external aggression. That Proclamation of emergency was the justification for the Act. The Act in fact recited the Proclamation in its preamble. Section 3 of the Act gave the Central Government power to make rules providing for the detention of persons without trial for various reasons there mentioned. Rule 30(1)(b) under which the order of detention of Dr. Lohia was made was framed under S. 3 and is in these terms: "The Central Government or the State Government, if it is satisfied with respect to any particular person that with a view to preventing him from acting in any manner prejudicial to the defence of India and civil defence, the public safety, the maintenance of public order, India's relations with foreign powers, the maintenance of peaceful conditions in any part of India, the efficient conduct of military operations or the maintenance of supplier, and services essential to the life of the community, it is necessary to do so, may make an order— (a)... (b) directing that he be detained." As I have said earlier, the order was made by the District Magistrate, Patna, to whom the power of the Government of the State of Bihar in this regard had been duly delegated under S. 40(2) of the Act.

Under this rule a Government can make an order of detention against a person if it is satisfied that it is necessary to do so to prevent him from acting in a manner prejudicial, among other things to public safety and the maintenance of public order. The detention order in this case is based on the ground that it was necessary to make it to prevent Dr. Lohia from acting in any manner prejudicial to public safety and the maintenance of law and order. I will, in discussing the contention of Dr. Lohia, proceed on the basis as if the order directing detention was only for preventing him from acting in a manner prejudicial to the maintenance of law and order. I will consider what effect the inclusion in the order of detention of a reference to the necessity for maintaining public safety has, later. The question is whether an order could be made legally under the rule for preventing disturbance of law and order. The rule does not say so. The order, therefore, would not be in terms of the rule unless it could be said that the expression "law and order" means the same thing as "public order" which occurs in the rule. Could that then be said? I find no reason to think so. Many of the things mentioned in the rule may in a general sense be referable to the necessity for maintaining law and order. But the rule advisedly does not use that expression.

It is commonplace that words in a statutory provision take their meaning from the context in which they are used. The context in the present case is the emergent situation created by external aggression. It would, therefore, be legitimate to hold that by maintenance of public order what was meant was prevention of disorder of a grave nature, a disorder which the authorities thought was necessary to prevent in view of the emergent situation. It is conceivable that the expression "maintenance of law and order" occurring in the detention order may not have been used in the sense of prevention of disorder of a grave nature. The expression may mean prevention of disorder of comparatively lesser gravity and of local significance only. To take an illustration, if people indulging in the Hindu religious festivity of Holi become rowdy, prevention of that disturbance may be called the maintenance of law and order. Such maintenance of law and order was obviously not in the contemplation of the Rules.

What the Magistrate making the order exactly had in mind, by the use of the words law and order, we do not know. Indeed, we are not entitled to know that for it is well-settled that courts cannot enquire into the grounds on which the Government thought that it was satisfied that it was necessary to make an order of detention. Courts are only entitled to look at the face of the order. This was stressed on us by learned counsel for the respondent State and the authorities fully justify that view: If, therefore, on its face an order of detention is in to of the rule, a court is bound to stay its hands and uphold the order. I am leaving here out of consideration a contention that an order good on the face of it is bad for reasons dehors it, for example, because it had been made *mala fide*. Subject to this and other similar exceptions—to which I have earlier referred and as to which it, is unnecessary to say anything in the present context and also because the matter has already been examined by this Court in a number of cases, court cannot go behind the face of the order of detention to determine its validity.

The satisfaction of the Government which justifies the order under the rule is a subjective satisfaction. A court cannot enquire whether grounds existed which would have created that satisfaction on which alone the order could have been made in the mind of a reasonable person. If that is so,—and that indeed is what the respondent State contends,—it seems to me that when an order is on the face of it not in terms of the rule, a court cannot equally enter into an investigation whether the order of detention was in fact, that is to say, irrespective of what is stated in it, in terms of the rule. In other words, in such a case the State cannot be heard to say or prove that the order was in fact made, for example, to prevent acts prejudicial to public order which would bring it within the rule though the order does not say so. To allow that to be done would be to uphold a detention without a proper order. The rule does not envisage such a situation. The statements in the affidavit used in the present case by the respondent State are, therefore, of no avail for establishing that the order of detention is in terms of the rule. The detention was not under the affidavit but under the order. It is of some significance to point out that the affidavit sworn by the District Magistrate who made the order of detention does not say that by the use of the expression law and order he meant public order.

It was said that this was too technical a view of the matter;

there was no charm in words used. I am not persuaded by this argument. The question is of substance. If a man can be deprived of his liberty under a rule by the simple process of the making of a certain order, he can only be so deprived if the order is in terms of the rule. Strict compliance with the letter of the rule is the essence of the matter. We are dealing with a statute which drastically interferes with the personal liberty of people, we are dealing with an order behind the face of which a court is prevented from going. I am not complaining of that. Circumstances may make it necessary. But it would be legitimate to require in such cases strict observance of the rules. If there is any doubt whether the rules have been strictly observed, that doubt must be resolved in favour of the detenu. It is certainly more than doubtful whether law and order means the same as public order. I am not impressed by the argument that the reference in the detention order to r. 30(1)(b) shows that by law and order what was meant was public order. That is a most mischievous way of approaching the question. If that were right, a reference to the rule in the order might equally justify all other errors in it. Indeed it might with almost equal justification then be said that a reference to the rule and an order of detention would be enough. That being so, the only course open to us is to hold that the rules have not been strictly observed. If for the purpose of justifying the detention such compliance by itself is enough, a non-compliance must have a contrary effect.

Carltona Ltd. vs. *Commissioners of Works* (1) is an interesting case to which reference may be made in this connection. It turned on a statutory Regulation empowering a specified authority to take possession of land for the purposes mentioned in it in various terms but which term, did not include the expression "national interest". Under this Regulation possession of certain premises of the Carltona Company was taken after serving a notice on it that was being done "in the national interest". It was contended by the Carltona Company that it had been illegally deprived of the possession of its premises because the notice showed that possession was not being taken in terms of the Regulation. This contention failed as it was held that the giving of the notice was not a prerequisite to the exercise of the powers under the Regulation and that the notice was no more than a notification that the authorities were exercising the powers. It was said that the notice was useful only as evidence of the state of the mind of the writer and, that being so, other evidence was admissible to establish the fact that the possession of the premises was being taken for the reasons mentioned in the Regulation. Our case is entirely different. It is not a case of a notice. Under r. 30(1)(b) a person can be detained only by an order and there is no doubt that the order of detention has to be in writing. It is not a case where the order is only evidence of the detention having been made under the rule. It is the only warrant for the detention. The order further is conclusive as to the state of the mind of the person who made it; no evidence is admissible to prove that state of mind. It seems to me that if the Carltona case was concerned with an order which alone resulted in the dispossession, the decision in that case might well have been otherwise. I would here remind, to prevent any possible misconception, that I am not considering a case where the order is challenged on the ground of *mala fides* or other similar grounds to which I have earlier referred. Before leaving this aspect of the case, it is necessary to refer to two other things. The first is a mistake appearing in the order of detention on which some argument was based by Dr. Lohia for quashing the order. It will be remembered that the order mentioned a certain Notification No. 180/CW. The Notification intended to be mentioned however was one No. II, 15/CW and the Notification No. 180/CW had been mentioned by mistake. It was under Notification No. II 15/CW that the power of the State Government to make an order of detention was delegated to the District Magistrate under the provisions of S. 40(2) of the Act to which I have earlier referred. The reference to the notification was to indicate the delegation of power. The Notification actually mentioned in the order did not, however, contain the necessary delegation. The result was that the order did not show on its face that the District Magistrate who had made it had the necessary authority to do so. This mistake however did not vitiate the order at all. Nothing in the rules requires that an order of detention should state that the authority making it has the power to do so. It may be that an order made by an authority to whom the Government's power has not been delegated, is a nullity and the order can be challenged on that ground. This may be one of the cases where an order good on its face may nonetheless be illegal. When the power of the person making the order is challenged, the only fact to be proved is that the power to make the order had been duly delegated to him. That can be proved by the necessary evidence, that is, by the production of the order of delegation. That would be a case somewhat like the Carltona case. In spite of the mistake in the order as to the Notification delegating the power, evidence can be given to show that the delegation had in fact been made. To admit such evidence would not be going behind the face of the order because what is necessary to appear on the face of the order is the satisfaction of the authority of the necessity for the detention for any of the reasons mentioned in r. 30(1)(b) and not the authority of the maker of the order. The second thing to which I wish to refer is that it appeared from the affidavit sworn by the District Magistrate that prior to the making of the order, he had recorded a note which read in these words: "Perused the report of the Senior S. P. Patna for detention of Dr. Rammanohar Lohia, M.P. under rule 30(1)(b) of the Defence of India Rules, on the ground that his being at large is prejudicial to the public safety and maintenance of public order. From the report of the Sr.S.P., Patna, I am satisfied that Dr. Rammanohar Lohia, M.P. aforesaid be detained under rule 30(1)(b) of the Defence of India Rules. Accordingly, I order that Dr. Rammanohar Lohia be detained ... am unable to see that this note is of any assistance to the respondent State in this case. It is not the order of detention. The respondent State does not say that it is. I have earlier stated that extraneous evidence is not admissible to prove that the rule has been complied with though the order of detention does not show that,. Indeed, this note does not even say that the District Magistrate was satisfied that it was necessary to make an order of detention to prevent Dr. Lohia from acting in a manner prejudicial to the maintenance of public order. It only says that the Superintendent of Police reported that he was so satisfied. The satisfaction of the Superintendent of Police would provide no warrant for the detention or the order; with it we have nothing to do.

For these reasons, in my view, the detention order if it had been based only on the ground of prevention of acts prejudicial to the maintenance of law and order, it would not have been in terms of r. 30(1)(b) and would not have justified the detention. As I have earlier pointed out, however, it also mentions as another ground for detention, the prevention of acts prejudicial to public safety. In so far as it does so, it is clearly within the rule. Without more, we have to accept an order made on that ground as a perfectly legal order. The result then is that the detention order mentions two grounds—one of which is in terms of the rule while the other is not. What then is the effect of that? Does it cure the illegality in the order that I have earlier noticed? This question is clearly settled by authorities. In*Shibban Lal Saksena* vs. *The State of Uttar Pradesh* (1) it *as held that such an order would be a bad order, the reason being that it could not be said in what manner and to what extent the valid and invalid grounds operated on the mind of the authority concerned and contributed to the creation of his subjective satisfaction which formed the basis of the order. The order has, therefore, to be held illegal though it mentioned a ground on which a legal order of detention could have been based. I should also point out that the District Magistrate has not said in his affidavit that he would have been satisfied of the necessity of the detention order only for the reason that it was necessary to detain Dr. Lohia to prevent him from acting in a manner prejudicial to public safety.

In the result, in my view, the detention order is not under

the Rules. The detention of Dr. Lohia under that order is not legal and cannot be justified. He is entitled to be set at liberty and I would order accordingly.

Hidayatullah, J.: Dr. Rammanohar Lohia, M.P., has filed this petition under Art. 32 of the Constitution asking for a writ of *Habeas Corpus* for release from detention ordered by the District Magistrate, Patna, under Rule 30(1)(b) of the Defence of India Rules, 1962. He was arrested at Patna on the night between 9th and 10th August, 1965. As it will be necessary to refer to the terms of the order served on him it is reproduced here

"ORDER

No. 3912 C. Dated, Patna, the 9th August 1965

Whereas I, J.N. Sahu, District Magistrate, Patna, am satisfied with respect to the person known as Dr. Rammanohar Lohia, Circuit House, Patna, that with a view to preventing him from acting in any manner prejudicial to the public safety and the maintenance of law and order, it is necessary to make an order that he be detained.

Now, therefore, in exercise of the powers conferred by clause (b) of sub-clause (i) of rule 30 of the Defence of India Rules, 1962, read with Notification No. 180/CW, dated the 20th March, 1964, of the Government of Bihar, Political (Special) Department, I hereby direct that the said Dr. Rammanohar Lohia be arrested by the police wherever found and detained in the Central Jail, Hazaribagh, until further orders.

Sd/-
J.N. Sahu,
9-8-1965
District Magistrate, Patna.

Sd/-
Rammanohar Lohia.
10th August-1.40."

Dr. Lohia was lodged in the Hazaribagh Central Jail at 3-30 p.m. on August 10, 1965. He sent a letter in Hindi together with an affidavit sworn in the jail to the Chief Justice, which was received on August 13, 1965, in the Registry of this Court. Although the petition was somewhat irregular, this Court issued a rule and as no objection has been taken on the ground of form we say nothing more about it.

In his affidavit Dr. Lohia stated that he was arrested at midnight on August 9, 1965 and was told that it was on charges of arson but later was served with the order of detention and that in this way his arrest for a substantive offence was turned into preventive detention. He further stated that the order of detention showed that he was to be detained in Bankipur Jail but the name of the Jail was scored out and "Central Jail, Hazaribagh" was substituted which led him to conclude that typed orders of detention were kept ready and that the District Magistrate did not exercise his mind in each individual case. He contended that his detention under Rule 30(1)(b) was illegal because, according to him, that rule dealt with prejudicial activities in relation to the defence of India and civil defence and not with maintenance of law and order of a purely local character. He alleged that the arrest was mala fide and malicious; that it was made to prevent him from participating in the House of the People which was to go into Session from August 16 and particularly to keep him away from the debate on the Kutch issue. He further alleged that he had only addressed a very large gathering in Patna and had disclosed certain things about the Bihar Government which incensed that Government and caused them to retaliate in this manner and that detention was made to prevent further disclosures by him.

In answer to Dr. Lohia's affidavit two affidavits were filed on behalf of the respondents. One affidavit, filed by the District Magistrate, Patna, denied that there was any malice or mala fides in the arrest of Dr. Lohia. The District Magistrate stated that he had received a report from the Senior Superintendent of Police, Patna, in regard to the conduct and activities of Dr. Lohia and after considering the report he had ordered Dr. Lohia's detention to prevent him from acting in any manner prejudicial to the public safety and maintenance of public order. He stated further that he was fully satisfied that the forces of disorder "which were sought to be let loose if not properly controlled would envelop the whole of the State of Bihar and possibly might spread in other parts of the country which would necessarily affect the problem of external defence as well in more ways than one". He said that the report of the Senior Superintendent of Police, Patna, contained facts which he considered sufficient for taking the said action but he could not disclose the contents of that report in the public interest. He sought to correct, what he called, a slip in the order passed by him, by stating that notification No. 11155C, dated 11th August 1964, was meant instead of the notification mentioned there. He stated further that as the disturbance was on a very large scale it was thought expedient to keep ready typed copies of detention orders and to make necessary alterations in them to suit individual cases, at the time of the actual issuance of the orders, and that it was because of this that the words "Central Jail Hazaribagh" were substituted for "Bankipur Jail". He denied that he had not considered the necessity of detention in each individual case. He repudiated the charge that the arrest was made at the instance of Government and affirmed that the action was taken on his own responsibility and in the discharge of his duty as District Magistrate and not in consultation with the Central or the State Governments. He denied that the arrest and detention were the result of anger on the part of any or a desire to prevent Dr. Lohia from circulating any damaging information about Government. The District Magistrate produced an order which, he said, was recorded before the order of detention. As we shall refer to that order later it is reproduced here

"9.8.65.

Perused the report of the Senior S.P., Patna, for detention of Dr. Rammanohar Lohia, M.P., under rule 30(1)(b) of the Defence of India Rules, on the ground that his being at large is prejudicial to the public safety and maintenance of public order. From the report of the Sr.S.P., Patna, I am satisfied that Dr. Rammanohar Lohia, M.P., aforesaid be detained under rule 30(1)(b) of the Defence of India Rules. Accordingly, I order that Dr. Rammanohar Lohia be detained under Rule 30(1)(b) of the Defence of India Rules read with Notification No. 180/CW dated 20.3.64 in the Hazaribagh Central Jail until further orders.

Send four copies of the warrant of arrest to the Sr. S.P., Patna, for immediate compliance. He should return two copies of it after service on the detenu.

Sd/-
J.N. Sahu,
District Magistrate, Patna."

The second affidavit was sworn by Rajpati Singh, Police Inspector attached to the Kotwali Police Station, Patna. He stated in his affidavit that the order was served on Dr. Lohia at 1-40 a.m. on August 10, 1965 and not at midnight. He denied that Dr. Lohia was arrested earlier or that at the time of his arrest, he was informed that the arrest was for an offence or offences of arson. He admitted, however, that he, had told him that cases of arson and loot had taken place. He affirmed that there was no charge of arson against Dr. Lohia.

Dr. Lohia filed a rejoinder affidavit and in that affidavit he stated that the internal evidence furnished by the order taken with the counter affidavits disclosed that his arrest and detention were patently illegal. He pointed out that while Rule 30(1)(b) provided that detention could be made for the maintenance of public order, the order stated that Dr. Lohia was arrested for maintenance of law and order. He characterised the counter affidavits as full of lies and narrated other facts intending to show that there was a conspiracy to seal his mouth so that disclosures against the Bihar Government might not be made. This represents the material on which the present petition is based or opposed. The petition was argued by Dr. Lohia in person though he was receiving assistance in constructing his arguments. His contentions are that he is not being detained under the Defence of India Rules but arbitrarily; that even if he is being detained under the said Rules the law has been flagrantly violated; that the order passed against him is *mala fide*; and that the District Magistrate did not exercise the delegated power but went outside it in various ways rendering detention illegal.

On behalf of the State a preliminary objection is raised that the application itself is incompetent and that by the operation of Art. 359 read with the President's Order issued under that Article on November 3, 1962, Dr. Lohia's right to move the Supreme Court under Art. 32 of the Constitution is taken away during the period of emergency proclaimed under Art. 352 as long as the President's Order continues. On merits it is contended on behalf of the State of Bihar that the petition, if not barred, does not make out a case against the legality of the detention; that this Court cannot consider the question of good faith and that the only enquiry open to this Court is whether there is or is not an order under Rule 30(1)(b) of the Defence of India Rules, 1962. If this Court finds that there is such an order the enquiry is closed because the petition must then be considered as incompetent. The State Government admits that the words of Rule 30(1)(b) and S. 3 of the Defence of India Act were not used in the order of detention but contends that maintenance of public order and maintenance of law and order do not indicate different things and that the area covered by maintenance of law and order is the same if not smaller than the area covered by the expression maintenance of public order. We shall go into the last contention more elaborately after dealing with the preliminary objection. Questions about the right of persons detained under the Defence of India Rules to move the Court have come up frequently before this Court and many of the arguments which are raised here have already been considered in a series of cases. For example, it has been ruled in *Mohan Choudhury* vs. *Chief Commissioner, Tripura* (1) that the right of any person detained under the Defence of India Rules to move any court for the enforcement of his rights conferred by Arts. 21 and 22 of the Constitution remains suspended in view of the President's Order of November 3, 1962. It has also been ruled that such a person cannot raise the question that the Defence of India Act or the Rules are not valid because, if allowed to do so, that would mean that the petitioner's right to move the court is intact. Other questions arising from detentions under the Defence of India Rules were further considered in*Makhan Singh* v. *The State of Punjab* (1). It is there pointed out that, although the right of the detenu to move the Court is taken away that can only be in cases in which the proper detaining authority passes a valid order of detention and the order is made *bona fide* for the purpose which it professes. It would, therefore, appear from the latter case that there is an area of enquiry open before a court will declare that the detenu has lost his right to move the court. That area at least embraces an enquiry into whether there is action by a competent authority and in accordance with Defence of India Act and the Rules thereunder. Such an enquiry may not entitle the court to go into the merits of the case once it is established that proper action has been taken, for the satisfaction is subjective, but till that appears the court is bound to enquire into the legality of the detention. It was contended that *Makhan Singh's (2)* case arose under Art. 226 and that what is stated there applies only to petitions under that article. This is a misapprehension. The ruling made no difference between the Art. 32 and Art. 226 in the matter of the bar created by Art. 359 and the President's Order. What is stated there applies to petitions for the enforcement of Fundamental Rights whether by way of Art. 32 or Art. 226.

Mr. Verma appearing for the State of Bihar, however, contends that the area of the enquiry cannot embrace anything more than finding out whether there is an order of detention or not and the moment such an order, good on its face, is produced all enquiry into good faith, sufficiency of the reasons or the legality or illegality of the action comes to an end, for to go into such matters is tantamount to allowing the petitioner to move the court which the President's Order does not permit. He contends that the courts' power to issue a writ of *Habeas Corpus* in such cases is taken away as completely as if cl. (2) of Art. 32 made no mention of the writ of*Habeas Corpus*. According to him, an order under Rule 30(1)(b) proper on its face, must put an end to enquiry of any kind. In view of this objection it is necessary to state the exact result of the President's Order for this has not been laid down in any earlier decision of this Court

The President declared a state of grave emergency by issuing a Proclamation under Art. 352 on October 26, 1962. This Proclamation of Emergency gave rise to certain extraordinary powers which are to be found in Part XVIII of the Constitution, entitled Emergency Provisions. Article 358 suspended the provisions of Art. 19 during the Emergency and Art. 359 permitted the suspension of the enforcement of the rights conferred by Part III. That article reads: "359. Suspension of the enforcement of the rights conferred by Part III during emergencies

(1) Where a Proclamation of Emergency is in operation, the President may by order declare that the right to move any court for the enforcement of such of the rights conferred by Part III as may be mentioned in the order and all proceedings pending in any court for the enforcement of the rights so mentioned shall remain suspended for the period during which the Proclamation is in force or for such shorter period as may be specified in the order.

(2) An order made as aforesaid may extend to the whole or any part of the territory of India.

(3) Every order made under clause (1) shall, as soon as may after it is made, be laid before each House of Parliament."

The President issued an order on November 3, 1962. The Order reads:

"ORDER

New Delhi, the 3rd November, 1962.

G.S.R. 1454.—In exercise of the powers conferred by clause (1) of article 359 of the Constitution, the President hereby declares that the right of any person to move any court for the enforcement of the rights conferred by article 21 and article 22 of the Constitution shall remain suspended for the period during which the Proclamation of Emergency issued under clause (1) of article 352 thereof on the 26th October, 1962, is in force, if such person has been deprived of any such rights under the Defence of India Ordinance, 1962 (4 of 1962) or any rule or order made thereunder. No. F. 4/62-Poll (Spl.)

V. VISWANATHAN, Secy."

As a result of the above Order the right of any person to move any court for the rights conferred by Arts. 21 and 22 of the Constitution remains suspended, if such person is deprived of any such rights under the Defence of India Ordinance, 1962 (now the Defence of India Act, 1962) or any rule or order made thereunder. No doubt, as the article under which the President's Order was passed and also that Order say, the right to move the court is taken away but that is in respect of a right conferred on any person by Arts. 21 and 22 and provided such person is deprived of the right under the Defence of India Ordinance (now the Act) or any rule or order made thereunder. Two things stand forth. The first is that only the enforcement in a court of law of rights conferred by Arts. 21 and 22 is suspended and the second is that the deprivation must be under the Defence of India Ordinance (now the Act) or any rule or order made thereunder. The word "thereunder" shows that the authority of the Defence of India Act must be made out in each case whether the deprivation is by rule or order. It, therefore, becomes necessary to inquire what are the rights which are so affected? This can only be found out by looking into the content of the Arts. 21 and 22. Article 21 lays down that no person is to be deprived of his life or personal liberty except according to procedure established by law. This article thinks in terms of the ordinary laws which govern our society when there is no declaration of emergency and which are enacted subject to the provisions of the Constitution including the Chapter on Fundamental Rights but other than those made under the powers conferred by the Emergency Provisions in Part XVIII.

When the President suspended the operation of Art. 21 he took away from any person dealt with under the terms of his Order, the right to plead in a court of law that he was being deprived of his life and personal liberty otherwise than according to the procedure established by the laws of the country. In other words, he could not invoke the procedure established by ordinary law. But the President did not make lawless actions lawful. He only took away the Fundamental Right in Art. 21 in respect of a person proceeded against under the Defence of India Act or any rule or order made thereunder. Thus a person so proceeded could not claim to be tried under the ordinary law or bring an action under the ordinary law. But to be able to say that the right to move the court for the enforcement of rights under Art. 21 is suspended, it is necessary to establish that such person has been deprived of any such right under the Defence of India Act or any rule or order made thereunder, that is to say, under the authority of the Act. The action of the authorities empowered by the Defence of India Act is not completely shielded from the scrutiny of courts. The scrutiny with reference to procedure established by laws other than the Defence of India Act is, of course, shut out but an enquiry whether the action is justified under the Defence of India Act itself is not shut out. Thus the State Government or the District Magistrate cannot add a clause of their own to the Defence of India Act or even the Rules and take action under that clause. Just as action is limited in its extent, by the power conferred, so also the power to move the court is curtailed only when there is strict compliance with the Defence of India Act and the Rules. The Court will not enquire whether any other law is not followed or breached but the Court will enquire whether the Defence of India Act or the Rules have been obeyed or not. That part of the enquiry and consequently the right of a person to move the court to have that enquiry made, is not affected.

The President's Order next refers to Art. 22. That Article creates protection against illegal arrest and detention. Clause (1) confers some rights on the person arrested. Clause (2) lays down the procedure which must be followed after an arrest is made. By cl. (3) the first two clauses do not apply to an alien enemy or to a person arrested or detained under any law providing for preventive detention. Clauses (4), (5), (6) and (7) provide for the procedure for dealing with persons arrested or detained under any law providing for preventive detention, and lay down the minimum or compulsory requirements. The provisions of Art. 22 would have applied to arrest and detentions under the Defence of India Act also if the President's Order had not taken away from such a person the right to move any court to enforce the protection of Art. 22.

The net result of the President's Order is to stop all claims to enforce rights arising from laws other than the Defence of India Act and the Rules and the provisions of Art. 22 at variance with the Defence of India Act and the Rules are of no avail. But the President's Order does not say that even if a person is proceeded against in breach of the Defence of India Act or the Rules he cannot move the court to complain that the Act and the Rules, under colour of which some action is taken, do not warrant it. It was thus that this Court questioned detention orders by Additional District Magistrates who were not authorised to make them or detentions of persons who were already in detention after conviction or otherwise for such a long period that detention orders served could have had no relation to the requirements of the Defence of India Act or the Rules. Some of these cases arose under Art. 226 of the Constitution but in considering the bar of Art. 359 read with the President's Order, there is no difference between a petition under that article and a petition under Art. 32. It follows, therefore, that this Court acting under Art. 32 on a petition for the issue of a *writ of Habeas Corpus*, may not allow claims based on other laws or on the protection of Art. 22, but it may not and, indeed, must not, allow breaches of the Defence of India Act or the Rules to go unquestioned. The President's Order neither says so nor is there any such intendment. There is, however, another aspect which needs to be mentioned here.

That is the question of want of good faith on the part of those who take action and whether such a plea can be raised. This topic was dealt with in *Makhan Singh's case (1)*. At page 828 the following observation is to be found:

> "Take also a case where the detenu moves the court for a writ of Habeas Corpus on the ground that his detention has been ordered mala fide. It is hardly necessary to emphasise that the exercise of a power mala fide is wholly outside the scope of the Act conferring the power and can always be successfully challenged. It is true that a mere allegation that the detention is mala fide would not be enough; the detenu will have to prove the mala fides. But if the mala fides are alleged, the detenu cannot be precluded from substantiating his plea on the ground of the bar created by Art. 359(1) and the Presidential order. That is an other kind of plea which is out side the purview of Art. 359(1)."

Mr. Verma, however, contends on the authority of *Smith* vs. *East Elloe Rural District Cormical and Others (1)* that the validity of the orders under the Defence of India Rules 1962 cannot be challenged on the ground of bad faith when the action is otherwise proper. That case dealt with the Acquisition of Land (Authorization Procedure) Act, 1946 (9 and 10 Geo 6 Ch. 49). Paragraph 15 (1) of Part IV of Schedule to that Act provided

> "If any person aggrieved by a compulsory purchase order desires to question the validity thereof ... on the ground that the authorization of a compulsory purchase thereby granted is not empowered to be granted under this Act he may, within six weeks from the date on which notice of the confirmation or making of the make an application."

The appellant more than six weeks after the notice had been published brought an action, claiming *inter alia* that the order was made and confirmed wrongfully and in bad faith on the part of the clerk. Paragraph 16 of that Act provided "Subject to the provisions of the last foregoing paragraph, a compulsory purchase order shall not ... be questioned, in any legal proceeding whatsoever.

The House of Lords (by majority) held that the jurisdiction of the court was ousted in such wise that even questions of bad faith could not be raised. Viscount Simonds regretted that it should be so, but giving effect to the language of paragraph 16, held that even an allegation of bad faith was within the bar of Paragraph 16. Lord Morton of Henryton, Lord Reid and Lord Somervill of Harrow were of opinion that Paragraph 15 gave no such opportunity. Lord Radcliffe dissented.

The cited case can have no relevance here because the statute provided for ouster of courts' jurisdiction in very different circumstances. Although this Court has already stated that allegations of bad faith can be considered, it may be added that where statutory powers are conferred to take drastic action against the life and liberty of a citizen, those who exercise it may not depart from the purpose. Vast powers in the public interest are granted but under strict conditions. If a person, under colour of exercising the statutory power, acts from some improper or ulterior motive, he acts in bad faith. The action of the authority is capable of being viewed in two ways. Where power is misused but there is good faith the act is only ultra vires but where the misuse of power is in bad faith there is added to the ultra vires character of the act, another vitiating circumstance. Courts have always acted to restrain a misuse of statutory power and the more readily when improper motives underlie it. The misuse may arise from a breach of the law conferring the power or from an abuse of the power in bad faith. In either case the courts can be moved for we do not think that Art. 359 or the President's Order were intended to condone an illegitimate enforcement of the Defence of India Act.

We now proceed to examine the contentions of Dr. Lohia by which he claims to be entitled to have the order of the District Magistrate set aside. It is convenient to begin with the allegation of want of good faith. Dr. Lohia alleges that there was a conspiracy between the Central Government, the State of Bihar, the Senior Superintendent of Police and the District Magistrate, Patna, to stifle his disclosures against the Bihar Government, the Chief Minister and others. He also alleges that he was arrested for a substantive offence under the Indian Penal Code but the arrest has been converted into preventive detention to avoid proof in a court of law. He says that he was about to leave Patna and if the train was not late he would have gone away and he hints that his detention was made to prevent him from taking part in the Session of Parliament. The District Magistrate and the Inspector of Police deny these allegations. The District Magistrate has given the background of events in which he made the order on his responsibility. On reading the affidavits on both sides, we are satisfied that the contentions of Dr. Lohia are ill-founded and that the order of detention was made by the District Magistrate in good faith.

There is no dispute that the District Magistrate was duly authorized to act under Rule 30 of the Defence of India Rules, 1962. Dr. Lohia, however, says that the order is in flagrant disregard of the requirements of the Defence of India Act, 1962 and the Rules. For this purpose he bases his argument on three circumstances:

(i) that the District Magistrate acted outside his jurisdiction as created by Notification No. 11155-C dated 11-8-1964 published in the Bihar Gazette Extra dated August 11, 1964;

(ii) that the District Magistrate's order is defective because he purports to derive power from notification No. 180 of March 20, 1964 which had been rescinded; and

(iii) the District Magistrate purports to act to maintain law and order when he can only act to maintain public order under the Defence of India Act and the Rules thereunder.

We shall now consider these grounds of objection. Before we do so we may read the provisions of the Defence of India

Act and the Rules to which reference may be necessary. The first part of the Defence of India Act we wish to read is the long title and the preamble. They are:

> "An Act to provide for special measures to ensure the public safety and interest, the defence of India and civil defence and for the trial of certain offences and for matters connected therewith.
>
> WHEREAS the President has declared by Proclamation under Clause (1) of Article 352 of the Constitution that a grave emergency exists whereby the security of India is threatened by external aggression;
>
> AND WHEREAS it is necessary to provide for special measures to ensure the public safety and interest, the defence of India and civil defence and for the trial of certain offences and for matters connected therewith;

We may next read section 3 which confers power to make rules:

> "3. **Power to make rules**.
>
> (1) The Central Government may, by notification in the Official Gazette, make such rules as appear to it necessary or expedient for securing the defence of India and civil defence, the public safety, the maintenance of public order or the efficient conduct of military operations, or for maintaining supplies and services essential to the life of the community."
>
> Then by way of illustration and without prejudice to the generality of the powers conferred by sub-section (1), certain specific things are mentioned for which provision may be made by rules. Clause 15 provides:
>
> "(15) Notwithstanding anything in any other law for the time being in force,—
>
> (i) the apprehension and detention in custody of any person whom the authority empowered by the rules to apprehend or detain (the authority empowered to detain not being lower in rank than that of a District Magistrate) suspects,

> on grounds appearing to that authority to be reasonable, of being of hostile origin or of having acted, acting, being about to act or being likely to act in a manner prejudicial to the defence of India and civil defence, the security of the State, the public safety or interest, the maintenance of public order, India's relations with foreign States, the maintenance of peaceful conditions in any part or area of India or the efficient conduct of military operations, or with respect to whom that authority is satisfied that his apprehension and detention are necessary for the purpose of preventing him from acting in any such prejudicial manner,
> (ii) the prohibition of such person from entering or residing or remaining in any area,
> (iii) the compelling of such person to reside and remain in any area, or to do or abstain from doing anything, and
> (iv) the review of orders of detention passed in pursuance of any rule made under sub-clause (1);"

We need not trouble ourselves with the other clauses. Section 44 next provides:

> "44. Ordinary avocations of life to be interfered with as little as possible.
> Any authority or person acting in pursuance of this Act shall interfere with the ordinary avocations of life and the enjoyment of property as little as may be consonant with the purpose of ensuring the public safety and interest and the defence of India and civil defence."

By virtue of the powers conferred by S. 3 of the Defence of India Ordinance, 1962 (now the Act), the Defence of India Rules, 1962 were framed. Part IV of these Rules is headed "Restriction of Movements and Activities of Persons" and it consists of Rules 25-30, 30-A, 30-B and 31-34. These rules provide for various subjects such as "Entering enemy territory" (Rule 25), "Entering India" (Rule 26), "Information to be supplied by persons entering India" (Rule 27) or "Leaving India" (Rule 28), "Regulation of Movement of Persons within India" (Rule 29), "Powers of photographing etc. of suspected person" (Rule 31), "Control and winding up of certain organisations" (Rule 32), provisions for "Persons captured as prisoners" (Rule 33) and "Change of name by citizens of India" (Rule 34). We are really not concerned with these rules but the headings are mentioned to consider the argument of Dr. Lohia on No. (1) above. Rule 30 with which we are primarily concerned consists of eight sub-rules. We are concerned only with sub-rule (1). That rule reads: "30. Restriction of movements of suspected persons, restriction orders and detention orders—

> (1) The Central Government or the State Government, if it is satisfied with respect to any particular person that with a view to preventing him from acting in any manner prejudicial to the defence of India and civil defence, the public safety, the maintenance of public order, India's relations with foreign powers, the maintenance of peaceful conditions in any part of India, the efficient conduct of military operations or the maintenance of supplies and services essential to the life of the community, it is necessary so to do, may make an order—
> (a)
> (b) directing that he be detained;
>
> Under S. 40(2) of the Defence of India Act, the State Government may by order direct that the powers conferred by the Rules may be exercised by any officer or authority in such circumstances and under such conditions as may be specified in the direction. A special limitation was indicated in S. 3(15) of the Act, where authority is given for making rules in connection with the apprehension and detention in custody of persons, that the delegation should not be made to an officer below the rank of a District Magistrate.

By virtue of these various powers the State Government issued a notification on March 20, 1964 authorising all District Magistrates to exercise the powers of Government under Rule 30(1)(b).

That notification was later rescinded by another notification issued on June 5, 1964. A fresh notification (No. 11155-C) was issued on August 11, 1964. This was necessary because of a mistake in the first notification. The new notification reads:

> "No. 11155-C.—In exercise of the powers conferred by sub-section (2) of section (40) the Defence of India Act, 1962 (Act 51 of 1962), the Governor of Bihar is pleased to direct that the powers exercisable by the State Government under clause (b) of sub-rule (1) of rule 30 of the Defence of India Rules, 1962, shall be exercised by all District Magistrates within their respective jurisdictions.
> By order of the Governor of Bihar M.K. Mukharji Secretary to Government".

Dr. Lohia contends that the District Magistrate in his affidavit says that he apprehended danger not only in his district but in the whole of Bihar State and even outside and hence he has not acted within his jurisdiction. His argument attempts to make out, what we may call, an exercise of extraterrestrial jurisdiction on the part of the District Magistrate. He contends also that the notifications are bad because although the Defence of India Act contemplates the imposition of conditions, none were imposed and no circumstances for the exercise of power were specified. In our judgment, none of these arguments can be accepted. Section 40(2) of the Act does not require the imposition of any conditions but only permits it. This is apparent from the words "if any" in the sub-section. The only condition that the State Government thought necessary to impose is that the District Magistrates must act within their respective jurisdictions. It cannot be said that this condition was not complied with. Dr. Lohia was in the Patna District at the time. There was nothing wrong if the District Magistrate took a broad view of his activities so as to weigh the possible harm if he was not detained. Such a viewing of the activities of a person before passing the order against him does not necessarily spell out extraterrestrial in the sense suggested but is really designed to assess properly the potentiality of danger which is the main object of the rule to prevent. We find nothing wrong with the order on the score of jurisdiction and argument No. (i) stated above must fail. Argument No. (ii) is up. C. & I./65-4 not of any substance. There was a clerical error in mentioning the notification and the error did not vitiate the order of detention.

This brings us to the last contention of Dr. Lohia and that is the most serious of all. He points out that the District Magistrate purports to detain him with a view to preventing him from acting in any manner prejudicial to the public safety and the maintenance of law and order and argues that the District Magistrate had misunderstood his own powers which were to prevent acts prejudicial to public order and, therefore, the detention is illegal. On the other side, Mr. Verma contends that the Act and the Rules speak of public order which is a concept much wider in content than the concept of law and order and includes the latter, and whatever is done in furtherance of law and order must necessarily be in furtherance of public order. Much debate took place on the meaning of the two expressions. Alternatively, the State of Bihar contends that the order passed by the District Magistrate prior to the issue of the actual order of detention made use of the phrase "maintenance of public order" and the affidavit which the District Magistrate swore in support of the return also uses that phrase and, therefore, the District Magistrate was aware of what his powers were and did exercise them correctly and in accordance with the Defence of India Act and the Rules. We shall now consider the rival contentions. The Defence of India Act and the Rules speak of the conditions under which preventive detention under the Act can be ordered. In its long title and the preamble the Defence of India Act speaks of the necessity to provide for special measures to ensure public safety and interest, the defence of India and civil defence. The expressions public safety and interest between them indicate the range of action for maintaining security, peace and tranquillity of India whereas the expressions defence of India and civil defence connote defence of India and its people against aggression from outside and action of persons within the country. These generic terms were used because the Act seeks to provide for a congress of action of which preventive detention is just a small part. In conferring power to make rules, S. 3 of the Defence of India Act enlarges upon the terms of the preamble by specification of details. It speaks of defence of India and civil defence and public safety without change but it expands the idea of public interest into "maintenance of public order, the efficient conduct of military operations and maintaining of supplies and services essential to the life of the community". Then it mentions by way of illustration in cl. (15) of the same section the power of apprehension and detention in custody of any person whom the authority empowered by the rules to apprehend or detain (the authority empowered to detain not being lower in rank than that of a District Magistrate), suspects, on grounds appearing to that authority to be reasonable

(a) of being of hostile origin; or
(b) of having acted, acting or being about to act or being likely to act in a manner prejudicial to—
  (i) the defence of India and civil defence;
  (ii) the security of the State;
  (iii) the public safety or interest;
  (iv) the maintenance of public order;
  (v) India's relations with foreign states;
  (vi) the maintenance of peaceful conditions in any part or area of India; or
  (vii) the efficient conduct of military operations

It will thus appear that security of the state, public safety or interest, maintenance of public order and the maintenance of peaceful conditions in any part or area of India may be viewed separately even though strictly one clause may have an effect or bearing on another. Then follows rule 30, which repeats the above conditions and permits detention of any person with a view to preventing him from acting in any of the above ways. The argument of Dr. Lohia that the conditions are to be cumulatively applied is clearly untenable. It is not necessary to analyse rule 30 which we quoted earlier and which follows the scheme of section 3(15). The question is whether by taking power to prevent Dr. Lohia from acting to the prejudice of "law and order" as against "public order" the District Magistrate went outside his powers.

The subject of preventive detention has been discussed almost threadbare and one can hardly venture in any direction without coming face to face with rulings of courts. These cases are now legion. It may be taken as settled that the satisfaction of the detaining authority cannot be subjected to objective tests, that the courts are not to exercise appellate powers over such authorities and that an order proper on its face, passed by a competent authority in good faith is a complete answer to a petition such as this.

The rulings in our country adopt this approach as do the English Courts. In England one reason given for the adoption of this approach was that the power was entrusted to the Home Secretary and to the Home Secretary alone. In India courts are ordinarily satisfied on the production of a proper order of detention made in good faith by an authority duly authorised and have not enquired further even though the power is exercised by thousands of officers subordinate to the Central and State Governments as their delegates. When from the order itself circumstances appear which raise a doubt whether the officer concerned had not misconceived his own powers, there is need to pause and enquire. This is more so when the exercise of power is at the lowest level permissible under the Defence of India Act. The enquiry then is not with a view to investigate the sufficiency of the materials but into the officer's notions of his power, for it cannot be conceived for a moment that even if the court did not concern itself about the sufficiency or otherwise of the materials on which action is taken, it would, on proof from the order itself that the officer did not realise the extent of his own powers, not question the action. The order of detention is the authority for detention. That is all which the detenu or the court can see. It discloses how the District Magistrate viewed the activity of the detenu and what the District Magistrate intended to prevent happening. If the order passed by him shows that he thought that his powers were more extensive than they actually were, the order might fail to be a good order.

The District Magistrate here acted to maintain law and order and not public order. There are only two possibilities: (i) that there was a slip in preparing the order, or (ii) that maintenance of law and order was in the mind of the District Magistrate and he thought it meant the same thing as maintenance of public order. As to the first it may be stated at once that the District Magistrate did not specify it as such in his affidavit. He filed an earlier order by him in which he had used the words "public order" and which we have quoted earlier. That order did not refer to his own state of the mind but to the report of the Senior Superintendent of Police. In his affidavit he mentioned "public order" again but did not say that the words "law and order" in his order detaining Dr. Lohia were a slip. He corrected the error about the notification but naively let pass the other, and more material error, without any remark. Before us every effort possible was made to reconcile "public order" with "law and order" as, indeed, by a process of paraphrasing, it is possible to raise an air of similitude between them. Such similitude is possible to raise even between phrases as dissimilar as "for preventing breach of the peace", "in the interest of the public", "for protecting the interests of a class of persons", "for administrative reasons" and "for maintaining law and order". We cannot go by similitude. If public order connotes something different from law and order even though there may be some common territory between them then obviously the District Magistrate might have traversed ground not within "public order". It would then not do to say that the action is deferrable to one power rather than the other, just as easily as one reconciles diverse phrases by a gloss. When the liberty of the citizen is put within the reach of authority and the scrutiny from courts is barred, the action must comply not only with the substantive requirements of the law but also with those forms which alone can indicate that the substance has been complied with. It is, therefore, necessary to examine critically, the order which mentioned "law and order" with a view to ascertaining whether the District Magistrate did not act outside his powers.

Before we do so we find it necessary to deal with an argument of Mr. Shastri who followed Mr. Verma. He contends that there is no magic in using the formula of the Act and Rules for the language of the Act and the Rules can be quoted mechanically. We regret such an attitude. The President in his Order takes away the fundamental rights under Arts. 21 and 22 from a person provided he has been detained under the Defence of India Act or the rules made thereunder. The Order is strict against the citizen but it is also strict against the authority. There can be no toleration of a pretence of using the Defence of India Act. The President's Order itself creates protection against things such as arbitrariness, misunderstood powers, mistake of identity by making his order apply only to cases where the detention is under the Act or the rules thereunder. No doubt, what matters is the substance but the form discloses the approach of the detaining authority to the serious question and the error in the form raises the enquiry about the substance. It is not every error in the order which will start such an enquiry. We have paid no attention to the error in the reference to the notification because that may well be a slip, and power and jurisdiction is referrable to the notification under which they would have validity. The other is not such a venal fault. It opens the door to enquiry what did the District Magistrate conceive to be his powers?

In proceeding to discuss this question we may consider a decision of the Court of Appeal in England in *Carltona Ltd.* vs. *Commissioners of Works and Others (1).* Curiously enough it was brought to our notice by Dr. Lohia and not by the other side. That case arose under Regulation 51(1) of the Defence (General) Regulations in England during the last World War. The Regulation read:

> "A competent authority, if it appears to that authority to be necessary or expedient so to do in the interests of the public safety, the defence of the realm or the efficient prosecution of the war, or for maintaining supplies and services essential to the life of the community, may take possession of any land, and may give such directions as appear to the competent authority to be necessary or expedient in connection with the taking of possession of that land."

There was an order against Carltona Ltd. by the Commissioner of Works requisitioning the factory. The order read:

> "I have to inform you that the department have come to the conclusion that it is essential, in the national interest, to take possession of the above premises occupied by you."

> It was objected on behalf of the Company that the mind was not directed to any one of the various heads mentioned in the Regulation which were put in the alternative. Lord Greene, M.R. speaking on behalf of Lord Goddard (then Lord Justice) and Lord du Parcq (then Lord Justice) observed: "It was said that it was the duty of the person acting in the capacity of 'a competent authority' to examine the facts of the case and consider under which, if any, of those various heads the matter came, and it is said that the assistant secretary did nothing of the kind. It is to be observed that those heads are not mutually exclusive heads at all. They overlap at every point and many matters will fall under two or more of them, or under all four. I read the evidence as meaning that the assistant secretary, seeing quite

clearly that the case with which he was dealing and the need that he wished to satisfy was one which came under the regulation, did not solemnly sit down and ask himself whether it was for the efficient prosecution of the war that this storage was required for maintaining supplies and services essential to the life of the community. He took the view that it was required either for all those purposes, or, at any rate, for some of them, and I must confess it seems to me that it would have been a waste of time on the facts of this case for anyone seriously to sit down and ask himself under which particular head the case fell. He regarded it, as I interpret his evidence, as falling under all the heads, and that may very well be having regard to the facts that these heads overlap in the way that I have mentioned. It seems to me, therefore, that there is no substance in that point, and his evidence makes it quite clear that he did bring his mind to bear on the question whether it appeared to him to be necessary or expedient to requisition this property for the purposes named, or some of them."

The case is distinguishable on more than one ground. To begin with, it dealt with an entirely different situation and different provision of law. No order in writing specifying satisfaction on any or all of the grounds was required. Detention under Regulation 18-B required an order just as detention under the Defence of India Act. The distinction between action under Regulation 51 and that under Regulation 18-B was noticed by the Court of Appeal in Point of *Ayr Collieries Ltd.* vs. *Lloyd-George(")*. It is manifest that when property was requisitioned it would have been a futile exercise to determine whether the act promoted the efficient prosecution of the war, or the maintaining of supplies and services. But when a person is apprehended and detained it may be necessary to set out with some accuracy what he did or was likely to do within the provisions of Rule 30, to merit the detention. The use of one phrase meaning a different thing in place of that required by the Act would not do, unless the phrase imported means the same thing as the phrase in the Act. Here the phrase used is maintenance of law and order and we must see how that phrase fits into the Rule which speaks of maintenance of "public order". The words "public order" were considered on some previous occasions in this Court and the observations made them are used to prove that maintenance of public order is the same thing as maintenance of law and order. We shall refer to some of these observations before we discuss the two phrases in the context of the Defence of India Rules.

Reliance is first placed upon a decision of the Federal Court in *Lakhi Narayan Das* vs. *Province of Bihar* (2) where the Court dealing with item 1 of Provincial List, 7th Schedule in the Government of India Act, 1935 which read—

> "Public order (but not including the use of His Majesty's naval, military or air-forces in aid of the civil power)."

observed that "Public Order" with which that item began was "a most comprehensive term". Reference is also made to*Ramesh Thapar* vs. *State of Madras* (1) where this Court dealing with the same subject matter also observed: "... Public order is an expression of wide connotation and signifies that state of tranquillity which prevails among the members of a political society as a result of internal regulations enforced by the Government which they have established it must be taken that 'public safety' is used as a part of the wider concept of public order and referring to Entry 3 in List III (Concurrent List) of the 7th Schedule of the Constitution which includes the "security of a State" and "maintenance of public order" as distinct topics of legislation, observed in the field of public order or tranquillity, marking off, may be, roughly, the boundary between those serious and aggravated forms of public disorder—which are calculated to endanger the security of the State and the relatively minor breaches of the peace of a purely local significance, treating for this purpose differences in degree as if they were differences in kind."

Fazl Ali J. took a different view which he had expressed more, fully in *Brijbhushan and Another* vs. *The State of Delhi* (2) but he also observed that "public safety" had, as a result of a long course of legislative practice, acquired a well rccognised meaning and was taken to denote safety or security of the State and that the expression "public order" was wide enough to cover small disturbances of the peace which do not jeopardise the security of the State and paraphrased the words 'public order' as public tranquillity."

Both the aspects of the matter were again before this Court in *The Superintendent Central Prison, Fatehgarh v. Rammanohar Lohia* (3) when dealing with the wording of clause (2) of Art. 19 as amended by the Constitution (First Amendment) Act, 1951, it fell to be decided what "public order" meant. Subba Rao J. speaking for the Court referred to all earlier rulings and quoting from them came to the conclusion that "public order" was equated with public peace and safety and said: "... Presumably in an attempt to get over the effect of these two decisions, the expression "public order" was inserted in Art. 19(2) of the Constitution by the Constitution (First Amendment) Act, 1951, with a view to bring in offences involving breach of purely local significance within the scope of Art. 19...."

Summing up the position as he gathered from the earlier cases, the learned Judge observed:

> "... Public order, is synonymous with public safety and tranquillity: it is thc abscnce of disorder involving breaches of local significance in contradistinction to national upheavals, such as revolution, civil strife, war, affecting the security of the State;...."

These observations determine the meaning of the words "public order" in contradistinction to expressions such as "public safety", "security of the State". They were made in different contexts. The first three cases dealt with the meaning in the legislative Lists as to which, it is settled, we must give as large a meaning as possible. In the last case the meaning of "public order" was given in relation to the necessity for amending the Constitution as a result of the pronouncements of this Court. The context in which the words were used was different, the occasion was different and the object in sight was different. We have here a case of detention under Rule 30 of the Defence of India Rules which permits apprehension and detention of a person likely to act in a manner prejudicial to the maintenance of public order. It follows that if such a person is not detained public disorder is the apprehended result. Disorder is no doubt prevented by the maintenance of law and order also but disorder is a broad spectrum which includes at one end small disturbances and at the other the most serious and cataclysmic happenings. Does the expression 'public order' take in every kind of disorder or only some? The answer to this serves to distinguish "public order" from "law and order" because the latter undoubtedly takes in all of them. Public order if disturbed, must lead to public disorder. Every breach of the peace does not lead to public disorder. When two drunkards quarrel and fight there is disorder but not public disorder. They can be dealt with under the powers to maintain law and order but cannot be detained on the ground that they were disturbing public order. Suppose that the two fighters were of rival communities and one of them tried to raise communal passions. The problem is still one of law and order but it raises the apprehension of public disorder. Other examples can be imagined. The contravention of law always affects order but before it can be said to affect public order, it must affect the community or the public at large. A mere disturbance of law and order leading to disorder is thus not necessarily sufficient for action under the Defence of India Act but disturbances which subvert the public order are. A District Magistrate is entitled to take action under Rule 30(1)(b) to prevent subversion of public order but not in aid of maintenance of law and order under ordinary circumstances. It will thus appear that just as "public order" in the rulings of this Court (earlier cited) was said to comprehend disorders of less gravity than those affecting "security of State", "law and order" also comprehends disorders of less gravity than those affecting public order". One has to imagine three concentric circles. Law and order represents the largest circle within which is the next circle representing public order and the smallest circle represents security of State. It is then easy to see that an act may affect law and order but not public order just as an act may affect public order but not security of the State. By using the expression "maintenance of law and order" the District Magistrate was widening his own field of action and was adding a clause to the Defence of India Rules. We do not know the material on which the District Magistrate acted. If we could examine the reasons we may be able to say whether the action can still be said to fall within the other topic public safety. That enquiry is not open to us. If we looked into the matter from that angle we would be acting outside our powers. The order on its face shows two reasons. There is nothing to show that one purpose was considered to be more essential than the other. We are not, therefore, certain that the District Magistrate was influenced by one consideration and not both. The order of detention is a warrant which authorises action. Affidavits hardly improve the order as it is. If there is allegation of bad faith they can be seen to determine the question of good faith. If mistaken identity is alleged we can satisfy ourselves about the identity. But if action is taken to maintain law and order instead of maintaining public order, there is room to think that the powers were misconceived and if there is such a fundamental error then the action remains vulnerable. It will not be possible to say that although maintenance of law and order were specified, what was considered was the problem of maintenance of public order. The error is an error of a fundamental character and unlike quoting a wrong notification. It is thus apparent why one error in the order of detention is admitted but not the other, and why with elaborate arguments it is attempted to establish that "public order" involves elements more numerous than "law and order" where, in fact, the truth is the other way.

It may be mentioned that Dr. Lohia claimed that the satisfaction of the President under Art. 359 is open to scrutiny of the court. We have not allowed him to argue this point which is now concluded by rulings of this Court. In our judgment the order of the District Magistrate exceeded his powers. He proposed to act to maintain law and order and the order cannot now be read differently even if there is an affidavit the other way. We have pondered deeply over this case. The action of the District Magistrate was entirely his own. He was, no doubt, facing a law and order problem but he could deal with such a problem through the ordinary law of the land and not by means of the Defence of India Act and the Rules. His powers were limited to taking action to maintain public order. He could not run the law and order problems in his District by taking recourse to the provisions for detention under the Defence of India Act. If he thought in terms of 'public order' he should have said so in the order or explained how the error arose. He does neither. If the needs of public order demand action a proper order should be passed. The detention must, therefore, be declared to be outside the Defence of India Act, 1962 and the Rules made thereunder. Dr. Lohia is entitled to be released from custody and we order accordingly.

Raghubar Dayal, J. : In this writ petition Dr. Lohia challenges the validity of the order made by the District Magistrate, Patna, dated August 9, 1965, under cl. (b) of sub-r. (1) of r. 30 of the Defence of India Rules, 1962, hereinafter called the Rules. This order is as follows:

"Whereas I, J. N. Sahu, District Magistrate, Patna, am satisfied with respect to the person known as Dr. Rammanohar Lohia, Circuit House, Patna that with a view to preventing him from acting in any manner prejudicial to the public safety and the maintenance of law and order, it is necessary to make an order that he be detained.

Now, therefore, in the exercise of the powers conferred by clause (b) of sub-rule (1) of rule 30 of the Defence of India Rules, 1962 read with Notification No. 180/CW dated the 20th March 1964 of the Govt. of Bihar, Political (Special) Department, I hereby direct that the said Dr. Rammanohar Lohia be arrested by the police wherever found and detained in the Central Jail Hazaribagh, until further orders."

If this order is valid, Dr. Lohia cannot move this Court for enforcement of his rights conferred by Arts. 21 and 22 of the Constitution, in view of the Order of the President dated November 3, 1962, in the exercise of powers conferred on him by cl. (1) of Art. 359 of the Constitution. Dr. Lohia has challenged the validity of this order on several grounds. I agree with the views expressed by Hidayatullah J., about all the contentions except one. That contention is that the appropriate authority is not empowered to order detention with a view to prevent a person from acting in any way prejudicial to the maintenance of law and order. It is urged that though the District Magistrate could order the detention of the petitioner with a view to prevent him from acting in any way prejudical to the public safety and the maintenance of public order, he could not order detention with a view to prevent the petitioner from acting prejudicially to the public safety and maintenance of law and order, as the latter object, being not synonymous with the object of preventing him from acting prejudicial to public order, is outside the purview of the provisions of r. 30(1) of the rules and that, therefore, the entire order is bad. I do not agree with this contention. Under r. 30(1)(b), the District Magistrate could have made the order of detention with respect to Dr. Lohia if he was satisfied that he be detained with a view to prevent him from acting in any manner prejudicial to public safety or maintenance of public order. Such satisfaction is subjective and not objective. The Court cannot investigate about the adequacy of the reasons which led to his satisfaction. The Court can, however, investigate whether he exercised the power under r. 30 honestly and bona fide or not i.e., whether he ordered detention on being satisfied as required by r. 30. What is crucial for the validity of the detention order is such satisfaction and not the form in which the detention order is framed. A detenu can question the validity of the detention order—valid on its face—on various grounds including that of *mala fides*. The onus will be on him to prove *mala fides*. He can question the validity of the detention order on the same ground when, on its face, it appears to be invalid. In such a case the onus will be on the detaining authority to establish that it was made *bona fide*.

An order is made *mala fide* when it is not made for the purpose laid down in the Act or the rules and is made for an extraneous purpose. The contention of the petitioner to the effect that the detention order cannot be made on the satisfaction of the detaining authority that it is necessary to prevent him from acting in a manner prejudicial to the maintenance of law and order, in effect, amounts to the contention that it is made *mala fide*.

The detaining authority is free to establish that any defect in the detention order is of form only and not of substance, it being satisfied of the necessity to detain the person for a purpose mentioned in r. 30 though the purpose has been inaccurately stated in the detention order. The existence of the satisfaction required by r. 30 does not depend on what is said in the detention order, and can be established by the District Magistrate by his affidavit. We have therefore to examine whether the District Magistrate was really satisfied about the necessity to detain Dr. Lohia with a view to prevent him from acting in a manner prejudicial to public safety and maintenance of public order.

The impugned order was passed under r. 30(1)(b) of the rules. The District Magistrate decided to detain the appellant with two objects, firstly, to prevent him from acting in any way prejudicial to public safety and, secondly, to prevent him from acting in any way prejudicial to the maintenance of law and order. The District Magistrate has—even in the absence of any such contention as under discussion and which was raised after the filing of the District Magistrate's affidavit—said that having regard to, *inter alia*, the circumstances which were developing in Patna on August 9, 1965, he was fully satisfied, in view of the report made by the Senior Superintendent of Police, Patna, in regard to Dr. Lohia's conduct and activities, that it was necessary to direct that he be detained in order to prevent him from acting further in any manner prejudicial to the public safety and maintenance of public order. There is no reason to disbelieve his statement. His original order, set out below, bears out this statement of his in his later affidavit:

> "Perused the report of the Senior S. P. Patna for detention of Dr. Rammanohar Lohia, M.P. under rule 30(1)(b) of the Defence of India Rules, on the ground that his being at large is prejudicial to the public safety and maintenance of public order. From the report of the Sr. S. P., Patna, I am satisfied that Dr. Rammanohar Lohia, M.P., aforesaid, be detained under rule 30(1)(b) of the Defence of India Rules. Accordingly, I order that Dr. Rammanohar Lohia be detained under rule 30(1)(b) of the Defence of India Rules read with Notification No. 180/CW dated 20-3-64 in the Hazaribagh Central Jail until further orders."

The District Magistrate's omission to repeat in the second sentence where he speaks of his satisfaction that Dr. Lohia be detained with a view to preventing him from acting prejudicially to the public safety and maintenance of public order, does not mean that he was not so satisfied when the earlier sentence makes reference to the report of the Senior Superintendent of Police for detaining Dr. Lohia on the ground of his being at large to be prejudicial to public safety and maintenance of public order.

The District Magistrate referred, in para 3 of his affidavit, to his satisfaction that the forces of disorder which were sought to be let loose, if not properly controlled, would envelop the whole State of Bihar and possibly might spread in other parts of the country which would necessarily affect the problem of external defence as well in more ways than one. The possibilities of such forces of disorder spreading to other parts of the country satisfied him with the necessity of taking immediate action to neutralize those forces. It appears from his statements in paras 6 and 7 of the same affidavit that actual disturbances took place at Patna that day and that he had to operate from the Control Room. In para 9 he states that the action taken against Dr. Lohia was purely for the purpose of maintenance of public peace in the circumstances stated by him earlier.

In his rejoinder affidavit Dr. Lohia states with reference to the alleged forces of disorder referred to by the District Magistrate that even if he was promoting what the executive would call 'forces of disorder', he was doing so not with a view to impair the defences of the country but further to strengthen them, that the various allegations made against him were extraneous to the scope and purpose of the legislative provisions of the proclamations of emergency which had no rational relationship to the circumstances which were developing in Patna on August 9, 1965.

Even in his original affidavit Dr. Lohia stated in para 6 that:

> "It is also revealing to note that after the events of the 9th August for which responsibility should have been sought to be fixed either through trial or enquiry, on me or Government or anybody else, I addressed a crowd of nearly a lakh for over an hour after seven in the evening."

The setting of the events that appear to have happened at Patna on August 9, 1965 further bear out the statement of the District Magistrate that he was satisfied of the necessity to detain Dr. Lohia in order to prevent him from acting in a manner prejudicial to public order. Further, the expression 'maintenance of law and order' is not used in cl. (1) of r. 30. The corresponding expression used therein is 'maintenance of public order'. The two expressions are not much different. The expression 'public order' has been construed by this Court in a few cases, the latest of them being *The Superintendent, Central Prison, Fatehgarh* vs. *Rammanohar Lohia* (1) wherein it was said at p. 839:

> "'Public order' is synonymous with public safety and tranquillity. It is the absence of disorder involving breaches of local significance in contradistinction to national upheavals, such as revolution, civil strife, war, affecting the security of the State." The expression 'maintenance of law and order' would cover 'maintenance of public safety and tranquillity'. It may be, as urged for the petitioner, an expression of wider import than public order but, in the context in which it is used in the detention order and in view of its use generally, it should be construed to mean maintenance of law and order in regard to the maintenance of public tranquillity. It is not usually used merely with reference to enforcement of law by the agency of the State prosecutting offenders against any of the numerous laws enacted for the purposes of a well-regulated society. Simple and ostensibly minor incidents at times lead to widespread disturbances affecting public safety and tranquillity.
>
> Reference may be made to the case reported as *Sodhi Shamsher Singh* vs. *State of Pepsu* (2). In that case certain persons were detained under an order under S. 3(1) of the Preventive Detention Act, 1950, on grounds which, in substance, were that one of them had published certain pamphlets whose circulation, in the opinion of the Government, tended to encourage the Sikhs to resort to acts of lawlessness and plunge the Hindus into a feeling of utter frustration and discouragement and consequently to make them take the law into their hands for the redress of their grievances. Section 3(1) of the Preventive Detention Act, 1950, reads: "The Central Government or the State Government may—
>
> (a) if satisfied with respect to any person that with a view to preventing him from acting in any manner prejudicial to—
>
> (i) the defence of India, the relations of India with

foreign powers, or the security of India, or

(ii) the security of the State or the maintenance of public order, or

(iii) ....

(b) ..., make an order directing that such person be detained."

This Court used the expression 'maintenance of law and order' in place of 'maintenance of public order' used in S. 3(1)(a)(ii) at three places in paras 4 and 5 of the judgment. I do not refer to these to show that the Court has construed the expression 'maintenance of public order' as 'maintenance of law and order' but to reinforce my view that the expression 'maintenance of law and order' is generally used for 'maintenance of public safety and tranquillity' which is covered by the expression 'public order'. When this Court used this expression in place of 'maintenance of public order' I cannot conclude, as urged by the petitioner, that the District Magistrate's using the expression 'maintenance of law and order' in place of 'maintenance of public order, is any indication of the fact that he had not applied his mind to the requirements of the provisions of r. 30(1) or had not actually come to the conclusion that it was necessary to detain Dr. Lohia with a view to prevent him from acting in any manner prejudicial to the maintenance of public order.

If the expression 'maintenance of law and order' in the impugned order be not construed as referring to 'maintenance of public order' the impugned order cannot be said to be invalid in view of it being made with a double objective, i.e., with the object of preventing Dr. Lohia from acting prejudicially to the public safety and from acting prejudicially to the maintenance of law and order. If the District Magistrate was satisfied, as the impugned order and the affidavit of the District Magistrate show that he was satisfied that it was necessary to detain Dr. Lohia with a view to preventing him from acting prejudicially to public safety, that itself would have justified his passing the impugned order. His satisfaction with respect to any of the purposes mentioned in r. 30(1) which would justify his ordering the detention of a person is sufficient for the validity of the order. There is no room for considering that he might not have passed the impugned order merely with one object in view, the object being to prevent Dr. Lohia from acting prejudicially to public safety. The entire circumstances in which the order has been made and which I have referred to earlier, point to that.

The question before us is not really at par with the question that arose in *Romesh Thappar* vs. *State of Madras* (1). In that case the provisions impugned were those of a statute whose language authorised the passing of orders which could be constitutional in certain circumstances and unconstitutional in others. In such a context, it was said that where a law purports to authorize the imposition of restrictions on a fundamental right in language wide enough to cover restrictions both within and without the limits of constitutionally permissible legislative action affecting such right, it is not possible to uphold it even so far as it may be applied within the constitutional limits, as it is not severable; so long as the possibility of its being applied for purpose not sanctioned by the Constitution cannot be ruled out, it must be held to be wholly unconstitutional and void. It was so held as, otherwise, the orders passed for purposes not sanctioned by the Constitution would have been in accordance with the law held valid. The validity of the orders passed under a valid law—the Defence of India Act and the rules have to be assumed to be valid—depends on their being made by the appropriate authority in accordance with the law empowering it to pass the orders.

The question before us is also not at par with the question which often arises in construing the validity of detention orders passed under the Preventive Detention Act for the reason that some of the grounds for the satisfaction of the appropriate authority were irrelevant or non-existent. The presence of such grounds raised the question whether the remaining good grounds would have led the authority to the requisite subjective satisfaction for ordering detention. In the present case, however, the question is different. The question is whether the District Magistrate would have made the order of detention on his satisfaction merely to the effect that it was necessary to detain Dr. Lohia with a view to prevent him from acting in a manner prejudicial to public safety. It is not that his satisfaction is based on two grounds, one of which is irrelevant or non-existent.

Even in such cases, this Court has held in *Dwarka Das* vs. *State of J & K* (1):

> "The principle underlying all these decisions is this. Where power is vested in a statutory authority to deprive the liberty of a subject on its subjective satisfaction with reference to specified matters, if that satisfaction is stated to be based on a number of grounds or for a variety of reasons, all taken together, and if some out of them are found to be non-existent or irrelevant, the very exercise of that power is bad. That is so because the matter being one for subjective satisfaction, it must be properly based on all the reasons on which it purports to be based. If some out of them are found to be non-existent or irrelevant, the Court cannot predicate what the subjective satisfaction of the said authority would have been on the exclusion of those grounds or reasons. To uphold the validity of such an order in spite of the invalidity of some of the reasons or grounds would be to substitute the objective standards of the Court for the subjective satisfaction of the statutory authority. In applying these principles, however, the Court must be satisfied that the vague or irrelevant grounds are such as, if excluded, might reasonably have affected the subjective satisfaction of the appropriate authority. It is not merely because some ground or reason of a comparatively unessential nature is defective that such an order based on subjective satisfaction can be held to be invalid."

As stated earlier, there does not appear to be any reason why the District Magistrate would not have passed the order of detention against Dr. Lohia on his satisfaction that it was necessary to prevent him from acting prejudicially to public safety. On such satisfaction, it was incumbent on him to pass the order and he must have passed it.

I am therefore of opinion that the District Magistrate made the impugned detention order on his being satisfied that it was necessary to do so with a view to prevent Dr. Lohia from acting in a manner prejudicial to public safety and maintenance of public order and that the impugned order is valid. Consequently, Dr. Lohia cannot move this Court for the enforcement of his rights under Arts. 21 and 22 of the Constitution in view of the President's Order under Art. 359(1) of the Constitution. I would dismiss this petition.

Mudholkar, J.: I agree that the petition of Dr. Rammanohar Lohia under Art. 32 of the Constitution be granted and would briefly indicate my reasons for granting it. At the outset I shall consider an objection of Mr. S. P. Varma on behalf of the State as to the tenability of the petition. The objection is two-fold. In the first place, according to him, in view of the Proclamation made by the President under Art. 359 this Court has no jurisdiction to entertain it. In the second place his contention is that the order of detention made against the petitioner being one under the Defence of India Rules, he cannot challenge the validity of his detention thereunder in any court. In support of these contentions Mr. Varma relies on the decision of this Court in *Mohan Choudhury* vs. *Chief Commissioner, Tripura* (1). In that case this Court has, while holding that the right of a person whose detention has been ordered under the Defence of India Rules to move any court for the enforcement of his rights under Art. 21 of the Constitution is suspended during the continuance of the emergency declared by the President by a Proclamation under Art. 352, held that the powers conferred on this Court by Art. 32 of the Constitution are not suspended. It is true that where a person has been detained under the Defence of India Rules he cannot move this Court under Art. 32 for the enforcement of his right under Art. 21 and so there will be no occasion for this Court to exercise its powers under that article in such a case. But what would be the position in a case where an order for detention purporting to be made under the Defence of India Rules was itself one which was beyond the scope of the Rules? For, before an entry into the portals of this Court can be denied to detenu. He must be shown an order under r. 30(1) of the Defence of India Rules made by a competent authority stating that it is satisfied that the detenu is likely to indulge in activities which will be prejudicial to one or more of the matters referred to in the rule. If the detenu contends that the order, though it purports to be under r. 30(1) of the Rules, was not competently made, this Court has the detenu contends that the order, though it purports to be under order if the Court finds that it was not competently made or was ambiguous it must exercise its powers under Art. 32 of the Constitution, entertain his petition thereunder and make an appropriate order.

In this case the District Magistrate, Patna purported to make an order under r. 3 0(1) of the Defence of India Rules. The State has placed on record copies of two orders: one is said to have been recorded by the District Magistrate on his file and another which was served on Dr. Lohia. We are not concerned with the former because the operative order must be the one served on the detenu. The District Magistrate may well keep the former in the drawer of his table or alter it as often as he likes. It cannot, therefore, be regarded as anything more than a draft order. The order which finally emerged from him and was served on the detenu would thus be the only one which matters. The grounds for detention given in the latter order are that Dr. Lohia's being at large is prejudicial to public safety and maintenance of law and order. Under r. 30(1) an order of detention of a person can be made "with a view to preventing him from acting in any manner prejudicial to the defence of India and civil defence, public safety, the maintenance of public order, India's relations with foreign powers, the maintenance of peaceful conditions in any part of India, the efficient conduct of military operations or the maintenance of supplies and services essential to the life of the community". I find it difficult to accept Dr. Lohia's argument that the appropriate authority must entertain an apprehension that the person to be detained is likely to participate in every one of the activities referred to in the rule. To accept it would be, apart from making a departure from the rules of grammar, (for doing which no valid grounds exist), making not only the rule in question but also s. 3 of the Defence of India Act where similar language is used almost ineffective. What has, however, to be considered is his other argument. The question posed by the argument is whether an authority competent to make an order under the aforesaid provision can make such an order on the ground that the authority feels it necessary to prevent a person from acting in any manner prejudicial to the maintenance of law and order. The expression 'law and order' does not find any place in the rule and is not synonymous with 'public order'. It is to me that 'law and order' is a comprehensive expression in which would be included not merely public order, but matters such as public peace, tranquillity, orderliness in a locality or a local area and perhaps some other matters. "Public order" is something distinct from order or orderliness in a local area. Under r. 30(1) no power is conferred upon that authority to detain a person on the ground that it is necessary so to do in order to prevent that person from acting in a manner prejudicial to the maintenance of order in a local area. What is it that the District Magistrate, Patna had in mind when he ordered the detention of the petitioner? Was the apprehension entertained by the District Magistrate that Dr. Lohia, if left at large, was likely to do something which will imperil the maintenance of public order generally or was it that he apprehended that Dr. Lohia's activities may cause disturbances in a particular locality? There is thus an ambiguity on the face of the order and, therefore, the order must be held to be bad. No doubt, the order also refers to the apprehension felt by the District Magistrate about Dr. Lohia's acting in a manner prejudicial to public safety. But then the question arises, what is it that weighed with the District Magistrate, the apprehension regarding public safety or an apprehension regarding the maintenance of law and order? Again, would the District Magistrate have made the order solely on the ground that he felt apprehension regarding the maintenance of public safety because of the activities in which he thought Dr. Lohia might indulge? It could well be that upon the material before him the District Magistrate would have refrained from making an order under r. 30 solely upon the first ground. Or on the other hand he would have made the order solely upon that ground. His order, however, which is the only material on the basis of which we can properly consider the matter gives no indication that the District Magistrate would have been prepared to make it only upon the ground relating to public safety. In the circumstances I agree with my brethren Sarkar and Hidayatullah that the order of detention cannot be sustained. I have not referred to any decisions because they have already been dealt with fully in the judgments of my learned brethren. In the result, therefore, I allow the petition and direct that Dr. Lohia be set at liberty.

ORDER

In view of the majority opinion, we allow the Petition and order that the petitioner be set at liberty.

5. RAMMANOHAR LOHIA AND OTHERS vs. STATE OF U.P. AND OTHERS

JUDGMENT
15/3/1967

Gangeshwar Prasad, J.

1. This is a petition for writ of *Habeas Corpus* by seven persons who were confined as undertrial prisoners in the district Jail of Agra at the time of making the petition. Petitioner No. 1 is Dr. Rammanohar Lohia who is a member of the Lok Sabha; petitioner No. 2 is Sri Brij Raj Singh who, according to the petition, is an old worker of the Samyukta Socialist Party and who was member of the Lok Sabha from 1957 to 1962; petitioner No. 3 is Sri Baloji Agarwal, who is a member of the Uttar Pradesh Vidhan Sabha from the Agra City Constituency; and the remaining petitioners are Sri Hukum Singh Parihar, Sri Ram Sanehi Lal Yadava, Sri Kitab Singh Yadava and Sri Ganga Prasad Sharma who, according to the petition, are active workers of the Samyukta Socialist Party. The opposite parties to the petition are the State of Uttar Pradesh, Sri Ravi Shanker Johri, District Magistrate Agra, and Sri K.C. Seth, Additional District Magistrate (Judicial), Agra.

2. The facts which led up to the petition are briefly as follows: Some political parties including the Samyukta Socialist Party were trying to organise 'U.P. Bandh' on July 12, 1966. In view of this situation, Opposite party No. 2, the District Magistrate of Agra, acting under Section 144 Cr.P.C. passed an order the relevant portions of which are as follows:

"To

The General Public residing or frequenting Agra District.

Whereas information has been received that in connection with U.P. Bund Agitation there is likelihood of some sections of the public indulging in violence and lawlessness to force the closure of shops, offices etc. and thereby causing breach of the peace and

Whereas immediate prevention and speedy remedy is desirable for maintaining public peace and tranquillity;

Now, Therefore in exercise of the powers under Section 144 of the Code of Criminal Procedure 1898, I. R.S. Johri District Magistrate, Agra hereby order as follows:

(i) No procession or demonstration of any kind shall be organised or taken out anywhere in the district without a special permit from me or from the Sub-Divisional Magistrate concerned or the Superintendent of Police Agra.

(ii) No assembly of five or more persons shall gather together at any public place. Any such assembly shall be deemed to be unlawful and shall be liable to be dispersed by necessary force without further warning if it does not disperse upon command by a Magistrate or an officer in charge of the Police Station. Exception—This prohibition does not apply to bona fide religious assemblies at places of worship like temple, mosque, gurdwara, church, etc.

(iii) ...

(iv) ...

(v) ...

(vi) No person shall indulge in any inflammatory speech as may likely to cause disturbance of the public peace.

(vii) ...

(viii) No person shall shout or make use of any slogans in public street of public places likely to cause a breach of the peace.

(ix) This order shall come into force at once and shall remain in force for a period of 15 days unless withdrawn earlier.

(x) This order is passed ex parte in view of the emergency.

(xi) This order shall apply to the limits of Agra District;

(xii) A breach of any of the provisions of this order is punishable under Section 188 of the Indian Penal Code.

(xiii) ...

Given under my hand and the seal of the Court this Tenth day of July 1966.

Sd/-
R.S. Johri,
District Magistrate, Agra.

A public meeting in connection with the observance of U.P. Bundh Day had been arranged to be held in the evening of July 11, 1966 in Phulatti Bazar, Agra and it was to be addressed by Dr. Rammanohar Lohia. Dr. Rammanohar Lohia arrived at Rajamandi Railway Station Agra in the afternoon of July 11, 1966 by the Toofan Express and when he came out of the railway station he was arrested by the Police. The other petitioners, who were present at the railway station to receive Dr. Rammanohar Lohia, were also arrested by the police at the same time. These arrests were for alleged violation of the above order of the District Magistrate of Agra. Counter-affidavits filed on behalf of the opposite parties do not disclose the acts which the petitioners are said to have committed in violation of the order of the District Magistrate, but they may be gathered from Annexure '4' to the counter-affidavit of Shri J.P. Srivastava, Assistant Public Prosecutor, Agra. The annexure purports to be a copy of a report made in the General Diary of Police Station Hariparvat, Agra on July 11, 1966, at 5.00 p.m. by Kr. Tej Pal Singh, Inspector in charge, who effected the arrests of the petitioners with the help of other police officers. It has been stated in the report after getting down from the train. Dr. Rammanohar Lohia delivered an objectionable speech at the platform of Rajamandi Station stressing that the Bundh had to be organised at all costs, and that the speech created a fear in the public mind. It has further been stated in the report that the other petitioners formed a procession and joined Sri Rammanohar Lohia in shouting slogans of various kinds. Mention may also be made of the fact that in paragraph 14 of their petition the petitioners say that at the time of his arrest Dr. Rammanohar Lohia asked the police officers who had arrested him as to whether they were imposing restrictions on freedom of speech and they replied that he had already delivered a speech. However, whether the petitioners did the acts alleged to have been done by them and whether those acts constituted violation of the order of the District Magistrate are questions which are not to be determined in this proceeding and, indeed, neither Sri S.N. Kacker, learned counsel for the petitioners, nor Dr. Rammanohar Lohia who addressed the Court also in person dealt with these questions.

3. The arrest of the petitioners took place at about 2.45 p.m. The same day at about 4.00 p.m. they were produced before Sri S.N. Sharma, Judicial Officer Agra, who remanded the petitioners to jail custody up to July 12, 1966. Till then no complaint had been filed against the petitioners. On July 12, 1966, however, opposite party No. 2, the District Magistrate of Agra, filed a complaint against the petitioners before Sri A.N. Kapoor, Magistrate 1st Class Agra, stating that the petitioners had contravened his prohibitory order under Section 144 Cr.P.C. dated July 10, 1966 and the contravention was punishable under Section 188 I.P.C. The petitioners were not brought to court from jail on that date and an application, copy of which is Annexure '5' to the counter-affidavit of Sri J.P. Srivastava, was moved on behalf of the State before Sri A.N. Kapoor stating that due to heavy law and order duties it was not possible to arrange escort for bringing undertrials from jail and requesting him that proceedings in the case against the petitioners be taken in the jail premises. The Magistrate accepted the request, but reached the jail at about 5.00 p.m. The petitioners were produced before him and copies of the complaints filed against them by the District Magistrate of Agra, and, according to the counter-affidavit of Sri J.P. Srivastava,

Assistant Public Prosecutor Agra copies also of the General Diary report made by Kr. Tej Pal Singh in police station Hariparvat on July 11, 1966, at 5.00 p.m. were furnished to them. The petitioners made an application, copy of which is Annexure '6' to the counter-affidavit of Sri J.P. Srivastava, praying that further proceedings in the case be taken forthwith and the statements of the petitioners and the prosecution witnesses be recorded. The Magistrate, however, adjourned the hearing of the case to July 16, 1966 with the direction that it would take place in court. Meanwhile, on July 13, 1966, the petitioners applied to the Additional District Magistrate (Judicial), Sri Chitrangad Singh, for the transfer of the case from the court of Sri A.N. Kapoor. The application was allowed on July 14, 1966 and the Additional District Magistrate (Judicial) transferred the case from the court of Sri A.N. Kapoor to his own court. On July 16, 1966 an application was moved on behalf of the State before the sessions Judge Agra for the transfer of the case from the court of Sri Chitrangad Singh, Additional District Magistrate (Judicial), and for staying proceedings meanwhile. While this application was pending Sri Chitrangad Singh was transferred from Agra and Sri K.C. Seth took over charge as Additional District Magistrate (Judicial) Agra on July 18, 1966. The State did not thereafter press its application for transfer. On July 20, 1966 the petitioners sent this petition from jail. A day later, i.e. on July 21, 1966, the petitioners were released from jail on their furnishing personal bonds of Rs. 200/- each as directed by the Sessions Judge Agra by his order dated July 16, 1966. The position, therefore, is that a case under Section 188 I.P.C. for the alleged infringement of the above quoted order of the District Magistrate passed under Section 144 Cr.P.C. is pending against the petitioners and they have been released from jail on their executing personal bonds.

4. The writ petition, as originally presented by the petitioners, contains the following prayers:

(1) Section 144 Cr.P.C. or that part of it which relates to

disturbance of the public tranquillity or a riot or an affray be struck down as unconstitutional, and

(2) as a consequence of the grant of the above prayer the petitioners be released but even if the State withdraws the case against the petitioners, the question of the constitutionality of Section 144 Cr.P.C. be determined.

In the course of the hearing of the petition the petitioners made an application for amendment of their petition seeking to add the prayer that Section 188 I.P.C. also be declared unconstitutional and the application was allowed. The petition thus challenges the validity of Section 144 Cr.P.C. under which the order of the District Magistrate of Agra which the petitioners are alleged to have contravened was passed and also the validity of Section 188 I.P.C. under which a prosecution is pending against the petitioners.

5. On behalf of the State the learned Govt. Advocate raised a preliminary objection to the hearing of the petition. He urged that since the petitioners have been released from jail their petition has become infructuous and no writ of *Habeas Corpus* can now be issued. The objection is plainly untenable. The petitioners have been released, on their furnishing personal bonds as required by the order of the Sessions Judge of Agra. The release has not, therefore, restored the petitioners to their liberty and they are subject to the restraint of the bonds that they have furnished and may again lose the limited freedom granted to them on breach of the conditions of the bonds. In the case of *Babulal Parate* vs. *State of Maharashtra*, AIR 1961 S.C. 884 the Supreme Court had before it a petition under Article 32 of the Constitution praying among other things for a writ of *Habeas Corpus* by a petitioner who was released on bail by the trying Magistrate after the proceedings pending against him had been stayed by the Supreme Court, but the Supreme Court did not on account of the release of the petitioner, treat the petition as infructuous but disposed it of on merits after a determination of the questions raised in the petition. The

question whether a person who has been released on bail can present a petition for a writ of *Habeas Corpus* was specifically raised before a Division Bench of this Court in *Zahir Ahmad* vs. *Ganga Prasad*, 1962 All LJ 654 (AIR 1963 All 4) and it was held that such a person remains under the control of the court and notionally in the custody of the court and he can, therefore, present a petition for a writ of *Habeas Corpus*. The learned Government Advocate sought to distinguish these cases on the basis that the petitioners therein had been released on bail whereas the petitioners in the instant case have been released only on their executing personal bonds. This cannot, however, be any basis for distinction. A personal bond, as a condition of release, involves restrictions on liberty just as bail does, and if a person already on bail may present a petition for a writ of Habeas Corpus or a person released on bail subsequent to the presentation of such a petition may have his petition decided on merits, there appears to be no reason why a person who has been released on his furnishing a personal bond may not present a petition, or a person, upon his release on furnishing personal bond subsequent to the presentation of a petition for Habeas Corpus, may not obtain a decision on the questions raised in his petition, if he is otherwise entitled to do so. The preliminary objection must, therefore be overruled and the petition must be decided on merits.

6. The constitutionality of Section 144 Cr.P.C. has been challenged on behalf of the petitioners on two grounds: firstly, that the section authorises the imposition of restrictions on the right to freedom of speech and expression. In the interests of things which are not covered by Article 19(2) of the Constitution, and restrictions on the right to assemble peaceably and without arms in the interests of things which are not covered by Article 19(3) of the Constitution; and secondly, that the powers which are exercisable under the section are so wide that the restrictions which it has the effect of imposing upon the fundamental rights are unreasonable. In view, however, of the pronouncement of the Supreme Court in the case of AIR 1961 SC

884 it is on the first ground that emphasis has really been laid.

7. It is indisputable that the second ground of challenge is clearly ruled out by the decision of the Supreme Court in the above mentioned case. The question of the vires of Section 144 Cr.P.C. was raised in the case on a petition under Article 32 of the Constitution and the main contention on behalf of the petitioners was that the section places unreasonable restrictions on the rights guaranteed under Article 19(1)(a) and (b) of the Constitution. After an exhaustive consideration of the provisions of Section 144 Cr.P.C., the Supreme Court repelled the contention and held that 'it cannot be said that by reason of the wide amplitude of the power which Section 144 confers on certain Magistrates it places unreasonable restrictions on certain fundamental rights.' The second ground taken on behalf of the petitioners must, therefore, be rejected at once and it does not call for any further comment.

8. The question, then is whether the law laid down by the Supreme Court in the above case also precludes the first ground of attack on the constitutionality of Section 144 Cr.P.C. Before proceeding to consider that question, however, it is necessary to make a few matters clear. The petitioners in this case are concerned with the constitutionality of only that part of Section 144 which relates to the power of issuing a direction of the nature specified therein if the direction is considered likely to prevent or tends to prevent disturbance of the public tranquillity. The prohibitory order which the petitioners are said to have contravened shows in unmistakeable terms that it was on that part of the section that the District Magistrate based his order. According to the preamble of the order, there were two reasons for passing it. Firstly, information had been received that in connection with the U.P. Bundh Agitation there was likelihood of some sections of the public indulging in violence and lawlessness in order to force the closure of shops, offices etc. and thereby causing breach of the peace Secondly, immediate prevention and speedy remedy was desirable for maintaining public peace and tranquillity. The first reason only expressed

the information received by the District Magistrate and even if it may be said that the District Magistrate appears to have accepted the information as correct it merely furnished at the occasion for passing the order, but the object intended to be achieved by the order was contained only in the second reason. It is true that the words used in the order, in this connection, are—'desirable for maintaining public peace and tranquillity', but there can be no doubt that the word 'public' governs both 'peace' and 'tranquillity' and this has not been disputed on behalf of the petitioners. The position, therefore, is that the order of the District Magistrate was founded on that part of Section 144 which empowers the issue of a certain direction if the Magistrate authorised to issue it considers that such direction is likely to prevent or tends to prevent disturbance of the public tranquillity and since that part alone affects the petitioners their challenge must be confined to that part of Section 144 Cr.P.C. and it cannot extend to the entire section. At one stage of his argument Sri S.N. Kacker, learned counsel for the petitioners, suggested that if any of the objects for which an order under Section 144 Cr.P.C. may be passed falls outside the saving provisions of Article 19(2) and (3) of the Constitution the whole section becomes ultra vires. He also drew attention to the case of *Sri Raj Narain Singh* vs. *District Magistrate, Gorakhpur*, AIR 1956 All 481 where it was held that some of the clauses of the section were in excess of the limits permitted by Article 19(2) of the Constitution. Later, however, this argument was not pressed by the learned counsel and he confined himself to that clause of the section which relates to disturbance of the public tranquillity. I may, however, observe that the various activities for the prevention of which a direction under Section 144 Cr. P.C. may be issued are quite separate and distinct, and the clauses relating thereto are not inextricably mixed but capable of surviving independently of one another. Bearing in mind the test of severability laid down by the Supreme Court in *State of Bombay* vs. *F.N. Balsara*, AIR 1951 SC 318 and *State of Bihar* vs. *Sir Kameshwar Singh*, AIR 1952

SC 252, it must be held that even if clauses relating to some of the above mentioned activities are found to offend against the Constitution, the whole of Section 144 Cr.P.C. would not on that account become unconstitutional and void. In AIR 1956 All 481 (supra) also the various clauses relating to the purposes for which an order under Section 144 Cr.P.C. may be passed were held to be severable.

9. The alternative prayer in the first relief claimed by the petitioners in their petition is that such parts of Section 144 Cr.P.C. as relate to the public tranquillity, riot and affray be struck down, and Dr. Rammanohar Lohia in the course of this argument on the constitutionality of Section 144 Cr.P.C. dwelt at length on those parts of the section also that relate to riot and affray, besides the part relating to the public tranquillity. I, however, think that in this case the vires of only that part of Section 144 has to be determined which relates to disturbance of the public tranquillity, because the order by which the petitioners are affected has that part alone as its basis. Nowhere in the order passed by the District Magistrate is there any reference to riot and affray, and even the first reason given for the order which, as I have already said, was only the information received by the District Magistrate—there is nothing that may relate the order to prevention of a riot or an affray.

10. I may now briefly set forth the argument advanced on behalf of the petitioners for attacking the constitutionality of that part of Section 144 which relates to disturbance of the public tranquillity and examine whether, in view of what has been laid down by the Supreme Court in AIR 1961 SC 884 (supra), the argument is still open or whether the matter should be regarded as settled in favour of the section, so far as this Court is concerned.

11. The argument on behalf of the petitioners is this. Clauses (2) and (3) of Article 19 of the Constitution do not extend their protection to a law imposing on the rights respectively mentioned therein restrictions in the interests of the public tranquillity. 'Public order' which is one of the things

mentioned in Clause (2) and the only thing mentioned in Clause (3) is not synonymous with the public tranquillity, and public disorder connotes a disturbance much graver in nature and magnitude and much larger in extent than a disturbance of the public tranquillity. A law authorizing the passing of an order for preventing disturbance of the public tranquillity is not in relation to the right guaranteed under Article 19(1)(a) of the Constitution, saved by Clause (2) of Article 19 because, if 'public order' is left out of consideration, there remains nothing in that clause which may be said to cover 'the public tranquillity': and in relation to the right guaranteed by Article 19(1)(b), it is not saved by Clause (3) of Article 19, because that clause mentions 'public order' alone. In regard to the Supreme Court decision in *Babulal Parate's* case, AIR 1961 SC 884 it was submitted on behalf of the petitioners that in that case the validity of Section 144 Cr.P.C. was not challenged on the ground that the section was outside the saving categories mentioned in Clauses (2) and (3) of Article 19 and the challenge to the validity of the sections was limited to the ground that the restrictions placed by it on certain fundamental rights are unreasonable. In the present case, it was contended, the constitutionality of the very power to place restrictions, irrespective of their reasonableness, is in question. It was also said that the question of the power to place restrictions was not considered by their Lordships in *Babulal Parate's* case, AIR 1961 SC 884 and in any event, such observations as were made in that case on matters not covered by the ground on which the validity of Section 144 was challenged are in the nature of obiter and are not binding. Great reliance was placed on behalf of the petitioners on the case of *Rammanohar Lohia* vs. *State of Bihar*, AIR 1966 SC 740 and it was urged that the first ground of the petitioners' attack on the relevant clause of Section 144 is supported by what has been laid down there regarding the meaning of the expression 'public order'.

12. It is no doubt true that in *Babulal Parate's* case, AIR 1961 SC 884 it does not appear to have been contended on

behalf of the petitioners that the power conferred by Section 144 Cr.P.C. is not in the interests of things specified in Clauses (2) and (3) of Article 19 of the Constitution and the section is, therefore, ultra vires, irrespective of the fact whether the restrictions it imposes are reasonable or not. But it is not possible on that basis to contend that the Supreme Court did not consider the constitutionality of the section from that point of view also. The question of the reasonableness of restrictions could arise only when the power to impose restrictions was found to be present and, therefore, the contention that the Supreme Court did not consider whether such a power really existed is unacceptable. Para 16 of the report of the judgment in that case clearly indicates that their Lordships considered the question whether the activities with regard to which the Magistrate is entitled under Section 144 Cr.P.C. to place restraint are such that their prevention would be in the interests of public order and held that they are such activities. If any doubt is still left about the scope and effect of this decision it should be dispelled by the final conclusion reached by their Lordships. That conclusion has been stated in para 34 of the report and is as follows:

> "We have, therefore, reached the conclusion that the order of the District Magistrate is not unconstitutional either because Section 144 is itself violative of fundamental rights recognised in Article 19 or on the ground that it is vague and places unreasonable restrictions on those fundamental rights."

The opinion expressed in the case by their Lordships, therefore, is that section 144 Cr.P.C. does not violate Article 19 of the Constitution, and it necessarily means that such parts of the section as may have the effect of placing restrictions on the rights guaranteed under Article 19(1)(a) and (b) are respectively protected by Clauses (2) and (3) of Article 19. This being the law declared by the Supreme Court it is binding on this Court under Article 141 of the Constitution and even the first ground on which the validity of Section 144 has been challenged on behalf of the petitioners must accordingly be rejected.

13. The contention that such observations of the Supreme Court in the above case as cover matters beyond the reasonableness of the restrictions placed on certain fundamental rights by Section 144 Cr.P.C. are obiter and, therefore, of no binding effect is wholly misconceived. A declaration of law made by the Supreme Court is not a mere precedent and the necessity of the declaration is not a condition of its binding effect. Even if such a declaration is in the nature of an obiter Article 141 of the Constitution makes it binding on all courts. But quite apart from this, it is obvious that the question whether Clauses (2) and (3) of Article 19 at all permit the imposition of restrictions is logically prior to the question of the reasonableness of the restrictions, and no part of the observations of their Lordships relating to the constitutionality of Section 144 Cr.P.C. was, therefore incidental or unnecessary for the decision of the case and no part of the observations can be regarded as obiter. It is a matter of no consequence that the constitutionality of Section 144 Cr.P.C. was challenged in that case only on the narrow ground of the reasonableness of the restrictions placed by it and not also on the wider ground of the total absence of the power to place restrictions. A declaration of law made by the Supreme Court remains a binding declaration, irrespective of the fact whether all the pros and cons of the matter to which it relates were put forward and argued before it. And this would be specially so when the law declared is in regard to the constitutionality of a statute or a rule, and in such a case the binding effect of the declaration cannot be measured by or limited to the points raised on behalf of the parties or to which express reference is made in the judgment. In this connection I may refer to the following cases:

14. In *Sharda Prasad Srivastava* vs. *Accountant General Uttar Pradesh Allahabad,* AIR 1955 All 496 the constitutional validity of a contract of service was in question. In a very similar earlier case the Supreme Court had declared a contract of that nature

valid. Dealing with a new line of attack taken on behalf of the person challenging the validity of the contract. V. Bhargava, J. observed:

> "Secondly, once the Supreme Court has declared that such a contract of service is valid, it is not open to me to examine the validity of that contract even on any ground which may not, have been considered by the Supreme Court. The law declared by the Supreme Court is binding whether the declaration is made after discussing all possible aspects or without doing so."

15. In *Commr. of Income Tax U.P. and V.P.* vs. *Man Mal Uttam Chand*, (1961) 42 I. T. R. 203 (All), a Division Bench of this Court had before it a reference under Section 66(1) of the Indian Income Tax Act 1922 where one of the points involved in the case had previously been decided by the Supreme Court under the Travancore Income Tax Act in which the relevant provisions were similar. V. Bhargava J., who delivered the judgment of the Bench, observed as follows in regard to the effect of the decision of the Supreme Court:

> "In that case their Lordships did not consider the effect of Section 14(2)(c) of the Indian Income Tax Act, as it stood at the relevant time, but we think that in spite of the fact that that provision was not considered that decision given by the Supreme Court is binding on us and is a declaration of law under Article 141 of the Constitution. Consequently we are bound to follow that decision."

16. In *Harkishan Das* vs. *Emperor*, AIR 1944 Lah 33 the vires of certain provisions of Defence of India Act was challenged. Adverting to a Federal Court decision and dealing, in the light of Section 212 of the Government of India Act 1935, with the effect of that decision on a contention raised in support of the challenge Munir. J said:

> "To this contention the preliminary objection of the Advo-

cate-General is that it cannot be raised in view of the Federal Court decisions in AIR 1943 F.C.I. and *Emperor* vs. *Sibnath Banerjee* (not yet reported) in which that Court has held that the Defence of India Act is intra vires the Indian Legislature. By reason of Section 212, Government of India Act, the law declared by the Federal Court so far as applicable has to be followed by us and in the two decisions of the Federal Court relied on by the learned Advocate-General the law declared by the Federal Court is that Section 2, Defence of India Act, is not ultra vires the Indian Legislature. It is contended by Mr. Sikri that the precise point urged before us was not taken before the Federal Court in those cases and that consequently there is no adjudication by the Federal Court on the point in question. This is correct but that does not mean that the Federal Court did not declare Section 2 to be intra vires. In our opinion the declaration by the Federal Court that Section 2 is intra vires is binding on us and precludes us from considering the point raised. The Federal Court may have the power, on this point being taken before it, to revise its view but so far as we are concerned we are bound by these decisions."

17. In my opinion, the Supreme Court decision in *Babulal Parate's* case, AIR 1961 SC 884 also precludes the controversy raised in the first ground urged on behalf of the petitioners for challenging the constitutionality of Section 144 Cr.P.C. But even assuming that this ground of challenge is still open I find it altogether unsustainable.

18. The meaning and the scope of the expression 'public order' have been the subject matter of decisions of the Supreme Court and the Federal Court and it has to be seen whether in the light of these decisions, 'public order' in Clauses (2) and (3) of Article 19 should be regarded as synonymous with or as including 'public tranquillity' In AIR 1966 SC 740, Hidayatullah, J. has in his judgment referred to the earlier decisions, giving at one place passages from each of them bear-

ing on the interpretation of the expression 'public order' along with their context. I may, therefore, quote below that portion of his Lordship's judgment in full which deals with them. His Lordship has observed:

> "Reliance is first placed upon a decision of the Federal Court in *Lakhi Narayan Das* vd. *Province of Bihar,* 1949 FCR 693 at p. 704 = AIR 1950 FC 59 at p. 63, where the Court dealing with Item 1 of Provincial List. 7th Schedule in the Government of India Act, 1935 which read—
>
>> 'Public order' (but not including the use of His Majesty's naval, military or air forces in aid of the civil power' observed that 'public order' with which that item began was 'a most comprehensive term'. Reference is also made to *Romesh Thapar* vs. *State of Madras,* 1950 SCR 594 at p 598=AIR 1950 SC 124 at p. 127, where this Court dealing with the same subject matter also observed:
>>
>>> '... 'Public order' is an expression of wide connotation and signifies that state of tranquillity which prevails among the members of a political society as a result of internal regulations enforced by the Government which they have established ... it must be taken that 'public safety is used as a part of the wider concept of public order....'
>>>
>>> and referring to Entry in List III (Concurrent List) of the 7th schedule of the Constitution which includes the 'security of the State' and 'maintenance of public order' as distinct topics of legislation, observed—
>>>
>>>> '... The Constitution thus requires a line to be drawn in the field of public order or tranquillity marking off may be, roughly, the boundary between those serious and aggravated forms of public disorder which are calculated to endanger the security of the State and the relatively

> minor breaches of the peace of a purely local significance, treating for this purpose differences in degree as if they were differences in kind.'

Fazl Ali, J. took a different view which he had expressed more fully in *Brij Bhushan* vs. *State of Delhi*. 1950 SCR 605 = AIR 1950 SC 129, but he also observed that 'public safety' had, as a result of a long course of legislative practice, acquired a well-recognised meaning and was taken to denote safety or security of the State and that the expression 'public order' was wide enough to cover small disturbances of the peace which do not jeopardise the security of the State and paraphrased the words 'public order' as 'public tranquillity'.

Both the aspects of the matters were again before this Court in *Supdt., Central Prison, Fatehgarh* vd. *Rammanohar Lohia*, (1960) 2 SCR 821-AIR 1960 SC 633, when dealing with the wording of Clause (2) of Article 19 as amended by the Constitution (First Amendment) Act, 1951, it fell to be decided what 'public order' meant, Subba Rao, J. speaking for the Court referred to all earlier rulings and quoting from them came to the conclusion that 'public order' was equated with public peace and safety and said:

> '... Presumably in an attempt to get over the effect of these two decisions, the expression 'public order' was inserted in Article 19(2) of the Constitution by the Constitution (first Amendment) Act, 1951, with a view to bring in offences involving breach of purely local significance within the scope of Article 19....'

Summing up the position as he gathered from the earlier cases, the learned Judge observed:

> '... 'Public order' is synonymous with public safety and tranquillity; it is the absence of disorder involving breaches of local significance in contradistinction to national upheavals, such as revolution, civil strife, war, affecting the security of the State....'

These observations determine the meaning of the words 'public order' in contradistinction to expressions such as 'public safety', 'security of the State'. They were made in different contexts. The first three cases dealt with the meaning in the legislative Lists as to which, it is settled, we must give as large a meaning as possible. In the last case the meaning of 'public order' was given in relation to the necessity for amending the Constitution as a result of the pronouncements of this Court. The context in which the words were used was different, the occasion was different and the object in sight was different."

19. Besides the passages quoted in the above decision from (1960) 2 SCR 821= AIR 1960 SC 633 (supra), I think it necessary to draw attention to one more passage from that case which runs as follows:

> "But in India under Article 19(2) this wide concept of 'public order' is split up under different heads. It enables the imposition of reasonable restrictions on the exercise of the right to freedom of speech and expression in the interests of the security of the State, friendly relations with foreign states, public order, decency or morality, or in relation to contempt of court, defamation or incitement to an offence. All the grounds mentioned therein can be brought under the general head 'public order' in its most comprehensive sense. But the juxtaposition of the different grounds indicates that, though sometimes they tend to overlap, they must be ordinarily intended to exclude each other. 'Public order' is therefore something which is demarcated from the others. In that limited sense, particularly in view of the history of the amendment, it can be postulated that 'public order' is synonymous with public peace, safety and tranquillity."

20. The conclusions deducible from these decisions appear to be these; that the expression 'public order' is a comprehensive expression and it should be given a large meaning, though not as large as would be given to it in the legislative Lists of the

Constitution; that 'public order' at least comprehends within itself 'public tranquillity' even if it cannot be equated with 'public tranquillity' and that public disorder, unlike national upheavals affecting the security of the State, are of local significance and, as compared to them, less serious. It was urged on behalf of the petitioners and particularly by Dr. Rammanohar Lohia that public disorder connotes a disturbance much graver in character than a disturbance of the public tranquillity, and that there can be situations in which public tranquillity is disturbed but not 'public order'. It was said that this contention is supported by the observations of Hidayatullah, J. in AIR 1966 SC 740 (supra) and reliance was placed on paras 51 and 52 of the report of his Lordship's judgment. I however, do not find that the observations made by his Lordship support the contention which has been put forward. The question involved in that case was whether the expression 'law and order' used by a District Magistrate in an order purporting to have been passed by him under Rule 30(1)(b) of the Defence of India Rules meant the same thing as 'public order' for maintaining which an order of that kind could be passed under the said provision. His Lordship held that 'public order' and 'order' are not identical and explained that distinction between the two concepts. In para 51 of the judgment his Lordship summed up the distinction in the following words:

> "The contravention of law always affects order but before it can be said to affect public order, it must affect the community of the public at large."

His Lordship then proceeded to point out in para 52 the comparative degrees of gravity involved in disturbances of 'law and order', 'public order', and 'security of the State' and observed:

> "It will thus appear that just as 'public order' in the rulings of this Court (earlier cited) was said to comprehend disorders of less gravity than those affecting 'security of State',

'law and order' also comprehends disorders of less gravity than those affecting 'public order'. One has to imagine three concentric circles. Law and order represents the largest circle within which is the next circle representing public order and the smallest circle represents security of State. It is then easy to see that an act may affect law and order but not public order just as an act may affect public order but not security of the State by using the expression 'maintenance of law and order' the District Magistrate was widening his own field of action and was adding a clause to the Defence of India Rules."

21. The position, therefore, is that while 'public order' is included in and is a part of 'order' it does not cover the entire area of 'order', with the result that although all public disorders are certainly disorders, all disorders are not public disorders, the latter being those aggravated forms of disorders which affect the public at large. What makes this difference in the ideas conveyed by the expressions 'order' and 'public order' is obviously the word 'public' in the latter expression. Since, however, that word is common to both 'public order' and 'public tranquillity', it is clear that the distinction between 'order' and 'public order' cannot hold good between 'public tranquillity' and 'public order'. The question involved in the present case is whether public tranquillity has the same connotation as 'public order' or is at least included in it, but on that question his Lordship has expressed no opinion, and in answering it we have to be guided by the earlier, decisions which have been referred to in his Lordship's judgment and also by a later decision of the Supreme Court to which I shall presently refer. Besides the observations quoted by Hidayatullah, J. from the earlier decisions I may draw attention to two other observations made by Subba Rao, J. (as his Lordship then was) in (1960) 2 SCR 821 = (AIR 1960 SC 633). In para 11 of the report his Lordship said that "it can be postulated that 'public order' is synonymous with public peace, safety and tranquillity" and in para 18 of the

report his Lordship summed up the position by laying down that "'public order' is synonymous with public safety and tranquillity". Observations to a similar effect were made in the later case of *O.K. Ghosh* vd. *E.X. Joseph*, AIR 1963 SC 812 where Gajendragadkar, J. (as his Lordship then was), speaking for the Supreme Court, said that in Clause (2) of Article 19 public order is 'virtually synonymous with public peace, safety and tranquillity'. It is not necessary to determine whether, in the light of these decisions, 'public order' and 'public tranquillity' should be regarded as interchangeable terms and public tranquillity, by itself and without anything else, may be equated with 'public order', or whether a 'public order' has some other requisites besides public tranquillity. Even if 'public order' and 'public tranquillity' are not entirely co-extensive in content the decisions do not, in my opinion, leave any room for doubt that public tranquillity is at least an essential constituent of 'public order' and that 'public order' is a comprehensive concept including within itself as one of its integral parts public tranquillity. The contention of Dr. Rammanohar Lohia that disturbance of the public tranquillity cannot in all cases result in the disturbance of 'public order' could have been acceptable if it had been possible to say that 'public order' can in some cases dispense with the public tranquillity and exist without it. Since, however, 'public order' is inconceivable in the absence of the public tranquillity, whatever has the effect of disturbing the public tranquillity must necessarily disturb 'public order' and it is not possible to say of any situation that although the public tranquillity has been disturbed 'public order' has remained unaffected. The obvious corollary is that whatever is done for preventing disturbance of 'the public tranquillity' must be regarded as done for preventing disturbance of the 'public order' and, hence, in the interests of 'public order'. The restrictions which Section 144 Cr.P.C., permits to be imposed for preventing disturbance of the public tranquillity are, therefore, restrictions within the limits of the saving provisions of Article 19(2) and (3).

22. The view that I take in regard to that part of Section 144 Cr.P.C. which relates to the public tranquillity was also the view taken by this Court in AIR 1956 All 481 to which I have already referred in another connection. The Division Bench which decided that case held that to the extent to which Section 144 allows the placing of restrictions for preventing disturbance of the public tranquillity or a riot or an affray, it is within the limits permitted by Article 19(2), (3), although it also expressed the opinion that some of the purposes for which restrictions are allowed to be placed by the section are in excess of the said limits. In the instant case, however, the constitutionality of only that part of Section 144 is involved which relates to the public tranquillity, because the order affecting the petitioners was based on that part alone. It is, therefore, unnecessary to express any opinion on any other part of the section.

23. Before leaving this aspect of the case I must note that in the course of arguments on behalf of the petitioners it was not urged that the prohibitory order passed by the District Magistrate of Agra was not an order which could be validly passed under Section 144 Cr.P.C. or that the order suffered from any other defect. In fact, Sri S. N. Kacker, learned counsel for the petitioners, and also Dr. Rammanohar Lohia, explicitly stated that they pressed the petition only on the basic question of the constitutionality of Section 144 Cr.P.C. and Section 188 I.P.C. and they did not want any other matter to be gone into by this Court in these proceedings.

24. I now proceed to consider the challenge to the vires of Section 188 I.P.C. The arguments which Dr. Rammanohar Lohia, who alone addressed the Court on this part of the case, advanced in support of the challenge were two; firstly, that Section 188 I.P.C. is inconsistent with Section 144 Cr.P.C. inasmuch as disturbance of the public tranquillity is not mentioned in the former section and this omission leads to the anomaly that while an order under Section 144 Cr.P.C. may be passed in the interests of the public tranquillity a disobedience of that order is not punishable if it merely causes or tends to

cause a disturbance of the public tranquillity; and secondly, that Section 188 I.P.C. makes the disobedience of an order passed under Section 144 an offence if the disobedience causes or tends to cause any of the results mentioned in the section, but none of the result not even riot or affray is such that the fundamental rights of freedom of speech and peaceable assembly may be restricted for the purpose of avoiding it, and, therefore, by reason of the fact that the section makes the exercise of even the aforesaid fundamental rights punishable it is void.

25. It is certainly true that although Section 188 I.P.C. mentions, in the same words and in the same sequence, all other things for preventing which a direction may be issued under Section 144 Cr.P.C., it does not mention, disturbance of the public tranquillity. About the reason for the absence of these words in Section 188 I.P.C. one can only speculate. Section 62 of the Code of 1861, Section 518 of the Code of 1872, and Section 144 of the Code of 1882 which were provisions analogous to Section 144 of the present Code of Criminal Procedure did not contain the words 'disturbance of the public tranquillity', and it was in Section 144 Cr. P.C. of the present Criminal Procedure Code of 1892 that these words were for the first time introduced. No corresponding amendment was, however, made in the Indian Penal Code. It may be that the necessity of amending Section 188 I.P.C. and adding therein the said words was overlooked and the mistake has not been detected by the legislature so far. But it may also be that the omission to make a corresponding change in Section 188 I.P.C. was deliberate. The legislature might have thought that causing or tending to cause disturbance of the public tranquillity, as an ingredient of an offence, would not be sufficiently definite for positive proof or disproof, and the disobedience of an order lawfully promulgated by the public servant should be made an offence only if it causes or tends to cause the comparatively more definite and determinate results mentioned in Section 188 I.P.C. To whatever reason, however, the absence of the

words 'disturbance of the public tranquillity' in Section 188 I.P.C. might be due, there appears to be no inconsistency between Section 144 Cr.P.C. and Section 188 I.P.C., and even if there may be some inconsistency it cannot, to my mind, make either of the sections unconstitutional.

26. Prevention of the disturbance of the public tranquillity is one of the objects for which the competent Magistrate may pass an order under Section 144 Cr.P.C., but in determining whether a person disobeying the order has committed an offence punishable under Section 188 I.P.C. what has to be seen is not whether the disobedience caused or tended to cause disturbance of the public tranquillity, but whether it caused or tended to cause any of the results mentioned in the second and the third clauses of Section 188 I.P.C. Disobedience of an order passed under Section 144 Cr.P.C. for preventing disturbance of the public tranquillity would not, therefore, constitute an offence under Section 188 I.P.C. if it does not cause any of the results mentioned in the latter section, although it may cause or tend to cause a disturbance of the public tranquillity. This may only have the effect of frustrating in some cases a part of the purpose for which an order under Section 144 Cr.P.C. is passed, but it does not create any conflict between the two sections or lead to any anomalous result, unless the frustration to any extent of the object of the order is itself called an anomaly. I say 'part of the purpose of the order' because the things enumerated in the second and the third clauses of Section 188 I.P.C. are not unrelated to the public tranquillity and, it will be noted, riot and affray are included in Chapter VIII of the Indian Penal Code which deals with what have been described by the Code as offences against the public tranquillity. However the fact that in some circumstances an act which was intended to be prevented by an order under Section 144 Cr.P.C. may not be covered by Section 188 I.P.C. and may go unpunished cannot be said to introduce any element of constitutional infirmity in either of the two sections.

27. Coming to the second argument of Dr. Rammanohar

Lohia regarding Section 188 I.P.C., I may mention that the complaint filed by the District Magistrate of Agra against the petitioners states only the alleged fact of disobedience of the directions issued by him under Section 144 Cr. P. C, and there is nothing in it to show the results, if any, the disobedience caused or tended to cause. However, Sri S. N. Kacker and Dr. Rammanohar Lohia stated in the course of their argument that they did not seek to support the petition on this feature of the complaint. The argument of Dr. Rammanohar Lohia was that the whole of Section 188 I.P.C. was unconstitutional although he laid special emphasis on that part of it which relates to riot and affray, presumably because he thought that the other things mentioned in the second and the third clauses of Section 188 I.P.C. could not possibly have any relation to 'public order'. In my opinion, there is a basic misconception involved in the argument. Section 188 I.P.C. does not make punishable any act as such but only when it is done in disobedience to an order duly promulgated by a public servant lawfully empowered to do so. In the absence of such an order the act would remain altogether unaffected by the provisions of the section and it is the order prohibiting that act that has the effect of attaching to it the penalty of the section. What is, therefore, made punishable under Section 188 I. P. C, when an order placing constitutionally permissible restrictions on certain fundamental rights is disobeyed, is not the exercise of the fundamental rights but the transgression of the constitutionally valid restrictions imposed upon the exercise of the rights. There can be no doubt that if Section 188 I.P.C. had made mere disobedience of an order of the above character an offence, even though the disobedience was not attended by anything else, it would have been open to no objection on the score of constitutionality. Does the section, then, suffer from the vice of unconstitutionality, because it makes the disobedience punishable only under certain conditions? In so far as Section 188 I.P.C. requires something more than mere disobedience of an order imposing permissible restrictions on fundamental rights before an act can become an offence under that section, it only mitigates the rigour of the restrictions. It is, therefore, incorrect that Section 188 I.P.C. makes the exercise of the fundamental rights guaranteed under Article 19(1)(a) and (b) punishable in the interests of things other than 'public order'. If an order under Section 144 Cr.P.C. imposing restrictions on such rights is constitutional by reason of its being in the interests of 'public order', a law punishing its disobedience would also be constitutional, irrespective of the presence or absence of any other requisite for making the disobedience punishable. The second argument which has been advanced for challenging the constitutionality of Section 188 I.P.C. is also therefore, untenable.

28. As a result of the foregoing discussion, I am of the opinion that Section 144 Cr.P.C., in so far as it empowers the issue of directions which are likely to prevent or tend to prevent a disturbance of the public tranquillity, is constitutional and not ultra vires. I express no opinion on any other part of Section 144 Cr.P.C. because it is not necessary to do so. I am also of the opinion that Section 188 I.P.C. is constitutional and not ultra vires.

29. The points raised in support of the petition fail and the petition should accordingly be dismissed.

Mahesh Chandra, J.

30. The facts leading to the arrest of the petitioners are very simple. They have been given in detail in the judgment of my learned brother and need not be repeated. The District Magistrate of Agra issued an order on 10-7-1966 under Section 144, Criminal Procedure Code. In the preamble of the order he mentioned that from the information received in connection with the U.P. Bundh agitation there was likelihood of some sections of the public indulging in violence and lawlessness to force the closure of the shops, offices, etc. and thereby causing breach of the peace. Immediate prevention and speedy remedy was considered desirable for maintaining public peace and

tranquillity. Consequently he issued a number of directions under Section 144, Criminal Procedure Code. In connection with the observance of the U.P. Bundh Day a public meeting had been arranged for the evening of April 11, 1966 in Phulatti Bazar Agra. It was to be addressed by Dr. Rammanohar Lohia, who arrived at Raja Mandi Railway station by the Toofan Express at 2.45 p.m. on July 11, 1966 and was arrested by the police when he came out of the railway station. The other petitioners who had come to receive Dr. Lohia, were also arrested at the same time. It was alleged that Dr. Lohia delivered an objectionable speech on the platform of the Railway Station and that objectionable slogans of various kinds were shouted by the petitioners. All these arrests were alleged to be in violation of the order of the District Magistrate, Agra. A case under Section 188, I.P.C. for the infringement of the District Magistrate's order is pending against the petitioners who have been released on execution of personal bonds.

31. The petitioners pray that Section 144, Criminal Procedure Code or that part of it which related to the disturbance of public tranquillity or a riot or affray be struck down as unconstitutional and that the petitioners be released. They prayed further that even if the case against the petitioners is withdrawn by the State the question of the constitutionality of Section 144, Criminal Procedure Code should be determined. By an amendment they have also been allowed to add the prayer that Section 188 Indian Penal Code be also declared unconstitutional.

32. I agree with my learned brother that the preliminary objection of the learned Government Advocate that the petition has become infructuous because of the release of the petitioners from Jail is untenable. The petitioners have not been restored to their liberty for they are subject to the restraint of the bonds furnished by them. The petition of *Babulal Parate*, AIR 1961 SC 884 was disposed of by the Supreme Court on merits even though the petitioner had been released on bail, vide AIR 1961 SC 884. In 1962 All LJ 654 (AIR 1963 All 4) this Court held

that a person remains under the control of the Court and notionally in its custody even after release on bail and could consequently present a petition for a writ of *Habeas Corpus* The mere fact that the petitioners in the present case have been released on execution of personal bonds does not create any difference. The restrictions on liberty are there whether it is a release on only a personal bond or on bail.

33. It was contended by the learned counsel for the petitioners that the powers which are exercisable under Section 144 Criminal Procedure Code are so wide that the restrictions had the effect of imposing restrictions upon the fundamental rights are unreasonable. In *Babulal Parate's* case, AIR 1961 SC 884 (supra) the Supreme Court held that the section does not confer an arbitrary power on the Magistrate in the matter of making an order and that the power of the Magistrate under the section is not unlimited or untrammelled. It is true that the judgment is to be of the Magistrate whether in the peculiar circumstances of a case an order in exercise of these powers should be made or not. But the Court was entitled to assume that power would be exercised legitimately and honestly and the section could not be struck down on the ground that the Magistrate might possibly abuse his powers. The fundamental rights guaranteed under Article 19(1) of the Constitution were subject to the restrictions placed in the subsequent clauses of Article 19 permitting reasonable restrictions on the exercise of the right to freedom of speech and expression in the interest, among other things, of public order. The action permissible under Section 144, Criminal Procedure Code is an anticipatory action and cannot be said to be impermissible under Clauses (2) and (3) of Article 19 merely because it is anticipatory. The Supreme Court also held that the remedy of Judicial review cannot be said to be illusory. Mudholkar, J., speaking for the Supreme Court, observed; "We would also like to point out that the penalty for infringing an order under Section 144 is that provided in Section 188 Indian Penal Code. When, therefore, a prosecution is launched thereunder, the validity of

the order under Section 144 Criminal Procedure Code could be challenged."

Mudholkar. J. further observed:

> "Further since the propriety of the order is open to challenge it cannot be said that by reason of the wide amplitude of the power which Section 144 confers on certain Magistrate it places unreasonable restrictions on certain fundamental rights."

34. I agree that these observations are binding on this Court under Article 141 of the Constitution even though they may be in the nature of obiter.

35. It was also contended by the learned counsel for petitioners that the purposes for which the section authorises the imposition of restriction on the right to freedom of speech and expression and a right to assemble peaceably and without arms are not covered by Article 19(2) and (3) of the Constitution and that Section 144. Criminal Procedure Code was consequently unconstitutional. The order of the District Magistrate of Agra in the present case recited the apprehension that section of the public were likely to indulge in violence and lawlessness in order to force closure of shop offices, etc. and thereby cause breach of the peace. It also mentioned the desirability for immediate prevention and speedy remedy for maintaining public peace and tranquillity. This was thus the sole object for which the order of the District Magistrate was made. We are consequently concerned in this petition with only that part of Section 144, Criminal Procedure Code which empowered the Magistrate to issue a certain direction which he considered likely to prevent or tend to prevent disturbance of public tranquillity. There is not the slightest doubt that the various activities for the prevention of which a direction may be issued by a Magistrate under Section 144, Criminal Procedure Code are separate and distinct and consequently that part of the section which relates to a direction likely to prevent or stand to prevent disturbance of public tranquillity is

clearly separable from the other part of the section. I would, therefore, agree with my learned brother that in this case it is not necessary to express any opinion on any other part of Section 144, Criminal Procedure Code.

36. I would also agree with the conclusion of my learned brother that Section 144, Criminal Procedure Code in so far as it relates to a direction which is likely to prevent or tends to prevent a disturbance of public tranquillity is not ultra vires. I would, however, hesitate to use any phrase or expression which might be taken to justify in the name of public order any unreasonable restriction on the right to freedom of speech and expression and to assemble peaceably and without arms. True, reasonable restrictions in the interest of public order have to be permitted. But it is equally true that democracy is based on the light to freedom of speech and expression. Without this elementary right democracy is bound to perish or degenerate into autocracy. Nor can it be said that a mere disturbance of the tranquillity of a great number of people amounts to a disturbance of public order.

37. Dr. Lohia in his arguments translated the word "tranquillity" as शान्ति and the word "order" as व्यवस्था I would agree with him that the Hindi equivalents suggested by him give us a correct idea of the implications of the two words. We should not forget that a democracy functions in a manner entirely different from autocracy Radical progress in democracy is bound to give rise to discussions in press and on platform involving disturbance of tranquillity of a vast number of people. For instance, preparation of the people for land reforms involving the abolition of zamindari necessarily disturbed the tranquillity of great number of the people of the States of U.P. and Bihar, since it was to affect not only the Talukdars and big zamindars but also the small zamindars. But it could not be said to have disturbed public order. It cannot be denied that the people were agitated and agitation is disturbance of tranquillity, for tranquillity शान्ति is that serenity and calmness which is bound to be disturbed and agitated when any radical reforms

are about to be launched against vested interests and established views about certain state of affairs are challenged and canvassed against. Again, in an enlightened democracy tranquillity of the people may be disturbed even without speech and expression. For instance, prices of food rising with an inordinately high speed would disturb the tranquillity of the people and agitate their minds even though discussions in press and on platform may be completely curbed. But really no such complete stoppage of discussion could be possible in an enlightened democracy, which works by persuasion, and after persuasion even by change of government by one party to government by another party. It would not, therefore, be correct to give the phrase "in the interests of public order" a meaning which would abolish all canvassing of a progressive reform or criticism and discussion of action of government and consequent agitation of the mind of the people.

38. I would not, therefore, be prepared to go beyond the extent to which their Lordships of the Supreme Court have gone, and would not give to "public order" a meaning more comprehensive than that given by them. They have themselves made a distinction between maintenance of "law and order" and "public order". Mudholkar, J. observed in AIR 1966 S.C. 740 at p. 763.

> "The expression "Law and order" does not find any place in the rule and is not synonymous with "public order". It seems to me that "law and order" is a comprehensive expression in which would be included not merely public order but matters such as public peace, tranquillity, orderliness in a locality or a local area and perhaps some other matters. "Public order" is something distinct from order or orderliness in a local area."

39. In the same case Hidayatullah. J observed at page 758

> "Does the expression "public order" take in every kind of disorders or only some of them? The answer to this serves

> to distinguish "public order" from "law and order" because the latter undoubtedly takes in all of them. Public order if disturbed, must lead to public disorder. Every breach of the peace does not lead to public disorder. When two drunkards quarrel and fight there is disorder but not public disorder. They can be dealt with under the powers to maintain law and order but cannot be detained on the ground that they were disturbing public order. Suppose that the two fighters were of rival communities and one of them tried to raise communal passions. The problem is still one of law and order but it raises the apprehension of public disorder. Other examples can be imagined. The contravention of law always affects order but before it can be said to affect public order, it must affect the community or the public at large...." The Supreme Court has thus refused to make "public order" as comprehensive as "maintenance of law and order"."

40. Relying on the observations of Hidayatullah, J. Dr. Lohia however contended that the decision in AIR 1966 SC 740 (supra) in 1966, modified the earlier view of the Supreme Court that "public order" was synonymous with public safety and tranquillity. This contention is without force. In the judgment of Hidayatullah, J. in AIR 1966 SC 740 (supra), the judgment of Subba Rao, J. in AIR 1960 SC 633, was mentioned and the specific observations of Subba Rao, J. quoted were—

> "public order" is synonymous with public safety and tranquillity;...". Hidayatullah, J. did not dissent from these observations in so far as the meaning of the phrase "public order" used in Article 19(2) of the Constitution was concerned. Consequently, whatever meaning might be attached to the word "tranquillity" standing alone, when the word "tranquillity" is qualified by the word "public" in Section 144, Criminal Procedure Code, we are clearly bound by the decision of the Supreme Court in (1960) 2 SCR 821: AIR 1960 SC 633 (supra) that "public order" is synony-

mous with public safety and tranquillity. Hidayatullah, J. himself went on to place "law and order" in the largest concentric circle and "public order" in the next circle and security of State in the smallest circle and the reason for placing "public order" in a smaller circle than that of "law and order" was the use of the word "public" before the word "order".

41. While on the one hand the necessity for the right to freedom of speech and expression and to assemble peaceably and without arms in a democracy is there, it cannot be denied that this right itself cannot be properly exercised by all without permitting a law which imposes reasonable restrictions in the interests of public order. No democracy can exist if "public order" is freely allowed to be disturbed by a section of the citizens. That was the background in which Clauses (2) and (3) of Article 19 of the Constitution had to be amended by insertion of the words "public order". In view of the decision of the Supreme Court equating "public order" with "public safety and tranquillity" the provisions in Section 144, Criminal Procedure Code for issue of directions which are likely to prevent or tend to prevent a disturbance of the public tranquillity cannot be said to be ultra vires.

42. Dr. Rammanohar Lohia also contended that Section 188 Indian Penal Code itself was ultra vires. For the reasons mentioned by my learned brother and which I need not repeat I am also of the view that Section 188, Indian Penal Code is constitutional and not ultra vires.

43. I would, therefore, agree that the petition be dismissed.

BY THE BENCH

ORDER

44. We dismiss the petition.

Appendix

The Struggle for Civil Liberties

Rammanohar Lohia

With a Foreword by
Jawaharlal Nehru

FOREWORD

There has been much talk of civil liberties in India during recent months. That is not surprising for the suppression of civil liberty here has assumed prodigious proportions and become a public scandal of the first magnitude. It effects all of us intimately and mere self-interest would prompt us to combat this suppression. And yet, in spite of all this talk and interest, there are not many persons who think clearly about it or are aware of the full significance of the idea. Questions are frequently put to us which betray an amazing ignorance of the subject, and economic and social questions are mixed up with it. Dr. Rammanohar Lohia has done well to prepare this pamphlet on the subject, to tell us what the concept of civil liberty is and how it has grown in western countries. I hope that many will read it and that it will help us in combating the suppression of civil liberties here and the ever-increasing encroachment by the State on what little remains.

December 21, 1936 **Jawaharlal Nehru**

1. CIVIL LIBERTIES IN FRANCE

"The League was born out of a revolt of conscience against the will fanatically to maintain an illegal and unjust condemnation. It was founded with the object to defend, against the spirit of caste and race and reasons of State, all survivals of a remote past, the Rights of Man as affirmed by the French Revolution." So begins a resolution of the 1935 Congress of the French League of Rights of Man.

Dreyfus is a household word in France. It is almost a synonym of the tyranny of a ruling caste and the vain and futile prejudices on which such tyranny rests. It awakens men to the dangers and the horror of a judiciary that is associated with the ruling caste. At the same time, it is a by-word for the dogged determination of the people to fight against tyranny and injustice. No matter if miscarriage of justice is oft repeated, Dreyfus is the word that denotes final victory of injustice through persistence and continued effort.

Dreyfus was a Jew and an officer in the French Army. A very capable man, he succeeded in arousing the ire of the caste that considered the army its preserve. Important army secrets were leaking out to Germany and the responsibility was naturally fastened on Dreyfus. Dreyfus was dishonoured, sentenced to hard labour and transported to the Devils Isle. Time after time, true facts were brought before the courts, which were none too pleasant for the army aristocracy, but reasons of State and the prestige of the French army decided the verdict against Dreyfus. The conscience of the French nation was convulsed and Emile Zola made a spirited attack on the culpabihty of the Courts. Twelve years of persistent effort, 1894-1906, succeeded in the rehabilitation of Dreyfus.

In 1898, the League of Rights of Man was founded. Men had harboured the fond illusion that, with the end of the

Dreyfus case, ignorance and prejudice and miscarriage of justice had been finally overcome. The League has since had to defend several cases against persecution of opinion, illegal detention, arbitrary action of the Government, tyrannous laws and such other attacks upon the Rights of Man.

The League has to-day a membership of over 160,000 which is spread over a territory of 96 departmental federations and 2,490 sections. Each section has its own executive and the right to convene conferences and public and private meetings. It may intervene on behalf of victims of injustice and arbitrary action and report to the higher Committees for the organisation of national agitation on certain issues. The League meets once a year in an annual Congress, reports on the work done, elects a central Executive and raises issues of changes in existing laws or of their maladministration. It is not difficult to imagine the extent to which the League, with its large membership and marvellous territorial reach, has become a part of French national life.

The more important of the Statutes of the League are:

1. A French Association to defend the principles of Liberty, Equality and Justice laid down in the "Declarations of the Rights of Man" of 1789 and 1793.

2. The League intervenes on every occasion where an injustice, an arbitrary act, an abuse of power or an illegality is done against the individual, the associations and the peoples. Its action consists in appeal to pubhc conscience, presentations to public authorities, petitions to Parlianient, publication of liter- ature, conferences and demonstrations.

3. No member of the Central Committee can assume Governmental functions.

4. An annual subscription of 10 Francs is levied on each member.

The concept of civil rights in any clear form arose first out of the French Revolution. In their fight against the Bastille where countless men were made to suffer and die without justice and without law, except an order of the Government, the French gave to the world a concept of what no Government dare do to its citizens and what is the right of every man. "Men are born and live free and equal before law;" "The aim of all political association (the State) is the conservation of natural rights of man; these rights are liberty, property, security and resistance to oppression"; "Sovereignty resides in the nation. No group or individual dare exercise authority which does not emanate expressly from the nation"; "Law is an expression of general will. All citizens are equally admissible to public employment and dignities"; "No man may be accused, arrested or detained out of the scope of the law and the prescribed forms"; "The free communication of ideas and opinion is a very precious right of man"; are a few of the articles laid down by the French Constitution of 1789. This statement of human rights is among the first points of departure for modern civilisation in the regulation of relations between the citizen and the Government. The French League through its incessant and numerous activities, attempts to pattern real life on the ideal and, also, to chisel the ideal brighter and clearer.

What this ideal is like, is evidenced in an extract from a speech Monsieur Guernut, an ex-General Secretary, made in Rumania in 1925:

> "It is said that Mr. Caillaux, while the war was on, wanted a piece of compromise. That is bad, but, then, it is his right to say so".
>
> "It is said that M. Caillaux, even during the war, wanted to change the Constitution. That is bad, but it is his right."
>
> "It is said that M. Caillaux beUeved tliat peace was possible in 1917. Perhaps an absurd idea, but that is his right." Monsieur Caillaux, who had to sujBFer a preventive detention of 27 months, is one of those whom the Civil Liberties Unions of the World seize upon as an "affair" around which to rouse a terrific campaign against executive encroachment on human rights.

Before, however, we fully understand the League's concept of civil rights, let us examine how it seeks to adapt judicial and executive action to its principles. In order that justice is done from day to day to individual sufferers, the League makes representations on their behalf. So, during the fortnight ending on 24th September 1936, the numerous Sections and Federations of the League intervened for about 50 individual cases with either the Minister of Justice, of Public Health, of Education or of Interior. Authentic information on each individual case is collected and documented dossiers prepared. The League and its Sections, also, pronounce their judgment on cases involving breach of civil rights in the form of resolutions and national campaign is sometimes organised. The sympathetic section of the daily press and journals, to whom communiques are furnished, assist the League in agitating public opinion in the necessary direction. The League itself issues a fortnightly periodical "Les Cahiers Des Droits De L'Homme", (Sheets of the Rights of Man), which surveys its work, resolutions and conferences and is generally educative on human rights. It publishes and distributes a large number of brochures of information and education and tracts, such as, "The Dreyfus Affair", "Democracy and War", "The Present Duty of the League", "Problems of Nationalities", "Colonel Picart in Prison", "Declarations of Rights of Man and of Citizens", "Fascism in Italy". Further, the League seeks to touch public conscience by organising mass meetings as also educative conferences. The mass meetings dramatise certain broad ideas and the educative conferences are designed for a deeper and more detailed impression. Vigilance, publicity and doggedness seem to be the League's eminent qualities.

The League does not confine its attention to France but is vigilant on the suppression of civil rights in the colonies and of other peoples. Monsieur Moutet, the present Secretary of State for Colonies, is a member of the League. In the course of a letter to the President of the League recounting his achievements during two months, Moutet says, "Since the advent to power of the new Government, the dossiers of 1871 political prisoners in Indo-China have been examined. For over 68 per cent of these, for 1277, interventions (mostly unconditional release) have been effected." In like manner the League carries on agitation for sufferers in other countries, particularly those under Fascist Regime.

The French League has rolled on from milestone to milestone on the road towards greater human dignity. Its tasks are not confined to the defence of human rights against the overt attacks of laws of sedition, of press, of restrictions on freedom of association and those of arbitrary executive action or of miscarriage of justice. Its concept of civil rights is wider. The League seeks also to fight all ultimate sources of mischief and to provide all citizens with a solid base from where they may ward off attacks on their rights. Democracy and peace are, therefore, essential items in the League's propaganda; the former to safeguard and extend the sovereignty of the people and the latter to secure its unbroken enjoyment. In the absence of democracy, the League rightly fears, human liberties stand in danger of being engulfed by dictatorial authority.

In a message of greetings to the Deputies of the People's Front, the League defines its task as the defence of democratic liberties conquered by the people, provision of bread to workers and labour to youth and the conferment of the grand human peace on the world. The League reminds the Deputies of their pledge that they will abolish the infamous laws of restrictions on public opinion and work for the liberty of conscience and encouragement of non-denominational public schools. They will ensure the Hberty of the working class to organise and to strike. They will seek to deliver the State and the organs of information of the democracy, press, etc. from the tyranny of money and financial oligarchies. They will effect an increase in the people's purchasing power, nationalise the Bank of France and the Arms Industry and take the world from armed peace to peace without arms. Further, the League draws the attention of the Deputies to its own demands for curtailment of the powers of the judiciary and police and the grant of freedom to the colonial peoples and the extension of franchise to women.

In the words of an ex-President, Ferdinand Buisson, the League is an advocate of the Little Man, of the working class, of the colonial peoples and oppressed nationalities and the organiser of public conscience.

The League to-day makes an approach to public conscience not merely on the judicial plane but also on the political. It is no mere revolt against miscarriage of justice or the existing penal laws but a positive defence of democracy and republicanism. The League does not directly participate in the elections but devotes itself to delineating the grand directions in which public authority. Government and Parliament a like, should engage itself.

An ex-General Secretary of the League once proclaimed that the League shall continue till "the last knot of the last chain of the last slave" is broken as under. Its President declares, "We are the vanguard of the Republic, the defence of democracy."

No greater tribute could be paid to the oldest of the Civil Rights Leagues in the world than that its President, Monsieur Victor Basch, is also the President of the People's Front, the power behind the Blum Government.

2. CIVIL LIBERTIES IN AMERICA

In the theoretical justification of extensive civil liberties and, in particular, of the rights of the citizen in opposition to the Government, the United States of America easily holds the palm in the world. The unlimited moral and legal freedom of the individual to express by speech, if he so chooses his revolt against the existing social order and the Government has met with an openhearted and an un- hedged assent. Thomas Jefferson, Patrick Henry, Benjamin Franklin and Abraham Lincoln, in pre-war times, ex-Governor Smith, Senator Borah and Justice Holmes, in recent years, to select only a few, have expressed noble sentiments in advocacy of unfettered freedom of opposition to the Government. Defending the 'field of opinion' against the magistracy, Thomas Jefferson declared in 1786 that it was time enough for the government to interfere when principles break out into overt acts against peace and good order.' A little earlier, Patrick Henry had advised the people to guard with zealous attention the public liberty' and to 'suspect everyone who approaches that jewel.' Admitting that abuses of freedom of speech ought to be suppressed, Benjamin Franklin retorted, 'to whom dare we commit the power of doing it.' Whenever the people shall grow weary of the existing government, said Abraham Lincoln in 1861, 'they can exercise their constitutional rights of amending it, or their revolutionary right of over- throwing it.' The United States Commission on Industrial Relations reported in 1914 that a government which could be maintained only by the suppression of criticism should not be maintained. Ex-Governor Smith of New York while pardoning prisoner Larkin in 1923, thought that 'an imprisonment of five years for the mere expression of an erroneous, or even an illegal, political doctrine unaccompanied by an overt act, was not at all required. Senator Borah said a year ago, "Repression is not only the enemy of free government, but it is the breeder of revolutions. It is the enemy of progress and human happiness. And above all, it is neither a test of error nor of truth.' In the course of an opinion, Justice Holmes remarked only recently, "those who won our independence by revolution were not cowards. They did not fear political change. They did not exalt order at the cost of liberty." For fear either that it will led to tyranny, that it will block progress and breed revolutions or that society will stagnate and experiments in better social forms stand outlawed, repression of opinion meets with unqualified condemnation at the hands of America's most eminent and respected men of affairs.

Still, in practice, America has its Tom Mooney and Billings, Tampa, Scottsboro, Sheriffs and vigilantes to put down rural agitation and smash workers' strikes, laws of sedition and criminal anarchy and suppression of freedom in education. Only with these 'affairs' and laws as the background, can one expect to understand the nature and extent of the American Civil Liberties movement.

The Mooney-Billings case, as has been suggested, is 'the civil counterpart of the great French military scandal,' the Dreyfus affair. Mooney and Billings were trade unionists before they were arrested on a charge of bomb-throwing in 1916. The industrialists, particularly the shipowners and the railway and electric corporations, of North California were then smarting under the 'closed shop' and the organisational strength of workers that were in no small measure due to Mooney.

During the days of war hysteria, a dynamite exploded in the rear of a patriotic parade in California and the crime was fastened upon Mooney and his associates. They were sentenced to a life term and it is now twenty years since they are held in prison. Prosecution witnesses, on whose evidence the original conviction followed, have been, one by one, proved to be unreliable and the presentation of testimony to be perjured. Congressional records and Federal enquiries reveal the then District Attorney as a crook who manufactured evidence. State officials have been shown up as men of the California Chambers of Commerce and the privateowned Railways. Positive photographic evidence of Mooney's alibi has been obtained by accident. Judge Griffin, who presided at Mooney's trial, says, "there can be no two opinions. There is now no evidence against him. There is not even a serious suggestion that it exists."

Still, Mooney and Billings continue to languish away in prison. The reason for this was recently given by a California editor, "It is quite beside the point whether or not they are guilty of the particular crimes of which they were charged and convicted. The question is: are Mooney and Billings the sort of people we want to run at large ? We have decided this in the negative and we have locked them up. We intend to keep them there."

Mooney and Billings are victims of case-fixing and frame-up and miscarriage of justice. They are symbolic of a judicial and political administration that is too blatantly on the side of big property.

Since March 25, 1931, nine Negro boys are held in an American prison on a charge of assault and rape on two white girls. They were travelling on a freight train when they were provoked to a fight by a few white boys. The white boys were thrown off the train, and, on their telephonic information, an infuriated mob met the train at Scottsboro in the State of Alabama. Two white girls, hoboing on the same train, lodged a complaint of rape in order to escape a charge of vagrancy. Race hysteria and Ku Klux Klan did the rest. Medical evidence showed that the girls had lied. One girl subsequently retracted her testimony. The United States Supreme Court has twice reversed previous convictions. And yet the Negro boys are held in prison.

In Alabama, the Courts and the State administration are ridden by race-hatred and the fiendish desire legally or illegally to lynch Negroes. The Negroes are underprivileged and live under the dictatorial rule of their economic masters, the former slave-owners of the South.

In Tampa, in the State of Florida, a man, who wanted to change the administration of the country and fought for the rights and liberties of the people, was illegally kidnapped and flogged to death by the regular State police. The Tampa Police and the ku-klux-klan knights of the whitehood deliberately burnt Joseph Shoe-maker and poured boiling tar on his body. The Committee for the Defence of Civil Rights in Tampa informed after Shoemaker's death has disclosed the widespread influence exercised by the gambling dens and the cigar manufactures and their hired gangmen on the State administration. No one who chooses to organise workers, employed and unemployed, for a better living and a superior Government is safe at their hands.

The suppression of civil liberties on the land, that is, in the villages is quite as widespread and acute. The fall in agricultural prices coupled with the heavy fixed charges of the monopolists, the railroad interests and the banking groups have reduced the farmers, particularly of South and West America, to dire straits. Out of these economic conditions ever since 1932, rural struggles have developed to an unprecedented extent and variety. There has been a corresponding increase in the use of repressive measures, private and official, directed against the farmers. Ground down by poverty and hunger, if the small land-owning farmers and farm labourers choose to agitate and struggle. they are confronted with a ferocious resistance. Mass movements, for example, against chattel-mortgage foreclosures appeared all over the country as early as February 1935 and auction sales became impossible. The organised and determined farmers succeeded in forbidding high bids and what is commonly known as "penny sales" took place. Farm machinery brought anything upto 8 cents (4 annas) an item and a team of horses went for 12 cents. Courts and officers sought to prevent this. Leaders of such protests against foreclosure sales were punished with fines or with imprisonment. In the year 1933, over 200,000 dairy farmers, oppressed by low prices paid them by monopoly milk companies, organised into new farmer groups and resorted to strikes. They picketed the roads leading into towns where creameries and cheese factories were located. Strike-breaking trucks were escorted by the hired gangmen of the milk companies as also the State militia. Armed encounters were a frequent occurrence I and a large number of farmers was thrown into jail.

In the Southern States of America, a vicious system of land tenure prevails which is commonly known as share-cropping. The share-croppers, of whom Negroes form a very high percentage, own neither land nor means of cultivation. They are virtually the serfs of the big landowner who is legally entitled to a one-half share of the produce but, in fact, extorts whatever he likes. Attempts to organise these share-croppers and tenants and awaken them to a sense of their rights have met with violent reprisals. The organisers are attacked by private guards of the ku-klux-klan and sheriffs together with the State judiciary have been fairly active with their prisons and lawcourts. Banning of meetings and their violent dispersal are frequent practices.

As the valuable brochure of the American Civil Liberties Union "The Struggle for Civil Liberty on the Land," puts it: Vigilantes, mobs, troops, sheriffs gunmen—legal and illegal agencies alike—have been brought into play against rural agitation.

In the American colonies Philippines, Puerto Rico, Virgin Islands, Hawaii, Samoa and Guam, Haiti peaceful assembly for the redress of grievances is often prohibited, the right of free speech is severely curtailed by laws of sedition and repressive measures such as use of military, banning of organisations and exiling of 'undesirables' are not an uncommon practice. In another brochure of the Union, the main causes of such restrictions are shown to be: (i) the imposition of an American culture, based on the assumption of the superiority of Anglo-Saxon civilisation (2) the penetration of American commercial interests and their support by the Government as against the interests of the colonial peoples, (3) centralised and arbitrary government by American officials, many either navy officers or with their mentality (4) absence of legislation in protection of civil rights such as the right to agitate for independence and that of peasants and workers to organise associations for the betterment of their conditions.

Laws of sedition and criminal anarchy and of compulsory patriotism in educational institutions very seriously suppress freedom of speech and of imparting of information in several States of America. In Indiana, for example, a statement that 'people can force Congress to change conditions' was construed as sedition and a heavy sentence was the outcome. In several States, teachers are required to take oaths of loyalty. Libraries are cleansed of books and text books of passages that are deemed objectionable by the State administration. Certain subjects of study are ruled out as vicious. Strict censorship over students' papers is attempted. Auditoriums of schools, which by right belong to the people for purposes of lawful meetings, are refused to poltical organisations of a radical profession.

This illustrative background of the wide array of affairs and laws in the United States of America will have shown the dangers to the civil liberties of the people, that lie or lurk in the Government of the country. The struggle for civil liberties on the land and in Tampa shows the extent of organised private violence that is tolerated and even encouraged by Governments of several States. The political machinery of numerous States is more or less in the employ of big interests and officers of Law and police are no better than case-fixers, oppressive gangmen and fabricants of evidence. Practically all the cases described here reveal the enormous miscarriage of justice. Scottsboro affair and repression in colonies demonstrate the ruthless oppression of imperialist interests when they find a convenient sanction in the mob hysteria of racial domination. And above it all, are the laws of sedition and of assembly, the restrictions on Negroes rights and on freedom in education, that choke all efforts for the reform of abuses in justice and administration and national economy.

Let us remember the exalted conception of civil rights held by eminent Americans in the past as also now. This conception is also enshrined in the following articles of the Bill of Rights of the Federal Constitution.

No law shall abridge the freedom of speech or of the press and of the right of the people peacefully to assemble. No warrant shall be issued but upon probable cause, supported by oath or affirmation, and particularly describing the place to be searched, and the persons or things to be seized. No person shall be deprived of life, liberty, or property, without due process of law. No person shall be denied the equal protection of laws. Excessive bail shall not be required, nor excessive fines imposed, nor cruel and unusual punishments inflicted. Why then is this inhuman variance of practice from the laws permitted ? Is it that pubhc vigilance is not sufficiently strong ? Or, is it, that the conception of civil rights first arose in the struggle between feudal absolutism and modern industry, which, Hke the poacher turned gamekeeper. has no use left for its former ideas, now that it is engaged in a deadly combat with the masses both at home and in the colonies? Perhaps, it is both.

No one can, however, accuse the American Civil Liberties Union of inactivity or lack of vigilance. In its annual story of the fight for civil liberty, which is a precious document of far-reaching social importance, it gives a close-up survey of all manners of suppression and of the forces ranged on the two sides. The Union plans its campaigns for the year and those of the running year further testify its vigilance. Under the four sections of Freedom of opinion. Rights of Labour, Censorship and Racial Minorities it evolved a fight on 14 different fronts. Under Freedom of Opinion, they comprise opposition to all forms to gag legislation and to restrictions on freedom in education and campaigns for the release of political prisoners, for changes in the immigration and deportation laws and for the setting aside of all recognised public places in all areas or cities for purposes of meetings and organisation. The Rights of Labour and Peasantry include the right to organise, strike and picket and the right of the unemployed to organise and demonstrate. Under the Section of Censorship is understood the fight for freedom of the radio by requiring equal facilities for all sides of controversial topics and opposition to Censor's control over motion pictures, books and plays and the post office. The fight for racial minorities consists of campaigns against lynching and for Negroes' civil rights and for civil forms of Government for the colonies.

Freedom of opinion is the rock-bottom of the concept of civil liberties held by the Americans Union. All through its various activities and the copious literature that the Union ceaselessly produces, there runs a single thread of the historic American position on the freedom of speech. No expression of opinion shall be punished, even if it extends up to the advocacy of violent overthrow of Government. Opinion to be punished must be accompanied by an overt act of revolt. It is easy enough to imagine the vast labour that must be undertaken in any country to approximate the actual practices of Government to this ideal concept of civil liberties. Laws of sedition have to be radically changed and a constant vigil kept on the decisions of law-courts. Public opinion is a potent instrument and the conscience of the people must not be allowed to relapse into a state of indolence or perversity, so that it may always revolt against laws and decisions contrary to the right of unlimited freedom of opinion. Dark interests will, of course, tenaciously cling to their power and raise scares of insecurity and violence and disloyalty and revolution to hack at the civil rights of the people. Lest the people should be deluded to forego their rights and, even, to support those who would restrict their freedom, these scares have to be exposed and fought against. On a more theoretical plane too attacks have been directed against the basic civil right of unrestricted freedom of opinion. It is argued that such freedom can be granted only to those who will secure it to their opponents when thay have attained control over the State. The American Union has rightly described this argument as highbrow; for, whatever the reasons adduced for the propriety of governmental control over opinion, all the corollaries of such a control, suppression and tyranny and social stagnation and blocking of progress, flow in as soon as its propriety is admitted. If society is to progress, no theory nor argument shall restrict the basic civil right of the people to express any opinion unaccompanied by an overt act. It is time enough to punish people when they actually resort to revolutionary action.

It will be seen that the American Union is not quite so extensive in its field of operations as the French League. It is, however, a very assiduous watch-dog of the civil rights of the people in the narrow sense of the term. No doubt, in its effort to secure freedom of speech and the right to organise and picket and proper dispensation of justice, it is faced with social and economic conditions which, as in France, are the roots of all mischief. No doubt every attack on civil liberties is but a reflection of certain basic social condition. A thorough going investigation into acts of suppression of civil rights has thrown very instructive sidelights on the economy and the political management of the country, as with Scottsboro, Tampa, Mooney and Sharecroppers. In so far, a campaign for civil liberties resolves indirectly into a campaign against social abuses. The concept of civil liberties, therefore, includes indirectly the campaigns for reform in administration, police and judiciary and for the suppression of private gangsterism.

The American Civil Liberties Union has over 3,000 members and contributors. Over 5,000 persons are active in one way or another in its work. This number includes 700 co-operating attorneys, 800 correspondents and investigators and 500 speakers, writers and churchmen who have volunteered their services. The ultimate control of policies rests in a National Committee which represents every shade of economic and political opinion and includes lawyers, teachers, clergymen, editors, businessmen and labour organisers. The Union is managed by a Board of Directors and the work of the national headquarters at New York is in the hands of a director, a staff counsel, a secretary and a publicity director. It has a re-presentative in Washington, State chairmen in 41 states, and branches in 25 cities. The operating expenses of the Union are about 20,000 dollars a year (Rs. 60,000) and its annual financial assistance in legal aid goes up to 10,000 dollars. Distributed all over the country, the co-operating attorneys assist in legal advice and defence; the correspondents investigate into breaches of civil rights as they arise from time to time, collect all relevant information and report to headquarters; the writers, speakers and clergymen make an appeal to public conscience and develop national campaigns. The Union was organised in 1920 and has issued over 40 brochures and other mimeographed material. Its Weekly Press Releases (Bulletins) which go out to several hundred newspapers and periodicals all over the country already amount to over 750.

Publicity is the soul of all civil liberties agitation and the American Union is keenly conscious of it. Aside of numerous publications and national campaigns, the Union makes an individual appeal to all who read its publications. In each of these, there is a series of "commandments" under "what you can do" exhorting readers to write to the editor of their newspaper asking for editorial comment on the subject matter of the particular pamphlet, to utilise the material in their conversations and speeches and to send protests, individually as also through their organisation, against the specific breach of civil liberties detailed in the pamphlet.

There are no doubt other sectional agencies like the International Labour Defence, the Association for the advancement of Coloured Peoples, Scottsboro Defence Committee, Defence of Civil Rights in Tampa, which engage in the defence of specific civil liberties. But the Civil Liberties Union is always there and it is a happy sign that of late sufficient goodwill and solidarity among all these organisations has come into being to give the civil liberties movement in America added strength and enthusiastic determination.

There is also the International Committee for Political Prisoners, which was formed in 1924 and which is designed solely to deal with appeals for protests and aid on behalf of victims of political persecution in other countries. In its annual survey of persecution abroad, the Committee estimated for 1933 a total of 230,000 political prisoners for the world, of which India contributed the very large number of 40,000. The Committee has published several brochures, such as, Political Persecution throughout the World and Venezuela Land of Oil and Tyranny.

Our account of the Civil Liberties Movement in America, will however, be incomplete, unless we pay a personal tribute to Roger N. Baldwin who is the chief of American libertarians and to whose untiring efforts and will is due the success and growth of the American Civil Liberties Union.

3. CIVIL LIBERTIES IN ENGLAND

It is only in recent years that the English citizen has begun to experience attacks upon his civil liberties. During the latter half of the nineteenth century and till before the outbreak of the world war, the Englishman had settled down to a comparatively unbroken enjoyment of the rights of free speech and assembly and association and equal justice which he had won after great efforts. Right from the days of the mediaeval Magna Carta upto the nineteenth century Chartist revolt for democracy and the Tolpuddle martyrdom of workers who had dared to form Trade Unions of the working-class, the fight for social changes and for civil rights had been waged. Social progress had later become possible in England without basic transference of power from one class to another. This was due to a variety of reasons such as the possession of the world's best industrial machinery and the largest colonial domains. What the American ruling caste did to the Negroes and the emigrant workers at home, the English could conveniently shift upon the colonial peoples. The English middle classes and the working class were fairly prosperous and participated, however meagrely, in the spoils of their ruling caste; they did not clamour for basic social changes and their civil rights were consequently untouched. Post-war England is, however, different. Social progress is now become dependent on disturbance in the control of political power. The fight for social progress, therefore, involves governmental attacks on the civil liberties of such citizens as seek such a progress and, therefore, a basic transference of political power. Civil Liberties have now acquired a new meaning and, though won after continuous sacrifices, they have to be fought for again. Whoever is for democracy as the basis of social progress, whatever liis other opinions on different economic and political systems may be, he lines up in this broad front of civil liberties against the autocracy and misuse of executive power.

In view of the fact that the traditions of civil liberties are particularly strong in the country and that a cry raised on an issue of freedom of opinion or organisation can rally large sections, flagrant breaches of the American or the colonial type are still uncommon. The attacks are directed more in isolated localities and on details of police and executive procedure and, oftener, in an indirect manner. Not that such indirect and subtler curtailment in the liberties of citizens does not take place in other countries and that the American and the French Civil Liberties Unions do not have to combat it with vigilance. But the activities of the British Union provide a more instructive field for the study of such subtle attacks of the Government on citizens' rights, even as the Union's major operations are directed against them.

Certain methods of the police securely sheltered from the public eye, which are quite contrary to law but are commonly practised, have of recent been widely talked about in England. They relate to the prevalent irregularities of wrongful arrests, of the questioning in regard to offences, of the influence on lower courts for refusal of bail and of wrongful detensions. "Suspected persons" are arrested on the flimsiest evidence of their "loitering with intent" and, it is believed, that the number of such wrongful arrests has increased in recent years. Individual policemen, often with an eye on promotion, effect the arrest of persons who, they allege, are loitering about suspiciously. To expose this police action of wrongful arrests, publicity in the newspapers and in the House of Commons has become necessary.

It is also the usual practice of the poHce to question a prisoner as to any offences of which he may be suspected other than that in connection with which he is in custody. That is clearly a violation of individual liberty. The Report of the Royal Commission on Police Powers and Procedure (1929) went so far as to recommend that the police should be rigidly instructed not to question a person in custody or in prison about any crime or offence with which he is or may be charged. There is a view, and that seems to be the proper view on civil liberties, that no statement, voluntary or otherwise, made to the police should be permitted as evidence. The police also exercises influence on the lower courts and police courts in the grant of bails. At the behest of the police, bails are either refused or excessive demands are made. This is a practice which requires a constant searchlight of publicity and exposure. In fact, so does the entire atmosphere of a police station which, as a Judge remarked sometime ago is "singularly conducive to confessions." The use by the police of agent provacateurs and the detention of arrested persons, while the police decide whether any charge shall be brought, are illegal practices and, yet, widespread.

Obsolete laws which have not been used for a century and over are now being revived. Legislation, in its executive application, is made to depart from its original designs and put to uses other than those intended by the legislators. Thus, for example, a law made a hundred years ago to prevent 'blowing a horn or a noisy instrument' was recently used by the police to prevent a loud speaker campaign for the Peace Ballot. At the same time, the commercial use of noisy instruments against wliich the law was directed is allowed without hindrance. An example of how an obsolete law is revived is the Statute of Edward III, passed in 1361, which has recently been used to imprison persons who have done nothing but who the Government suspect might say something dangerous. As the declaration of principles of the British Civil Liberties Union says, "These restrictions are the danger signals. The only way to preserve freedom of speech is to resist now, before it is too late, each individual infringement wherever it is attempted."

Police bans, departmental encroachments and local legislation, which have no legal validity, have, of recent, tended to restrict severely the right of free assembly and procession. The English law on processions has, through a continuous series of court decisions, become very liberal so that there is no legal justification for an advance ban by the police on processions nor is a subsequent conviction easily obtainable in the case of moving processions on a charge of obstruction to traffic. Recent attempts have, however, been made by the police to ban processions in advance or disperse them by force. One such attempt in Manchester aroused such a storm of protest from prominent politicians and publicmen of the country that the City Constable, despite his own ban, allowed the procession and demonstration to take place. An Armistice Day Procession in Blackburn, planned as a demonstration against War and Fascism, was banned by the local Chief Constable but, when the Council for Civil Liberties sent a telegram and a letter of protest, the ban was withdrawn on the following day. Certain other orderly processions have been dispersed with baton charges and arrests were made. The Council is following up the matter by interpellations in the House of Commons.

The law regarding meetings is not quite as liberal as that on processions. Still, there are traditional meeting-places in practically every area of the country where public gatherings have been held for generations. Of recent, the police has attempted to ban such meetings on the plea of obstruction to traffic. A serious interference with the right of assembly is the so-called "Trenchard Ban" on all meetings outside Labour Exchanges, where the unemployed pass in que for work or relief. The Council has helped in the organising of test meetings and contesting of test law-suits with varying success. There is the famous "Duncan Case" in which Mrs. Duncan is charged with obstructing a police officer in the execution of his duty, because she insisted on holding a meeting as there was no obstruction to traffic. The Council is assisting the case by way of press propaganda and arrangement of legal defence.

The Council also directs its campaigns against cases of political discrimination and victimisation. The refusal of the lessees of the Albert Hall, for example, to let their hall for a type of political meetings arouses protest from the Council as much as the victimisation of a professor or a teacher in an educational institution who is known to express pronounced views on such subjects as war and peace. The Council has often had to bring to light the opposition of the British Broadcasting Corporation to the judicial and fair presentation of differing views. That all this amounts to a curtailment of the freedom of thought and expression, there is no doubt. In some of these cases, the Government is directly involved. In view, however, of the subtle manner in which this censorship over thought is exercised, it is not strange that a higlily developed sense of civil rights is preliminary to preventing it.

England, however, is not altogether devoid of major attacks on her civil liberties. The Incitement to Disaffection Act of 1934, as it has passed both Houses of Parliament, is to an extent different in its scope and provisions from the original plans of its sponsors. Still, under pretext of safeguarding His Majesty's Forces from incitement to disaffection or rebellion, stringent clauses have been enacted which will tend to suppress freedom of opinion in the country. As it has been pointed out in a statement of the Council, it will be very difficult for the publisher of a book, pamphlet or newspaper to put in a strong defence, as the very existence of such literature, even though it may not have been expressly written for the army, might seduce a soldier. The Government had persistently refused to accept an amendment which would have limited the operation of the Act to literature devised and intended for the armed Forces. It is clear, therefore, that such literature as seeks to educate the public on the causes of war, the destruction that it effects and the measures to prevent such a calamity, though it may not contain a direct and special appeal to the soldiery, may be held objectionable under the scope of this Act. Moreover, the Act arms the magistracy with large powers of a general search. As the Council points out, such powers are capable of being used for political purposes, to enable the police to gain entry to the offices of political societies on which a single copy of an objectionable literature may be found. Assurances have of course been given by the Government that such wide powers will scarcely be used. But it is clear that behind the pretext of keeping intact the loyalty of the soldiery, a major attack on the freedom of opinion and its expression has been made by the Government through this Act. The Council has throughout the career of this legislation expressed a determined opposition to it and has succeeded in toning it down considerably. A much larger success achieved is the awakening of the consciousness of the British citizen to the menace of repression. This has been due largely to the vigilance of the Council which, within 48 hours of the publication of the text of the Bill, analysed its provisions and emphasised their dangerous character. This analysis was circulated to every member of the House of Commons. Meetings and demonstrations at which numerous political, religious, and other organisations participated were also organised. A Conference was organised in opposition to this legislation composed of 1600 delegates who were official delegates of societies representing every phase of progressive thought. A mass demonstration organised by the Council in Trafalgar Square was described by the press as having drawn together all progressive elements to a degree never known before. Whatever may be the provisions of this legislation, the British citizen is now definitely awakened to the danger that it represents to his liberty and will not so lightly tolerate its executive application. Already certain printers have refused to print entirely legal material in fear of possible punishment under this Act and the Council has made this an issue in its campaign against the Act.

In England a large mass of legal standards, regulating the relation between the government and the citizen, has grown up through a series of Parliamentary enactments and, more particularly, the decision of law courts. The National Council for Civil Liberties takes its stand on this heritage of liberty and has in its declaration classified this heritage under six heads. They are: freedom of speech, freedom of assembly, freedom of association, freedom of thought and expression, full rights for all peoples under the British Parliament, democratic control of

Government. We have already seen the manner in which the Government is seeking to curtail this freedom. The Council, therefore, has more ample opportunities than sister organisations in other countries of directing its attention to the details of executive and police procedure. It has, therefore, rightly stated in its declaration that "National Liberty is in a great measure the sum of local liberties and freedom as a whole will be preserved to the extent that men and women in their work and in their own localities resist legal encroachment upon their rights." In England it is not the law nor its judicial application that has yet become such a danger to civil liberties as it has in America. It is the irregular action of the police and other local bodies which though not so monstrously outspoken as a bad law or a bad decision hits at the liberties of the people. In so far the concept of civil liberties of the British Union is emphasised by this opposition to executive and police action contrary to due processes of law.

The Council has also stood up for democratic control over Government. It opposes the recent practices of the Executive to put into force its measures and, only subsequently, submit them to Parliament for necessary legislation. The Council considers that, in the measure legislative functions are assumed by the Government departments and the Civil Service, the liberty of the citizen is curtailed. The vigilance of the Council is not confined to England, for it espouses the cause of all peoples under British Parliament. In the colonies of Gambia, Nigeria, Trinidad, Sierra Leona and others and in India, political parties and meetings are banned and leaders arrested and imprisoned without trial. The extent of its activities in behalf of victims of colonial oppression is discernible in its statement, "History shows that attacks on the freedom of Englishmen at home are always preceded by attacks on the rights of British subjects abroad." Ronald Kidd, the present Secretary of the Council, is actively associating himself with the campaign in England for Indian Civil Liberties.

The National Council for Civil Liberties was formed at the

beginning of 1934, when the country was agitated on the provisions of the Incitement to Disaffection Bill. The need of a non-party and undenominational organisation was acutely felt. Such an organisation could concentrate into a single channel the diffused efforts of many political and other bodies.

The Council has an Executive Committee of not more than 24 members which controls its day to day action. It takes associate members on a minimum annual subscription of five shillings and has succeeded in es- tablishing several branches.

Among other activities the Council has developed a particular form of organisation, which it calls Vigilance Committees. These Committees consisting of prominent writers and publicmen are sent to act as observers on the spot when processions and demonstrations are organised by one political party or the other. This institution has considerably curbed the irregular activities of the police who are afraid of the evidence of distinguished men and women in the law courts. The Council for example organised a Vigilance Committee of 30 persons consisting of such prominent men as Prof. Laski, Mr. H.G. Wells, Mr. Nevinson, to report on cases of violence or irregularity on the occasion of simultaneous fascist and anti-fascist demonstrations in the Hyde Park of London. A temporary headquarter with a telephone was established for the day near the park and the Committee was to mix with the crowd in batches of two. Complaints of irregularities could thus be communicated at once on the telephone.

In its instructions to branches, members and affiliated societies, the Council has noted nine heads on which reports should be made. They relate to banning of or interferences with (i) meetings (2) processions (3) propaganda (leaflets, loud-speakers, etc.) (4) irregular police actions (5) censorship over literature, films, plays, radio, newspaper press and printers' refusal to print under Incitement to Disaffection Act, (6) victimisation for political, racial or religious reasons (7) cases of search or prosecution under the Disaffection Act (8) refusal of passport for political views. (9) unwarranted deportations for political views. The branches, members and others are required to report to the Council's Headquarters in England on any breaches of Civil Liberties under the foregoing heads and are at the same time expected to lodge complaints locally.

We have, until now, considered the civil liberties of the citizen. There are special societies all over the world to watch over the rights of the citizen when he is transformed into a prisoner. One such society, the British "Howard League for Penal Reform", Has been better publicised in India than such other organisations of a similar type as the "International Penal and Penitentiary Commission" of Berne. Standard Minimum Rules for the treatment of prisoners have been prepared and the League of Nations has accorded them its seal of approval. These rules relate to the prisoner's food, work, accommodation and bedding, health and medical services, punishments, prison staff etc. It is rather surprising that the Government of India should have declared in its 1935 report to the League of Nations that these rules are already in force in this country. The Howard League has, however, published a number of violations in different parts of the world without naming the countries and it will not be very misleading to imagine that India is included on the list of violaters. The Howard League works on an international scale and is ready to fight in the cause of prisoners anywhere.

4. THE CONCEPT OF CIVIL LIBERTIES

In order to arrive at an understanding of what civil liberties are, it is necessary to go into their conceptual extent, origins, present state and contemplated actions to maintain them. An enquiry under these four heads: What is the number and types of civil liberties ? How did they arise ? How and why are they attacked today? Why and how should they be defended ? will yield us the concept of civil liberties.

What is the number and types of civil liberties ? We have only to string together the epochal statements of state-builders and the basic doctrines of organic laws and court decisions. These doctrines and state- ments have related to various types of civil liberties. At the head of them all stands liberty of person and movement and the sanctity of dwellings. "The aim of the State is the conservation of natural rights of man; these rights are liberty, property, security and resistance to oppression," lays down an article of French Constitution of 1789. No one shall be arrested and detained or imprisoned without due processes of law. Such processes have gradually come to include an open trial by jury, whose predominating element is drawn out of the same class of men as the accused. Everyone shall be secure in his house, which will not be broken into and searched unless on charge of a definite and specified act of lawlessness. No restrictions shall be imposed on the freedom of a citizen to move about in the country and to obtain passports in order to travel abroad.

In this age of great mass efforts and people's awakening, the liberties of opinion and assembly are as important as those of person and dwellings. The standard in regard to freedom of expression by speech or press is the American dictum that no opinion, whatever its revolutionary import, may be punished unless it is accompanied by an overt act of revolt. The standard in regard to freedom of assembly and processions is the English doctrine that, unless serious obstruction to traffic can be proved, the police or the executive may not take any action. These doctrines imply the abolition of sedition laws and of censorship over press, books, post and radio. Ban orders on meetings and processions are also impermissible. Equal rights shall be granted to everyone to hold meetings in public halls and such areas in every town and village as are traditionally used for purposes of assembly.

Together with the two types of civil liberties relating to person and opinion, the freedom of association and organisation has been steadily acquiring a unique significance. In order that larger masses of men may translate their keen interest in State affairs and economic management into organised effort to remove existing evils, they must in no event be robbed of their precious freedom to organise and strike and picket. The executive might often pretend and advertise the fear that such strikes or organisations will eventually lead to breaches of peace and the spread of a revolutionary mentality and, thus, seek to interfere with this precious freedom. Such attempts have to be resisted and exposed and, short of an overt act, the freedom to organise and strike should not be allowed to be tampered with.

"Law is an expression of the general will" was laid down in an article of the 1789 French Constitution. State authority is to originate from the will of the people and thus democratic control over the Government is considered as an important type of civil liberties. The Government may not act secretly nor without the previous permission of a democratically elected assembly. In some form or the other the civil liberties unions of the world have accepted democratic control over the Government and even the republican form as one of their agitational planks.

The rights of racial minorities come within the extent and scope of a civil liberties agitation. The persecution of racial minorities is obviously a reflection of unequal laws as also unequal dispensation of justice and is therefore an attack on the civil liberties of a section of citizens. Thus, the Civil Liberties Union of America lays especial emphasis on the protection of Negroes and the British and French Unions on that of the colonial peoples.

Freedom of conscience and thought and education is properly speaking a part of liberty of opinion. This freedom must however be especially emphasised in so far as all interference takes place within the precincts of governmental or semi-governmental institutions. If a professor or a teacher is dismissed from his job for expressing opinions unsavoury to the administration and denominational or communal institutions are encouraged by the government, the liberties of free conscience and education are direcdy attacked without serious possibilities of appeal.

The demand for the release of political prisoners is yet another aspect of civil liberties. Most convictions are based on a legal and judicial system, which is too heavily weighted in favour of the government as against the citizen. A fight against this system would obviously entail protection of its victims and, therefore, the release of political prisoners is a demand of civil liberties. Pending such release, the rights of prisoners in relation to food, accommodation, punishments, intel- lectual provisions and the like have to be fought for.

The conceptual extent of civil liberties is now clear. It embraces the rights of the citizen in regard to security both of his person and of dwellings, to freedom of opinion and assembly, thought and organisation, to equal justice and control over the Government and to release from political convictions.

How did they arise ? The concept of civil liberties is an outcome of the struggle that the citizen has eternally waged against his State. Throughout history, the State and its laws have given rise to manifold types of abuses. Whether it was an oppressive tax system or a bloodthirsty landed aristocracy, the citizen groaned and attempted to resist. Wars and cultural stagnation were forced on him and he sought to end them. In his efforts, however, to end oppression and existing evils, he was met with stern repression. The authority in whom State-power was vested did not brook the defiance, wliich was naturally involved in the struggle against abuses and evils. The wrath of the State fell down on the citizen who tried to be critical. He suffered long and solitary confinements, quite often death, and his most precious possessions were snatched away from him. He, therefore, stood in need of a minimum basis of safety from where he could launch attacks on the abuses and evils of his times. The rights of the citizen in opposition to the Government, as enshrined in the organic and ordinary law of different lands, are an expression of such a minimum basis of safety. If a regime of civil liberties prevails, resistance to oppression is not attended with frightful consequences.

It is instructive to recall the occasions of the American and French Constitutions and the English Bills of Rights. In each case, much oppression and many social and financial abuses had preceded. Bastilles of one type or the other had been built to frighten people into submission and acceptance of conditions as they obtained. When finally the peoples had gathered sufficient strength to smash the State and its economic and social laws, they overthrew the Bastilles. On the ruins of the Bastilles was reared the imposing structure of civil liberties. It was an organic defence against the Having memory of persecutions and repression.

Civil liberties comparatively smoothen society's march towards progress. Society is being eternally pulled between reaction and progress and, often, degenerates into a state of stagnation. In this pull, the State has more often been controlled by forces of stagnation and reaction. There are, of course, brief interludes when former rebels, in the initial stages of their power, have used the State as an agency of progress. Soon however the rebels acquire a distaste and hatred of all changes and the powerful machine of the State is directed against the progressive efforts of the dispossessed. Lest the State should turn into a terrible obstruction to progress and continually block it by its repression, its supreme authority over the citizens stands in need of description and curtailment. The entire scheme of citizens' rights is an outcome of the effort to describe and curtail State-authority. In this manner, orderly social progress becomes possible and society is not continually faced with the choice between tyranny and revolution. The concept of civil liberties is thus essentially a liberal concept which acts as a shockabsorber of the cruel impact between State tyranny and mass revolts. It enables society's march towards progress to proceed on orderly lines. If a citizen chooses to be critical of the world in which he Uves, society permits him to question and test and experiment without fear of serious reprisals.

Why are civil liberties attacked today ? The answer is obvious. A titanic world struggle is going on before our eyes between the forces of status quo and reaction and those of progress. Whether in the colonies or among the masses in imperialist countries, banners of criticism and revolt have been raised against the prevailing economic and political system. This system has meant progressive deterioration in employment and living conditions and cultural attainments and is ever resulting in humiliations for the colonial peoples and barbaric wars. The whole world is a vast question mark and old social structures are being tested and found wanting. The colonial peoples and oppressed masses all over the world are thinking out an alternative Society and are propagating and organising and striking for its acceptance. And so the State is weighting the struggle in favour of the existing society and answers the cry for alternatives with stern arrests and bans.

It is instructive to remember that it is the national freedom movement in the colonies and the socialist and communist" parties of the world that are the worst sufferers. They suffer because they are voicing the demand for alternatives of the colonials and peasants and labourers of the world. Against them are pitted the powers of status quo, the force of finance and imperialist capital and landed aristocracy. The Governments throw overboard the concept of civil liberties and go out of the pale of their described and limited authority. And so attacks on the civil liberties of citizens have become a permanent instrument of the State and the class policy of finance capital and landed aristocracy.

It is desirable here to go into the stray enquiries, made for some time past in our country, that assume the function of civil liberties as being divided into a religious or a political or an economic scope. It is obvious that such enquiries rest on a misconception. There are no religious or political or economic civil liberties as such. The question of civil liberties arises only when the constituted authority of the State fails to safeguard them to its citizens either by acts of commission or, less often, through those of omission. Civil liberties are violated when the State either itself attacks the various freedoms of opinion and association of its citizens or permits private gangsterdom to do so. The basic factor in all such State and private violence is the fear of criticism and revolt against the existing system of laws and government.

How are Civil Liberties violated ? In the first instance, laws of detention, house-searches, sedition. censor and association and codes of criminal procedure practically all over the world militate against the fundamental guarantees of civil liberties. These laws and codes are either frankly repressive or deliberately vague. In either case they deluver the citizen to the caprices of the Executive. Secondly, the executive and judicial administrations of the world are trying increasingly to conquer every inch of territory that they had to concede to liberty and justice. This they do in all manner of ways. Justice is severely and often faultily applied; imprisonment and heavy sentences out of all proportion to the offence have become very usual. The executive issues edicts wliich could not be defended in a properly constituted court of law and, otherwise, seeks to corrupt and frighten public opinion by State subsidies, propagandist scares and secret action. Thirdly, in the dark chambers of the police, shielded from public eye, excesses are done and third degree methods used. Often, the police stretches the law much beyond its proper scope. Illegal detention and forced statements and threats of drastic action are usual. Fourthly, private violence in the employ of the State or of vested interests is permitted and encouraged. This is particularly done in the villages. In their total effect, the four types of violations restrict the right of the citizen to hold meetings and form associations and propagate thought through books, newspapers and radio. The citizen becomes an easy prey to dismissal from his job, police-torture, detention and heavy sentences.

How should civil liberties be defended ? The Civil Liberties Unions of the world have developed an efficient mechanism of branches and local correspondents who throw the searchhght of publicity on legal, judicial, executive, police and private excesses and prepare dossiers of each individual case. Action is taken on each individual report. Interventions on behalf of the victims are made with the authorities. With the voluntary aid of prominent speakers, writers, solicitors and public men, the national headquarters develop mass campaigns against specific laws, for individual affairs, for public enquiries and free trial and for release of detenus and political prisoners. They also organise legal defence. The publicity apparatus of special press releases, brochures and other publications is evolved.

Why should civil liberties be defended? The question is obviously absurd and yet it is not seldom asked. Why should we defend your civil liberties; would you, were you in power, safeguard these to us ? Again, the advice is often given to those, whose civil liberties are violated, to slow down their agitation against the existing order or, even, to stop it. It is easy to see the implications of both the rhetoric and the advice.

Both amount to an acceptance of the status quo and a falling in line with the forces of social reaction. Only the hard-boiled reactionary will not shrink before such a prospect. Whoever believes in orderly social progress, and the front extends in normal-times from the conservatives over the liberals to the radicals, lines up in a joint defence of civil liberties.

There is another type of argument, met with among a section of radicals, that seriously whittles down the importance of any special defence of civil liberties. It is asserted that there is not much use of fighting for civil liberties, for, ultimately it is a question of political power. Suppression and repression will willy-nilly take place, so long as criticism or an organised action against the existing order are attempted. The ultimate guarantee of civil liberties, therefore, lies in the overthrow of the existing State. The argument that civil liberties can finally be protected only under a different regime is true enough but there is a serious flaw in the deduction that it is not much use fighting for civil liberties.

The special front of civil liberties maintains the backbone of the people. The spirit of opposition against injustice is kept intact. The individual gets strength from the knowledge that his resistance to police or executive oppression will awaken common interest. Again, such a common interest serves to convulse the conscience of the people against encroachment on their liberties. The people are taught to be vigilant and, so they clear the road to progress.

The fight for civil liberties also lays bare political and social abuses which are the fountainhead of all suppression. As in the American fight for civil liberties in the countryside, facts of economic and political management, which would have otherwise remained unknown, come out in the open. An enquiry into a case of violation of civil liberties is simultaneously an enquiry into the particular abuse against which the individual had fought and for which the wrath of the State and other interests had descended upon him. Thus, the fight for civil liberties awakens the social conscience of the people.

We may not also forget that the front of civil liberties is more broad based and inclusive than that of freedom and progress. Among the ranks of freedom and progress, there may be differences of opinion on other matters but they will all unite on an issue of civil liberties. Their ranks are further strengthened by the inflow of such as have not yet turned into hardboiled reactionaries. Such a broad-based and inclusive front is a great moulder of public opinion and can also exercise much pressure on the State.

It is also incorrect to say, that, till the final objective of State power is achieved, nothing can be done towards the safeguarding of civil liberties. Such an argument assumes that the existing state-power can do whatever it likes until it is fully defeated. That may be a legal fiction and to a very large extent true, but even the State shrinks from doing certain things lest they should recoil on its head. To restrict, therefore, the factual authority of the State, all manners of trenches should be dug and citadels fortified in defence of people's freedom. The agitation for civil liberties is even such a trench and a citadel. In most cases, it may only stiffen public opinion but, in some, the State shall have to bend. There have been cases where previous orders of the Executive or subordinate officials were revoked and release of political prisoners effected in response to an insistent pubHc demand.

Violations of civil liberties are not restricted to this country or the other and a large part of the world is today more or less a prison-house. World opinion, as never before, is feeling its way towards an organised expression and speedily reacts to suppression of liberties, wherever that might take place. If a national Civil Liberties Union exists in different countries, it can also serve as an exchange bureau of international information and propaganda.

The concept of civil liberties is now clear. It defines State-authority within clear limits. It assigns well-defined liberties to the people. The task of the State is to protect these liberties. But the States usually do not like the task and act contrarily. Armed with the concept of civil liberties, the people develop an agitation to force the State to keep within clear and well defined limits. The agitation for civil liberties does not directly propagate a change of the existing order, but it attempts to keep the way clear for such as may.

5. CIVIL LIBERTIES IN INDIA

India has fought hard and bitter struggle to win her civil liberties. Modern India begins in the eighties of the last century with a fight on the issue of equal justice as between the Englishman and the Indian. It was the Ilbert Bill that sought to aboUsh the preferential justice meted out to Englishmen. The English bureaucracy and the commercial class were alarmed and launched on a violent campaign against the Bill. The Indian people answered by an equally resolute agitation in favour of the Bill and this agitation became the starting point for a sense of political rights in the country. Again, the period of submissive criticism ends and the era of a vigorous nationalism is ushered

in with a fight for civil liberties. Post-war India was made to suffer the Rowlatt Act and the denial of all human liberties, Jallianwala Bagh and crawling on all fours, that followed in its train. The first mass action that the country carried out to wrest its freedom from British Imperialism was largely inspired by its revolt against the Rowlatt Act and, consequently, the suppression of civil liberties. Since then, there has been no single year when all manner of repressive laws and Acts of the Government have not been a sore point with Indian Nationalism.

Even to ordinary law which governs the liberties of the people is viciously vague and being constantly put to a repressive use. The ordinary law of sedition, which governs freedom of opinion, punishes all expressions that bring the government of the country into hatred or contempt. Hatred or contempt are vague terms and the line, therefore, between legitimate criticism and seditious utterances is left to be drawn by the magistracy. It is said that the dictum which guides magistrates is that criticism of or protest against particular policies and measures of government is permitted, but any wholesale condemnation of government falls under the law. Here again, it is the magistrate who decides as to when the condemnation of a particular policy resolves into that of the entire government, and so the difficulty remains. The citizen has, thus, no constitutional nor legal guarantees to defend his freedom of opinion from executive and magisterial encroachment. His expressions need not have caused an overt act of revolt, nor is it necessary to show that he had attempted or even intended to do so, and yet he may be punished for breach of the law of sedition. The citizen's liberties of assembly and organisation are quite as precarious. Under Section 107 of the or- dinary Criminal Procedure Code, action is usually taken in the countryside against attempts to form associations on the charge that a breach of the peace was likely. In like manner, wide use is made of Section 144 which empowers the declaration of bans on specified areas and an assembly of more than five men is made punishable. These and several other sections of the criminal law militate against the ordinary liberties of the citizen and deliver him to the caprices of the police and the executive.

When this is the ordinary law, it is not difficult to imagine the deadly grip of emergency laws, variously known as the Criminal Law Amendment Acts, Public Security Acts and the like, on the civil liberties of the people. It is true that emergency laws, like the State Prisoner's Regulation of 1818, Press Acts of 1867 and 1910 and the Rowlatt Act of 1919, have been comparatively normal features of Indian administration also in the past. Today the grip is deadlier and, as the Lucknow Congress Resolution says, "at no period since the great Revolt of 1857 has the suppression of civil and personal liberties and the repression of the Indian people. . . . .been so great as it is now."

In several provinces, security of person and sanctity of dwellings and liberty of movement are practically non-existent. Indefinite detentions without trial, internment, and externment are common in Bengal and the Punjab. The number of Bengal's detenus is computed at over 2000 and, in the month of July alone, about 40 Socialist workers were home or village interned in the Punjab. It is made a crime, punishable with a sentence of 6 months, for boys of 12 and over to sit and loiter between sunset and sunrise in certain playgrounds, parks and public places of Dacca and Narainganj in Bengal. Large numbers of young men are not allowed to stir out of their houses between sunset and sunrise all over Bengal. The movements of a still larger number are strictly confined within narrow town limits and they are frequently required to report themselves to the police once a day. In order to travel to Darjeeling, a passport is necessary. In the town and the interior of the Midnapur district, a special police permit is necessary for riding bicycles. General search warrants are issued and warrantless searches are frequently instituted by subordinate police officers in their own judgment. Security of person is further jeopardised by granting large powers to the police of keeping suspects under prolonged custody. All over the country, visitations by the police at odd hours of the night and day and questionings and pestering are becoming alarmingly usual.

The ordinary law of sedition. Sea Customs Act and the Boards of Censors are in themselves sufficient to put a ban on all advanced opinion, thought and art. And yet there are the one time ordinances, designed to combat the Civil Disobedience and other revolutionary movements, which have been enacted into the ordinary law of the land. The Indian Press Act and other provincial Press Laws have made the freedom of press a mockery. Advance permission of the Government is necessary and security deposits for good behaviour are demanded before a newspaper or periodical may be published. Even the purely literary journals are a victim to this vexatious and embracing interference. Advance securities were demanded of "Hans" and "Bhartiya Sahitya" (Indian Literature), two purely literary monthlies devoted to building up a common platform for the various Indian languages and literatures. Subsequent forfeiture of securities is not rare. The latest instance is that of "Anand

Bazar Patrika", a Bengali daily, having to forfeit its security for commenting on "Official Tyranny on Literature." Aside of the Editor and Publisher, the owner of the printing press is also made responsible. It is with immense difficulty, therefore, that movements with scanty resources, such as those of labour, can persuade the owner of a press to print their official organs. The list of newspapers which had to cease publication in re- cent years because of these laws is formidable—the official number of such suppressions is 348. Imprisonment of violation of Press Laws is frequent. There have been instances when the publisher of a notice for a public meeting has been awarded a sentence of six months hard labour. Such a notice is a newssheet in the eyes of the law and, as such, requires previous permission of the Government before it can be issued. The Newsletter of the Foreign Department of the Indian National Congress also fell under the provisions of this law and the office of the All India Congress Committee was raided and a variety of mimeographed material seized.

Bengal suffers strangling restrictions in the shape of a Press Officer who casts his shadow over the entire Press and has constituted himself into a kind of editor-in-chief of aU newspapers. He interests himself not only in the views but the news and the method of display and issues warnings. With the threat of action under the Press laws and the judicious dispensation of ofBcial advertisements, he also carries on positive propaganda for the Government.

Advanced literature and books are frequently proscribed. There is the all India banning by the Government of India; in addition each provincial Government proscribes books within its own area. In Bengal, a whole class of literature is banned. A per- son found in possession of a book, which is not itself banned but which, in the opinion of a policeman or a subordinate magistrate, belongs to that dangerous class, is liable to a term of imprisonment. The usual sentence for possessing such a book is a year.

Throughout the country, the liberties of assembly and

association are constantly violated. Even under the ordinary Trade Union laws, workers are not permitted to strike unless they have, very much in advance, given individual notices to the management. Strikes for political ends are unlawful. Under the special laws of association. Trade Union organisations are speedily declared illegal and the Government is ably assisted by the Anglo-Indian Press in the spreading of scares. As soon as a workers' organisation shows signs of activity, the semi-official press comes out with stories of revolutionary mentality and communist influence and what follows is easy to imagine. In recent years, a larger number of Unions of railwaymen, tramways workers, textile workers, crew in inland navigation have come under the ban of the Government. The Bengal Publicc Security Act of 1932 was styled a "heavy roller" by a former Governor and yet a communique of the Government of Bengal has conferred, since September, 1936, additional powers, particularly in regard to meetings of industrial workers, on the Commissioner of Police in Calcutta and the neighbouring District Magistrates. The communique remarks on the increasing activity of organisations which use expressions commonly associated with violent revolutionary movements in other parts of the World.

In the countryside, meetings are forcibly dispersed and much private violence is permitted. These have become frequent in the proportion that the peasantry is agitating and organising against tax and rental demands, which bear no relation to its shrunken income. From the province of Behar, where the peasantry is growing restless, are reported recent instances of ele- phants being run on peaceful assemblies and assaults made on peasant leaders.

Among organisations, wliich were declared illegal during the civil disobedience movement and conti- nue to remain so, are several Congress Committees, Volunteer Corps, Students and Youth Unions. No definite reasons are ever advanced in support of the continuance of the ban, except that it is not in the interests of public peace to disclose them. In the North

Western Frontier Province and in parts of Bengal, no political work of any kind is possible. The permanent menace and frequent resort to aerial attacks on the civil population, officially known as war-like tribes, have completely crippled and paralysed the political life of the Frontier Province.

During the year 1936, enormous suppression of civil liberties has taken place in the country and there are a number of 'affairs' as great as those of Dreyfus and Tom Mooney to convulse the conscience of the nation. In the beginning of the year, Subhas Chandra Bose was arrested immediately he set his foot on Indian soil and has since been interned in the remote village of Kurseong. Despite repeated demands, the Government refuses to bring him before an open and free court of law. In the last sessions of the Central Legislature, the Government was asked if they shirked the trial, as they had no evidence to which, the Home Member made the eternally silly reply that an open trial was not desirable in the public interest. The cry of public interest has become a convenient smoke-screen under which the Executive lightly tampers with the personal liberties of the people. It accuses Subhas Bose of association with terrorist activities and holds him up as an efficient organiser. The people accept that Bose is an efficient organiser in the cause of the Congress and Indian freedom and suspect that to be the real reason of why the Government charges him with terrorist associations. "Subhas Bose is an undesirable person and, whether a particular charge against him stands or not, he ought to be where he is," seems to resemble closely the reasoning of the Californian editor on Tom Mooney. In a similar manner, declared communists and labour workers, who miss no chance of condemning terrorism, have fallen a prey to the charge of terrorist associations and so the punishment of detention. Muzaffar Ahmad, the Meerut case prisoner, came under the clutches of this law and Abdul Halim is still languishing away in prison. Khan Abdul Ghaffar Khan was, immediately upon his release on August 1, after serving out a two years' sentence, served with orders not to enter the jurisdiction of the Punjab and the Frontier Provinces. The Frontier Government is satisfied that there are reasonable and sufficient grounds for believing that Ghaffar Khan has "acted in a manner prejudicial to the public tranquillity." The Punjab Government prefers to be non-committal and vague and so "has reasonable grounds for believing that Khan Abdul Ghaffar Khan.... has acted or is about to act in a maimer prejudicial to the public safety or peace" M. R. Masani, on his arrival in Lahore on September 4, was served with an externment order for precisely the same reasons. Khan Abdul Ghaffar Khan is a member of the Congress Working Committee and M. R. Masani the General Secretary of the Congress Socialist Party, which are both open and legal organisations, and it is difficult to understand how the Punjab Government could so definitely speculate on other probable activities.

Three recent cases of alleged suicide amongst the Detenus of Bengal, each in September, October and November, have again brought their deplorable condition in painful prominence. Poet Rabindranath Tagore, President of the Indian Civil Liberties Union, in urging a public enquiry says, for many years Bengal has endured the agony of seeing thousands of her sons and daughters confined and crushed in detention camps without even the semblance of a trial. Their hves have been ruined, their families broken up, and the shadow of unending suffering has lain heavily over the province and over India." Naba Jiban Ghosh, one of the detenus who have committed suicide, belonged to a family which has suffered a particular and rather vengeful repression. Binoy Jiban Ghosh, an elder brother, was a Professor of History in the Midnapur College for three years, when he was summarily dismissed from his services in October, 1933. Nirmal Jiban Ghosh, another brother, was executed in connection with the Burge murder case in October, 1934. Yet another brother, Jyoti Jiban Ghosh, has been under detention since April, 1932.

In answer to a question in the House of Commons, it was

known that Parmanand must continue to be a prisoner, as he had not reformed sufficiently. Parmanand was arrested at Lahore on 22nd February 1915 and has now been 21 years in prison. Parmanand is one of the 62 who were arrested in connection with what is known as the First Lahore Conspiracy Case of these were sentenced to transportation for life and 8 who did not appeal for mercy were hanged. On the occasion of the amnesty, in December 1919, 28 of these were released and the prison authorities did not recommend the case of the rest. Out of the 15, who continued to be imprisoned, 14 were released in different years between 1925 and 1929, Parmanand alone continues to be a prisoner, though the sentence of transportation for life is usually commuted after the expiry of twenty years.

Jyotish Chandra Chakravarty was one of the countless little men of Calcutta, when he had a case of cholera in his house. He went out in the early hours to fetch some medicines. The suspicion of the police was as usual lightly, awakened and Chakravarty was clapped in the police prison. Not all his remonstrances were of any avail to him and his child died. A departmental enquiry was later ordered. The 8th of July was no extraordinary day in the history of administration of laws in Bengal. It is only with a view to show what any day has in store for the people that relevant clippings of Calcutta papers of that date are here reproduced. . . . Miss Lilavati Nag M.A., detenu since December, 193 1, who was transferred from the Midnapur jail to the Dacca jail in order that she may stay three hours daily with her parents for a period of two weeks, has been sent back to the Midnapur jail.... Manoranjan Guha of the district of Backerganj, who was recently released from the Andamans after serving out his sentence of 4 years' rigorous imprisonment, has been interned at Pirganj in the district of Midnapur. . . . Soumyendranath Tagore was sentenced to one year's rigorous imprisonment for a speech deli- vered on the 'Subhas Bose Day', organised in protest of detention without trial. In the course of his judgment, the magistrate said, "the language used is well-calculated to excite and promote disaffection." .... Surya Kumar Bhattacharya, formerly a teacher of a High English School, is appointed a peripatetic lecturer in the district of Noakhali. He tours the district and delivers speeches on the evils of terrorism, unemployment and agricultural and industrial enterprises. It requires no vivid imagination to picture the nature of this man's loyalist propaganda... The High Court of Calcutta rejected application of detenu Broja Madab Das, who was sentenced to one year's rigorous imprisonment by a lower court. The charge against him was that, in contravention of the order served upon him, he was found mixing or conversing with another detenu Kshitish Chandra Chakravarty on 20th October, 1935 Counsel for 65 accused charged with rioting in the Hoogly Jute Mills challenged the statement made by the Under-Secretary of State for India in the Commons wliich, he said, was based on the false and inaccurate message of Reuter's agency. He objected to inaccurate statement of facts of a case which was subjudice (a total sentence of nearly 20 years has since been awarded in this case.)... The Kotwali police raided three houses in Barisal and searched for proscribed literature. Nothing incriminating was found and no arrest was made.

It is obvious that to talk of the liberty of democratic control over the Government in this country is idle. Aside of the neglect with which resolutions of the Central Legislature are treated, the last sessions with be remembered for the number of adjournment motions that were disallowed by the Viceroy. Despite assurances to the contrary, official interference with elections under the New Government of India Act is continuing in a number of ways. Candidates are disqualified from contesting the election on the ground of their conviction for a period of more than a year. Circulars have been unearthed which instruct district and police officers to keep a close watch over the candidates in their area and to help defeat the Congress candidate. In United Provinces, Frontier Provinces and Madras, a number of meetings has been banned under one law or the other.

So all manner of violations of civil liberties take place. The law is repressive and loose. Justice is severe. The executive acts on speculation. Police excesses are manifold. Private violence is permitted. And none of the liberties is safe.

We may here remember the reasons given by the American Union for the repressive regime in the American colonies. They could as well be applied to the repressive administration in India. British commercial and capital interests have penetrated into the plantations, railways, jute and textile industry, inland navigation and the like and, so, the right to organise and strike, particularly of the industrial workers, is permanently attacked. The administration is actuated by the Indian civilian mentality, which is as bad as the American navy mentality, and carried on by subordinate executive and police officers, who are worse. The Indian freedom movement has entered the stage of frontal opposition to British Imperialism, which can now' have but scant regards for the liberties of the people. The increasing poverty and humiliation of the people motivates the nationalist movement, as never before, with the yearning for an alternative society and an uncompromising condemnation of the existing order. The yearning and the condemnation are met with stern arrests and bans.

There can be no talk, therefore, of a voluntary relaxation of the repressive regime in this country. The police state has come to stay. There is a show of re- leasing some detenus, mostly on conditions, or training them in industrial centres, but the heavy hand of fresh convictions and detentions, internments and externments knows no rest. Efforts of the Congress and other individuals to enquire into the working of repressive laws have come under the ban of the Government. The Law courts acquit but the executive detains, and so the seeming liberality of justice is fully offset by executive fiats. Only an insistent demand of the people for their civil liberties and an agitation to curtail State-authority can bring about the relaxation of the repressive regime in this country.

India lives today under the shadow of tyranny and what is worse, fear of tyranny. All manner of work, political and social, thought and art wastes and withers away. The Indian Civil Liberties Union is a new comer in the scheme of world defence of Civil Liberties. But its work is vaster than in other countries.